BRITISH CATHEDRALS

BRITISH CATHEDRALS

Paul Johnson

WILLIAM MORROW & COMPANY INC.
NEW YORK   1980

The book is dedicated to
Tom and Miriam Stoppard

House editor Anne Dobell
Designed by Sara Komar

First published in Great Britain by
George Weidenfeld and Nicolson Limited
91 Clapham High Street London SW4

ISBN 0-688-03672-4

Library of Congress Catalog Card Number 80-81171
Colour separations by Newsele Litho Ltd
Filmset by Keyspools Ltd, Golborne, Lancs
Printed and bound in Great Britain by
Butler & Tanner Ltd
Frome and London

Contents

But let my due feet never fail
To walk the studious Cloysters pale,
And love the high embowèd Roof,
With antick Pillars massy-proof,
And storied Windows richly dight,
Casting a dim religious light.

JOHN MILTON, *Il Penseroso*

Acknowledgments

The pictures in this book are reproduced by kind permission of the following (numbers refer to pages, italics indicate colour pictures:

ACL Brussels (Antwerp Museum) 172
John Bethell 49, *52 top and bottom*, 71, 89, 191, 198, 205 left and right (photo B. H. Cox), 214 bottom
Bibliothèque Nationale, Paris 171
British Museum (John Freeman) 20
Corpus Christi College, Oxford (CCC Oxf. Ms. 161) 180
British Insulated Callender's Cables Ltd 271
British Tourist Authority 87 bottom, 93 top, 95, 251
Cooper-Bridgeman Library *50–1, 90–1, 91, 230–1*
Courtauld Institute 7
Dean and Chapter, Westminster Abbey 124 bottom, 125 bottom
Dean and Chapter of the Cathedral Church of Exeter 11
Sonia Halliday *212 bottom*
Hereford Cathedral Library 224
Michael Holford *12–13, 70–1, 110–11, 111*
Angelo Hornak 69, 72, *109, 112, 203, 206 left, 206 right, 210–11, 212 top*
A. Kay 181
A. F. Kersting frontispiece, 5, 18, 21, 23, 29, 30, 33, 34, 36, 38, 39, 41, 43, 46, 53, 56, 57, 59, 65, 73, 74, 75, 80, 81, 82, 84, 87 top, 92, 93 bottom, 96, 98, 101, 107, 108, 114, 117, 127, 129, 130, 131, 135, 138, 140, 143, 144, 150, 154, 160, 163, 177, 185, 193, 199, *209*, 216 top and bottom, 219 top and bottom, 223, 225, 229, *232 top and bottom*, 233 top and bottom, 244, 247, 253 right, 254 top, 256 top and bottom, 257, 258, 263, 265, 270
Mansell Collection endpapers, 183, 227, 236 bottom
National Monuments Record 15, 47, 48, 116, 123 (Crown Copyright), 124 top, 152, 153, 156, 167, 168 (Crown Copyright), 192, 208, 213 left and right, 214 top left and top right, 215 top and bottom, 217 top and bottom, 218, 222 (Dean and Chapter of Liverpool), 253 left
The National Trust 200
Pitkin Pictorials (photo Sydney W. Newbery) 272
The Royal Institute of British Architects, London 66, 220, 236 top, 237 bottom, 237 top
Walter Scott 201
Crown Copyright: the Scottish Development Department 94, 157, 235
Edwin Smith 16, 27, 35, 44, 97, 99, 103, 105, 115, 120, 125 top, 126, 133, 149, 240, 241, 243, 254 bottom, 255 top and bottom, 266, 267
Trinity College, Cambridge 190
Victoria and Albert Museum 187
David Webster 262
Weidenfeld and Nicolson archives 26, 63
Welsh Office (Philip Micheu) 155
York Minster Library 196
The illustration on p. 176 is reproduced from *The Construction of Gothic Cathedrals* by John Fitchen by permission of The University of Chicago Press.

1
The Earliest Cathedrals of Britain

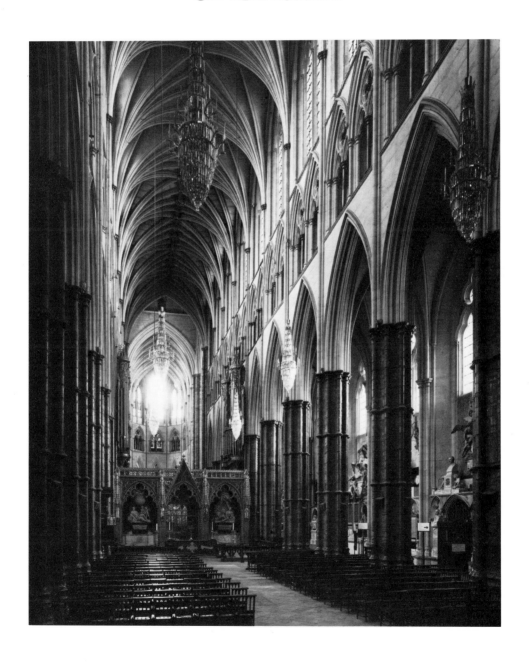

he cathedrals of North-West Europe are among the noblest of human artifacts, and within this larger collection the British cathedrals form a group of exceptional interest and distinction. But if we are to understand and enjoy to the full these splendid creations, it is important that we should grasp from the start that they were not, and are not, primarily works of art. A cathedral has a spiritual purpose. It is a statement of faith. It declares belief in a certain conception of man's relationship to his maker, and in a society which acknowledges this relationship to be the central fact of existence. Hence the design and fabric of a cathedral are shaped by function and ideology, rather than art, and the aesthetic of the cathedral, as it slowly evolved, was the product of these two factors. Always, when looking at a cathedral, we must start with the question: what did those who made this building believe? We shall, therefore, study the cathedrals of Britain in their religious and social context.

Cathedra is a Greek word for chair; originally any kind of chair, but later a specific type of chair used by rhetoricians and philosophers when discoursing. Such a chair was used by the bishops of the early church – that is, the men who claimed direct official descent from the Apostles – when instructing their flocks on faith and morals. A statement *ex cathedra*, 'from the chair', carried the highest authority; it was 'apostolic'. When making it, the bishop resembled the master of the house seated in the *solium* or place of honour, or the magistrate in court, whose chair was on a dais raised above the rest of the attendance. A bishop's *cathedra* was placed on a higher level than the seats of the presbyters, who were grouped about him in accordance with Revelations 4:4–5: 'And round about the throne were four and twenty seats: and upon the seats I saw four and twenty elders sitting. ... And out of the throne proceeded lightnings and thunderings and voices.' We have here the elements of the episcopal church: the bishop seated authoritatively on his raised throne in the choir, and the lesser clergy ranged in stalls on either side of him.

The earliest Christian bishops thus adopted the magisterial role from Roman civil courts; but they also echoed Jewish practice, by following the Jewish custom of remaining seated while delivering the sermon. St Chrysostom (347–407) was the first to preach from the *ambon*, or pulpit, in the body of the church, but here again he was following the ancient Jewish practice of reading the Scrolls of the Law from a desk. Originally the building where the bishop held court and pronounced judgement was of secondary importance; it was merely the *ecclesia cathedrae*, the church of the episcopal throne. But there was a tendency, which naturally became more marked when the Christian church was accorded legal status early in the fourth century, for such special churches to acquire grandeur, and to assume a specific architectural form. Civic practice provided a model – the basilica, or royal hall, to be found in the forum in every large town. In essence it was nothing but a meeting-hall, where the magistrate dispensed justice from his seat on a dais surmounted by a shrine which held the effigy of the emperor. The dais was at the top, or honourable end, which became the apse; the body of the hall constituted the nave, which when extended into the open (in sunny countries) constituted the open-air narthex of early churches.

Other religious sects of the Roman Empire adopted the basilica formula – the Jews for their synagogues, for example. Indeed, a reception-hall in any big aristocratic house was a basilica. The notion acquired a more distinctive Christian colouration, however, after Constantine presented the church with the

OVERLEAF The nave of Westminster Abbey. The vault, 102 feet from the nave floor, is exceptionally high for an English cathedral.

Lateran, one of his palaces, as a residence for the Bishop of Rome. The new *ecclesia cathedrae* of Rome, laid out on the site of a former cavalry barracks, was called the Basilica Constantiniana, and is now known as St John Lateran. This consisted of a vast aisled nave, 250 feet long by 180 wide, supported by two rows of fifteen green-marbled columns on high pedestals. The sanctuary, terminating in an apse, was a further 65 feet long, and held 200 clergy who attended the bishop on important feast-days. The great nave would hold several thousand layfolk, and they were already separated from the clergy by a silver screen on a double row of columns.

The notion that a cathedral-church was a long rectangle, oriented towards Jerusalem on a rough west-east axis, and terminating in a choir within an eastern apse, became the fundamental fact of cathedral architecture in the west. But superimposed on it was the idea of Hagia Sophia, a centralized church, under a vast dome, created at the instigation of the Emperor Justinian in Constantinople in AD 532–7 by the architects Anthemius of Tralles and Isidorus of Miletus. The shape was derived from the Pantheon in Rome and the vast thermal halls of the larger imperial cities. Hagia Sophia, or St Sophia, the cathedral of divine wisdom, gave expression to the caesaro-papalism of the Byzantine monarchy and imperial ceremonial in its religious aspect. Its aim was that every member of a vast congregation could see the mystery of the faith in the greatest possible splendour. It is not surprising that cathedrals in the west are now occasionally built on this principle (for example Brasilia, and the Roman Catholic cathedrals in Clifton and Liverpool), and are designed to ensure maximum visibility.

St Sophia's dome was never repeated on such a scale; but the centralized church, conceived as a cluster of domes in rough cruciform shape, covering a focal interior space, became the basis of Byzantine church architecture. It penetrated the Latin west to the extent that a central space, marking the point where the congregational part of the church met the sanctuary, was added to the rectangular basilican plan. Cathedral churches in the west became cruciform, but the cross was rectangular, the short eastern arm constituting the sanctuary, the congregational arm stretching away to the west. The north-south arms became transepts, and the central dome, over the crossing, was transformed into a tower.

Such an arrangement helped the authorities to distinguish between a parochial church, with a nave and chancel, and an episcopal church. The distinction was a real one in many ways. In large parts of the former imperial west, bishops were the source of secular as well as spiritual authority in the fifth and sixth centuries, and dispensed justice and administration, as well as divinity, from their *cathedrae*. The bishop's church was often an integral part of a fortified upper town. The bishop's church was also the only place where all the sacraments could be dispensed. Holy oils, waters and relics were kept there. In the early Dark Ages, only cathedrals had baptistries, often large affairs built for total immersion. Only the cathedral enacted the full liturgical cycle. It was therefore natural for the eastern arm to become the 'bishop's church', where his throne and attendant choir were to be found, the distinction emphasized by the crossing-space formed by the north-south transepts and eventually by a screen placed in front of the choir.

The ideology of an increasingly hierarchical church was thus stamped on ecclesiastical architecture in two ways: first by the nave-chancel division, marking the absolute distinction between clerics and layfolk; second, as a refinement of this principle, by the existence within the cathedral chancel of a specific bishop's church, containing choir and sanctuary, placed inside the fabric like an inner box. Since Christian churches, unlike Greek temples, were built from the inside outwards – their liturgical functions dictated the external architecture – the cathedral was essentially a building designed to accommodate an episcopal choir.

So much for the cathedral as such. The study of its British manifestation raises certain specific problems. The administrative divisions of the Latin church reflected Roman imperial arrangements: the bishop ruled over a diocese, and certain senior bishops, or archbishops, were awarded the *palium* (a fur tippet once worn by Roman officials) by Rome, and ruled over a province. As a rule, there was only one cathedral church in each diocese. The British dioceses were unusually large, and they have changed substantially in the course of time. We know practically nothing about church arrangements in Britain under the Roman Empire, though there were almost certainly cathedral churches in London and York. In Dark Age Britain, the church in the Celtic areas was administered from monastic centres, where power and authority rested with aristocratic abbots; bishops were mere functionaries, and their churches small affairs. Iona, from which Scotland and northern England were evangelized, was an abbey, not a cathedral, though a cathedral of sorts was built in Lindisfarne by the Iona monks. When southern England was evangelized by Rome in the late sixth century, it got the rudiments of a Roman-style diocesan system which was later extended to the whole country. The first Canterbury cathedral was built before 600, Rochester and London in 604, York in 627, Ripon in 678, Worcester and Hereford before 680. The ecclesiastical life of Mercia revolved around cathedrals at Lichfield and Leicester, and of Wessex around Sherborne and Winchester.

This Saxon diocesan system was substantially changed as a result of shifts in power and population and the Danish invasion. The bishoprics of Dunwich, Elmham, Lindsey, Hexham and Whithorn ceased to exist. Lindisfarne cathedral was moved to Durham. We have a rare and precious glimpse of such an administrative revision provided by Manuscript 2072 in the library of Exeter Cathedral. This is a charter of Edward the Confessor, dated 1050, which reads:

> This do I first make known to my lord Pope Leo, and confirm it by his attestation, and then to all the magnates of the English, that I deliver over the diocese of Cornwall ... with all its adjoining parishes to St Peter in the city of Exeter, to wit that it be one episcopal seat, one pontificate, and one ecclesiastical rule. And because of the fewness of the people and the devastation of their goods – for pirates have been able to plunder the churches of Cornwall and of Crediton – it has seemed clear that there is a safer defence against the enemies in the town of Exeter, and therefore I will that the See should be there: that is, that Cornwall, with its churches, and Devonshire, with its churches, should be in one bishopric, and should be ruled by one Bishop. And so I, King Edward, place this privilege upon the altar of St Peter with my own hand: and, leading Bishop Leofric by the right arm, whilst my Queen Edith leads him by the left, place him on his episcopal throne, in the presence of my great men and my kinsfolk, my nobles and chaplains.

This transfer from Crediton to Exeter left, however, other anomalies in the shape of rural cathedrals, anomalies which were gradually corrected after William I conquered the country. The see of Dorchester was removed to Lincoln, Elmham to Norwich, Sherborne to Salisbury, Selsey to Chichester, and new cathedral centres were created at Chester, Carlisle and Ely.

For most of the Middle Ages, England was served by seventeen cathedrals. Of these, nine were 'secular' cathedrals, that is served by chapters of canons who did not take special vows of poverty. They were Chichester, Exeter, Hereford, Lichfield, Lincoln, London, Salisbury, Wells and York, collectively known as the Old Foundation. Other Saxon cathedrals were served by chapters of Benedictine monks, a system continued under the Normans, and are known as Monastic Foundations: Bath (grouped with Wells in a single diocese), Canterbury, Durham, Ely, Norwich, Rochester, Winchester and Worcester. In addition there was Carlisle, served by Augustinian regular canons, from the twelfth century.

When Henry VIII destroyed the monastic system, he decided to compensate for the loss of ecclesiastical services by turning twenty-one of the old monastic churches into cathedrals. We possess his autograph list of these, which included Waltham, Thame, Dunstable, Newenham, Shrewsbury, Fountains and Leicester. Some of those on the list, such as Oseney and Westminster Abbey, became cathedrals for a short time in the sixteenth century. The Benedictine houses of Gloucester and Peterborough, and the Augustinian houses of Oxford, Bristol and Carlisle, were added permanently to the ranks of cathedrals, this group of five becoming known as the New Foundation. In the nineteenth and twentieth centuries, twenty new Anglican cathedrals have been created. Five are former monastic or collegiate churches: St Albans, Southwark, Ripon, Southwell and Manchester. Eleven are former parish churches: Birmingham, Blackburn, Chelmsford, Leicester, Portsmouth, St Edmundsbury, Bradford, Sheffield, Newcastle, Wakefield and Douglas. Four are new: Truro, Guildford, Liverpool,

Charter of Edward the Confessor in Exeter Cathedral Library, recording the foundation of the diocese.

Coventry. To these, for the purposes of this book, I have added Westminster Abbey and Beverley, both of which have served as cathedrals; the two surviving medieval cathedrals of the North, Glasgow and Kirkwall; the four ancient cathedrals of Wales, Bangor, St Davids, Llandaff and St Asaph; the cathedrals of the Episcopalian Church of Scotland; and the twenty-seven Roman Catholic cathedrals of England, Wales and Scotland – making a grand total of nearly ninety cathedrals.

We know very little about the earliest British cathedrals. The ruined church of North Elmham in East Anglia is the only Anglo-Saxon cathedral of which a part is still visible above the surface. The Saxon cathedral of York, the first in England to be built of stone, has not been located; an investigation carried out by Dr Brian Hope-Taylor, during the strengthening process carried out on the present Minster, 1966–71, revealed details of its Norman predecessor but concluded that the first cathedral must have been built on a different site. According to Alcuin, this cathedral was about 200 feet long. Offa built a cathedral of similar size at Lichfield, and the abbey church at Chichester was 175 feet long. At Canterbury, the original church consecrated by St Augustine was probably a reconstituted Roman building, only eighty feet long. It was replaced in the ninth century (we assume) by a cathedral of roughly the same size as York, and it was this building

S·EADWARDI·REGIS·AD·ECCLESIAM· PETRI

A section from the Bayeux Tapestry showing the body of Edward the Confessor being borne into his newly-built Abbey at Westminster in January 1066.

which was burned down in Norman times and described from memory by Eadmer in the twelfth century. Eadmer says it was like Old St Peter's in Rome, and it is possible that all the Saxon cathedrals were modelled on St Peter's for, despite the distance, the links between England and the See of Rome were firm.

The work of Martin Biddle at Winchester in the 1960s shows that a small cruciform church 60 feet long was built there *c.* 650; a free-standing tower was added later, and in the late tenth century the two were joined, the resulting cathedral being provided with a westwork and a new east end, forming a long, narrow building. Together with St Paul's Saxon cathedral in London, this was England's largest church, until Edward the Confessor, towards the end of his reign, built his new abbey at Westminster. The Confessor's cultural ties were with Continental Normandy, then at the beginning of a great religious and artistic revolution, and his fine new abbey marked a distinctive break with the Saxon past; had it survived, it must have ranked as the first of Britain's true medieval cathedrals. Excavations and the picture of it on the Bayeux Tapestry show that it was grander than anything which then existed on this side of the Channel, a Norman-type abbey with conventual buildings on the standard Cluniac plan. It had a nave of six double bays, transepts with a tall tower over the crossing, a pair of western towers and a triple-apsed sanctuary.

13

Precisely how this type of cathedral evolved in North-West Europe during the Dark Ages can only be a matter for conjecture, but here is a possible sequence. The central space needed for the grandeur of the episcopal church was created by an adoption of the Byzantine plan, either by creating a square based on four great wooden posts, or a stone square with arches punched into each side. In deference to Rome, and its long basilicas, the western arm was extended into a lengthy nave, the other arms becoming north-south transepts and an eastern chancel with the choir inside it. Often, however, it was difficult to extend the cathedral westward because the entrance to the church was a ceremonial open square. Instead, a new cruciform structure, on a bigger scale, was built to the east, crowned with a tower over the crossing, and linked to the old church by a rectangular portion which became a new, and even longer, nave. The old nave was then demolished to expand the ceremonial entrance square, and the old cruciform church was transformed into a westwork, often with two towers, one of which acted as a belfry. This composite building was neither exactly Byzantine nor basilican: its great crossing, with its four massive piers, reflected the splendours of Byzantium, which until the twelfth century was by far the richest and most advanced part of the Christian world; on the other hand, the long rectangular nave gave the cathedral the general appearance of a Roman basilica, and thus the reassurance of its Latin and papal orthodoxy. This pattern had already evolved in North-West Europe before the schism between the Greek and Latin churches became formal in 1054. Thereafter it enjoyed a life of its own as a standard cathedral plan, and it was to prove exceedingly resistant to change, as we shall see.

In Britain, certain marked regional characteristics were implanted on this standard pattern, almost from the start. Anglo-Saxon society evolved from the forest and its buildings were dominated by timber from first to last. Though the Saxons came to use stone in increasing quantities, especially for churches, their masonry tended to be a mere petrification, as it were, of wood, and carpenters played a much more important and adventurous role in the design and construction of buildings, including the largest cathedrals, here than on the Continent.

Second, Britain was a mission-territory in the early Dark Ages, and (like parts of Germany) was evangelized by Benedictine monks. Hence the monastic cathedral foundations. Archbishop Lanfranc of Canterbury, whom William the Conqueror put in charge of reorganizing the Saxon church, was himself a Benedictine monk. Instead, therefore, of abolishing the monastic cathedral as a Saxon aberration, he consolidated it, and it remained an important and distinctive feature of our church. It meant that many cathedrals were part of a large conventual complex; in England, indeed, most of the secular cathedrals were also provided with cloisters. Monastic cathedrals tended to emphasize the already profound distinction between the clerical and the lay areas of the building, for the monks were cut off from the world by their vows and the laity were not encouraged to penetrate their quarters. The choir was monks' territory and the laity did not normally pass beyond the crossing. The church of the people was the nave; hence its great extension in English cathedrals, where it was used for all major processions. Hence, too, the tendency to provide it with an elaborate westwork, for which the laity paid.

The monastic system also influenced the general character of cathedral settings. On the Continent, cathedrals spring dramatically from the clustering roofs of their cities. They are quintessentially urban protuberances. In the first decade of Norman rule, the decision was taken by the authorities to end the anomaly of the rural cathedral. But the monastic cathedral retained its semi-rural atmosphere, even when it was part of a thriving town. It constituted a distinct and exclusive *quartier*; and even new secular foundations, like Salisbury, were built on the outskirts of towns. The cathedral close thus became an important formative element in the social and aesthetic character of our cathedrals, an element which survived the dissolution of the monastic foundations and is still visible and palpable today.

The strongly collegiate character of British cathedrals, whether monastic or secular, was also expressed by magnificent display chapter-houses, sometimes square, more usually polygonal. At one time there were at least twenty-five polygonal chapter-houses in England and two in Scotland; more than half of these have been destroyed, but there are notable survivors at Salisbury, Wells and Westminster.

In doctrinal matters, the British churches tended to be strict: that is, they combined insularity with a self-conscious orthodoxy and strong links with Rome – the English church always made a direct payment to the papacy in the form of 'Peter's Pence'. They insisted their altars be orientated, extending the transepts so that altars could be built along their eastern walls, rather than setting them up in

The east end of Salisbury Cathedral.

the north-south aisles of the choir. Sometimes they built altars on the eastern side of the great nave piers, and the wall-paintings surmounting them can still be seen at St Albans. On the Continent, additional altars were provided by adding a series of projecting chapels to the processional ambulatory which surrounded the apsidal east end. These were known as 'chevets' or 'bed-heads'. In Britain they were disliked, partly because of their dubious orientation and partly because, under sunless skies, they produced dark altars. There is a chevet at Westminster, the most French of our great churches, though the centre of it was demolished to make way for Henry VII's magnificent chapel, and there are residual chevets at the monastic cathedrals of Norwich, Peterborough and Gloucester. However, most English east ends are square. They either fall away in steps, as at Winchester, Salisbury, Chichester, Wells, Exeter, Hereford, St Albans and Gloucester, or constitute sheer cliffs, as at York, Lincoln, Carlisle, Ripon, Worcester, Oxford and Bristol. This square east end is one of the most marked features of the English-type cathedral, which is sometimes provided with a double transept, making yet more space for properly orientated altars.

Finally, while English cathedrals are notable for the length of their naves, they are rarely very high, at any rate by the standards of France. Here again Westminster is the exception, with a vault 102 feet from the nave floor; but even this was low by the standards of the Isle de France, where the vault at Amiens was 140 feet and at Beauvais 154. But with lowish vaults, the English could risk the erection of high crossing-towers, which the French could not. English cathedrals are notable for their great stone towers and steeples – sometimes, as at Salisbury, both. The central tower at Lincoln is 271 feet high and its timber spire once made it, at 524 feet, the tallest cathedral in the world, visible from the Wash and parts of East Anglia. This spire came down in a great storm in 1548 and was not replaced (Lincoln lost its two western spires early in the nineteenth century). Tall stone towers surmounted by wooden spires cased in lead were once the most striking element in the English cathedral silhouette, but most of the spires have long since disappeared.

In judging the cathedrals of Britain as a historical phenomenon in architecture, it is useful to make some statistical comparisons. There are several ways of doing this. The great Oxford historian of English Gothic, Francis Bond, noted first that in total length English naves, whether Romanesque or Gothic, had no competitors on the Continent, the six longest in England easily leading the field:

Old St Paul's	586 feet	Milan	475 feet
Winchester	530	Florence	475
St Albans	520	Amiens	435
Ely	517	Rouen	435
Canterbury	514	Rheims	430
Westminster	505	Cologne	427

By contrast, in all other respects, English cathedrals were smaller than the Continental leaders. Thus in nave-spans we have:

York	45 feet	Gerona	73 feet
Ripon	40	Toulouse	63
Ely	39	Albi	58
Lincoln	39	Milan	56
Canterbury (choir)	39	Seville	56
Old St Paul's	36	Florence	55

OPPOSITE East end, central tower and spire of Norwich Cathedral.

For internal height, that is from pavement to apex of vault:

Old St Paul's (nave)	103 feet		Cologne	155 feet
Westminster	103		Beauvais	154
York (choir)	102		Bologna	150
Gloucester (choir)	86		Amiens	144
Salisbury	84		Bourges	117
Lincoln (nave)	82		Chartres	106

Francis Bond's method of calculating the ground plan area in square feet gives the following results:

Old St Paul's	72,460	square	Seville	150,000	square
York	63,800	feet	Milan	92,000	feet
Lincoln	57,200		Saragossa	80,000	
Winchester	53,480		Amiens	70,000	
Ely	46,000		Cluny	66,000	
Westminster	46,000		Toledo	66,000	

The ratio of height to span in England tends to be about two to one (somewhat higher in the choirs than in the naves), and is nearer to three in France, with Beauvais as high as 3.3 and Cologne 3.8. Bond noted one other important factor. Lichfield and Wells have nave-heights of twice the span, but they do not look low, as do the naves of Exeter and Lincoln, where the ratio is virtually the same. This depends on a further ratio, of the breadth of the bay to its height. At Exeter it is only 3.1; at Lichfield it is 3.5 and at Wells 4.0; in the choir of Westminster the enormous ratio of 5.5 is reached. Moreover, in addition, at Lichfield the shafts of the vault rise direct from the pavement, which makes the bay seem higher; at Exeter and Lincoln they start from the corbel half way up.

A somewhat different method of calculating the area, used by Professor E.S. Prior in *A History of Gothic Art in England* (London 1900), gave Old St Paul's 100,000 square feet, as against 90,000 for Cologne, 70,000 for Lincoln and slightly less for Bury St Edmunds, the largest of the English Benedictine houses. The most comprehensive comparative system, however, has been devised by Dr John Harvey, Britain's leading authority on Gothic architecture and Consultant Architect to Winchester College. This calculates the area of a rectangular plot of land needed to contain the ground-plan of the cathedral, not including subsidiary buildings. He gives Old St Peter's, Rome, which was accepted as standard for large cathedrals in Latin Christendom, the index figure of 126 (using as standard the other Roman pilgrimage church, St Paul's-Outside-the-Walls, at 100). The only cathedral of its age to rival it was St Sophia itself, with 110. Indeed, Old St Peter's, by this measurement, was larger than nearly all the buildings of antiquity, the Parthenon being 23, the Great Temple of Baalbek 47, the Temple of Artemis at Ephesus 82, and even the great secular basilica of Tragan being only 112. The great Moslem buildings of the Dark Ages were likewise smaller, the Damascus Mosque being 68 and the Dome of the Rock, Jerusalem, only 32. The one exception was the eighth-tenth century Mosque of Cordova, which Harvey gives as 169.

Britain's pre-Conquest cathedrals were tiny, Elmham being a mere 7 and St Augustine's Canterbury 19. But there was a progressive increase from the eighth to the eleventh centuries, and by the time of the Conquest abbey and cathedral churches were rivalling old St Peter's. Winchester (1079) was 122, Bury St

OPPOSITE The cliff-like east end of York Minster.

In the image: S. PAULES CHURCH, Bew Church, Hansted Mills, Hansted, the Water house, S. Brides, THAMESIS, The Eell Schyps, The belly fishe, Three Craves, The Shilbard, The Bear Gardne, The Globe

A detail from Jan Visscher's panoramic map of London, 1650, showing Old St Paul's on the north side of the river, after the central spire had fallen.

OPPOSITE The west towers of Lincoln Cathedral, seen from the roof of the south transept.

Edmunds (1081) 130, both about the same size as the largest French abbey, the third and biggest on the site of Cluny (1088), which was 125. Old St Paul's was by far the largest of the English cathedrals, at 203 much bigger than the successor-church built by Wren (143), though both were eclipsed by the new Renaissance St Peter's, Rome, at 354.

Harvey's index divides English cathedrals into three groups. Large (91 to 109) includes Salisbury, St Albans, Peterborough, Ely, Norwich, Canterbury and Durham. Medium (61 to 76) includes Wells, Worcester, Hereford, Chichester, Gloucester, Exeter, Chester and Lichfield. Small (21 to 47) comprises Ripon, Bath, Oxford, Bristol, Southwell, Rochester, Southwark and Carlisle, to which should be added the four Welsh cathedrals, Glasgow and Kirkwall.

Though some of the cathedrals were comparatively small, all of them dwarfed the other buildings of their time and district. In antiquity, the great public buildings of each city were designed to accommodate all of its citizens, and to some extent this principle was applied by medieval man to his cathedrals.

20

Cathedral cities were, of course, rich in parish churches: by the end of the medieval period, Norwich, for instance, had 50, Lincoln 49, and York 41. All the same, in these and other cities cathedrals were made big enough to hold all their inhabitants. The only exception was London, where Old St Paul's, vast though it was, could not keep pace with the ever-growing population. In general, though, the cathedrals were almost out of scale with their times; it is impossible for us to conceive the extent to which, in a literal sense, they loomed large in the lives and vision of medieval people, reducing all else (including themselves) to insignificance and providing inescapable and ocular evidence of the power and majesty of God. They were awesome and overwhelming.

Yet each was different, preserving its strikingly individual character through the work of many centuries. Each was an accretion of ages, yet in each a particular age and style of architecture was transcendental. Bearing this in mind, we will look at them more closely, using chronology and style as our organizational principle.

2
Cathedrals of the
Norman Age

ny investigation of Britain's medieval cathedrals must start with an examination of the impact of the Normans on church and state. They were one of the great races of history, and the hundred years 1050–1150 was the 'Norman Century'. Their effect on England was all the more striking in that England had had a quite separate social, political and legal development to that of her Continental neighbours. In military technology she lagged behind, and artistically she had strong and conservative traditions of her own. England, therefore, was slow to adopt the new type of architecture, which we call Romanesque, evolving in western Europe in the tenth-eleventh centuries and this natural conservatism and lethargy was increased by the ferocious assaults on the country by the Danish raiders of the late tenth and early eleventh centuries.

England was a comparatively rich country, with an excellent silver coinage, but the huge amounts paid in Danegeld, recorded in the Anglo-Saxon Chronicle and other documents, made a perceptible impact on the scale and number of the church-building projects in the years 1000–50. Thus England was slow to enter the Romanesque era, and she began to do so only tentatively in the last three decades of the reign of Edward the Confessor. The Confessor was linked by blood and inclination to the Norman court, and it was under Norman influence and with Norman assistance that the first motte-and-bailey castles were built in England, mainly on the Welsh border. The ground-plan of Westminster Abbey, England's first major exercise in the Romanesque, was laid down in 1054, and the building, modelled on a Norman abbey, was virtually completed by the time of the Conquest. However, this was the only large Romanesque church, so far as we know, built in Edward's time.

The year 1066, therefore, marks a great watershed in English architectural history, as in so many other things. William I was a great and audacious, but above all methodical and systematic, builder who put his trust in high palisades and strong stone walls. In this respect he did not draw an absolute distinction between castles, on the one hand, and churches, cathedrals and abbeys on the other. He entered, conquered and held down England with a following which never numbered more than 10,000. His means were the mobility of the armoured knight, raised by the feudal system of knight-service, which he imposed everywhere, and the static defences of the motte-and-bailey, erected at every large town and settlement.

This secular system was underpinned by an ecclesiastical one. William came to England not merely as a claimant to the throne, but as a crusader against a church branded as corrupt and schismatic. Saxon England had not accepted the Hildebrandine reforms of a newly invigorated papacy; her leading ecclesiastic, Archbishop Stigand, was an excommunicate, and many of her ecclesiastical arrangements were regarded as irregular by Continental standards. In Normandy, William had reinforced his power by a thorough reform of the church, and had recruited an able and vigorous band of young clerics (chiefly monks) in the process. He came to England with a papal mandate for root-and-branch reform on a still more comprehensive scale. Hence the changes in clerical personnel which he brought about were almost as rapid and sweeping as his destruction of the Saxon earls and thegns, and his replacement of them by a new military aristocracy. Since the new bishops and abbots owed the king knight-service for their lands and were expected to fight alongside him in battle, the

OVERLEAF The nave of Durham Cathedral, the first Romanesque cathedral to be stone-vaulted throughout.

distinction between the clerical and secular rulers imposed on the English was small. Moreover, in both cases, building programmes provided ocular evidence of the new power-structure.

William set up a prefabricated castle the very day he landed in Sussex, and he continued to build castles at breakneck speed throughout his reign – a policy also followed by his heir, William II. In addition to temporary wooden structures, he erected thirty-one permanent castles in the first five years after Hastings, and there were more than fifty by the time of Domesday Book in 1086. As fast as possible, these wooden castles were provided with stone keeps. Stone was shipped over from Caen and other Norman quarries controlled by the King, and English quarries, on river-sites, opened up at Barnack, Quarre, Maidstone and elsewhere.

This castle-building programme was the biggest concerted enterprise of its kind since the Romans built the great forts of the Saxon Shore. But it was accompanied by an ecclesiastical building programme which was, in many respects, even more remarkable. William restructured the bishoprics and dioceses, founded and refounded abbeys, and introduced a much stricter system of appointment and discipline. The change was emphasized by the building of cathedrals and abbeys on the vast new Norman model. Like the castles, they were intended to fill the Saxon beholder with awe and wholesome terror; and, like the castles, they were built to be defended. They used the same stone; they were planned by the same designers and made by the same carpenters and masons; they were decorated by the same artists and covered in the same ubiquitous whitewash. There can be no doubt, for instance, that the master-mason who carved the delicate blind arcading on Norwich Castle also worked on the nearby cathedral. The decorative elements of castles were much more prominent than they appear today, and were further emphasized by whitewash and painting, so that to the contemporary eye castles and cathedrals would have seemed unmistakably part of the same programme, reflecting the authority of the new master-race. Indeed, the siege-towers used to build, as well as destroy, castles, were also employed in cathedral construction.

If anything, the cathedrals were technically in advance of the castles, and as a rule on a much bigger scale. Work began on the Conqueror's own thanksgiving foundation of Battle Abbey immediately after the Conquest in 1066. By 1070, the Normans were rebuilding Canterbury Cathedral and the nearby abbey of St Augustine. Then we have Bury (1070), Lincoln (1072), Old Sarum (1076), Rochester (1077), St Albans (1077), Winchester (1079), Worcester (1084) and, shortly after the Conqueror's death, Gloucester (1087), Norwich and Ely (both in 1090) and Durham (1093). Nothing like these buildings had been seen before in England, or indeed anywhere. They were bold and simple in design and execution, and on the whole uniform in concept. But their most impressive feature was sheer size – long naves, massive transepts, ponderous piers of great width, often rounded and carved, and noble arches everywhere. On the great saints' days an episcopal procession making its way up one of these dramatically long naves, attended outside the narthex by the full panoply of the bishop's temporal power, gave the spectators an overwhelming sense of the majesty and rule of the church, in this world as well as in the next, and emphasized the permanence and durability of Norman power, lay and ecclesiastical.

The economics and finance of this enormous building programme were possible only in the context of a social revolution, in which nine-tenths of the land changed hands in less than a generation. The tendency was for estates to be regrouped in a smaller number (about 300) on much bigger holdings, lay and clerical. The crown, which now held over a fifth of the land, was the greatest beneficiary and also the greatest contributor to the building programme; bishops and abbots also did well, and many richly-endowed lay barons proved munificent benefactors to the church. With fewer but much larger estates, surpluses were available for building investment; but there is little doubt, also, that the 'Norman Yoke' – the phrase was still part of folk-memory at the time of the Civil War six centuries later – forced the peasants to work harder, as the Domesday Book provides mute testimony and as the Anglo-Saxon Chronicle angrily complained. The first generation of great English cathedrals was built by the sweat of a conquered people, as well as by the audacity of a gifted and ruthless oligarchy.

St Albans is the best introduction to the Norman version of Romanesque architecture, because it shows the style and concept at its most elemental. Its long, low silhouette, broken only by the massive stump of the central tower, crowns the hill overlooking the delectable valley where the Romans built their town and where the eponymous martyr was killed. It is still very largely a medieval landscape, and the looming majesty of the church, which overshadows St Albans town even today, symbolizes the dominance of the monks over the citizens. Such urban monasteries (Bury St Edmunds, Reading and Glastonbury were other outstanding examples), with their great economic power and armoury of legal privileges, stunted the civic growth of the towns which were attached to them, and were increasingly resented in the later Middle Ages. There were anti-monastic riots, and the monks, to protect themselves, built high crenellated walls and massive gatehouses. At St Albans the gatehouse is still standing (as at Bury, where it constitutes virtually all that is left of the medieval fabric), but the other monastic buildings, to the south of the cathedral, have been cleared away, leaving a spectacular park-like approach to the grim cathedral walls.

St Albans did not actually become a cathedral until 1877, when the new diocese was created, but throughout the Middle Ages it was one of the most important

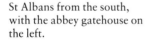

St Albans from the south, with the abbey gatehouse on the left.

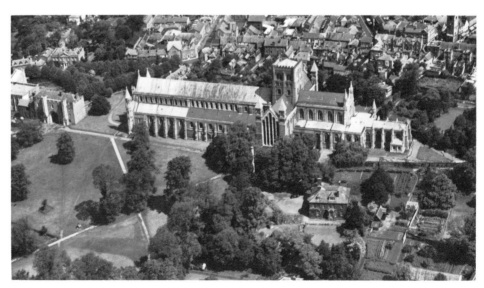

OPPOSITE St Albans: the chancel and crossing.

26

ecclesiastical centres in the country. It lay on the great north road and had the duty of accommodating the king on his journey; in return, it was given special royal protection and unrivalled access to news. The St Albans chronicles series is the finest we possess, and Matthew Paris and Thomas Walsingham, its two outstanding contributors, are among the greatest of the medieval historians. Nicholas Breakspeare was born within its liberties and after he became England's only pope, as Adrian IV, he gave the abbey (in 1154) the Bull *Incomprehensibilis*, which placed St Albans at the head of all English monasteries, its abbot outranking all other abbots in parliament.

There is no stone locally, and no navigable river up which to ship it. As at the Tower of London and Colchester Castle, the Normans fell on the ruins of the Roman city and built the cathedral of its bricks, supplemented by local flint. The absence of stone left little opportunity for carving. The internal walls were plastered with mortar, whitewashed and painted, and some of these murals (of the thirteenth and fourteenth centuries) were recovered in the nineteenth century. Externally, the absence of detail is very striking: it tends to bring out the big, bold character of this brick monster, especially the insolence and *hubris* of its blunt central tower, identical in essentials to a Norman castle keep. Although much wider windows were later punched in the fabric, enough remains of the original fenestration to show what a tiny proportion of the surface area they occupied – arches and windows were mere slits in the dark red mass of wall and pier. It would have been exceedingly difficult to undermine these thick, compacted walls, bound in mortar, and the narrow openings constituted a planned defensive system.

Inside St Albans it is still possible to conjure up the feeling of a great Norman church. Essentially, it is built outwards from the four massive piers which hold the tower and created a monumental central space, spanned by the arches of the crossing. With its paintwork and torches, this formed a dark and glittering cavern, or a stage on which the ecclesiastical drama was enacted. This stage was reserved for the greatest feast-days. Normally the populace only penetrated the long nave; they had their own altar on the west of the rood-screen, which itself is west of the crossing. All the rest of the building was the monks' church, so that when the procession reached the people's rood-altar, it separated and passed through doors on either side into the sacerdotal area.

St Albans is one of the few places where this arrangement was kept. The nave is immensely long – thirteen bays – and could accommodate a multitude. The monks never thought it necessary to rebuild it *in toto*, though it has been added to and patched up over the centuries and puzzles the visitor with a variety of styles, more instructive than harmonious. More important, the church had from the start a long eastern arm of five bays, so when the choir was rebuilt in Gothic times, there was no need to lengthen it by moving it to the east; it is still in its eleventh-century position west of the crossing-tower. Hence, though St Albans has been battered by neglect and vandalism over the centuries and, perhaps worse, subjected to crude and radical cosmetic surgery at the hands of its Victorian benefactor, Lord Grimthorpe, it retains to a remarkable extent its Norman core: it is plain, massive, harsh, inelegant, and has the purity of its primitive sincerity. It is a cathedral in which the bones of its structural necessities are always visible, never fleshed out by decorative contrivance, and it stands out on its hill like a primordial patriarch, the first-born of its kind.

Peterborough, by contrast, is evidently not a first-born; it is a rarified and

The west front of Peterborough.

sophisticated exemplar of the same model. Here we have another Benedictine abbey church on a grand scale. Henry VIII, when he suppressed the monastery, raised the church to cathedral status partly because he considered it 'one of the goodliest monuments in Christendom', and partly because his first wife, Catherine of Aragon, is buried there (for a time it also held the trunk and severed head of Mary Queen of Scots, until James I moved them to the splendour of Westminster Abbey in 1612).

It is fit to be a cathedral. Though built on essentially the same plan as St Albans, it is a generation later – work began in 1118 – and during that lifetime, the Normans had effected immense improvements in their method of building. To begin with, Peterborough is in stone, and stone of superlative quality. The town lies on the edge of the great limestone belt which stretches across England diagonally from Lincoln through Northamptonshire and the Cotswolds to the Dorset coast. It is only nine miles from the historic quarry at Barnack, exploited as long ago as Roman times, reopened by the Normans and in use from then until it was exhausted in the early eighteenth century. Only four-and-a-half miles away was the complementary quarry at Alwalton, which supplied marble for the abbots' tombs and other luxurious embellishments.

The stone at Peterborough retains its buff-and-white crispness and gives to the decorations of the interiors a wonderful fresh glow, almost as though they were carved yesterday. But what transforms this admirable stone into great architecture is the stylish and authoritative design of each bay. The bay was the basic unit of medieval cathedral architecture, in that each of the four arms of the church was constructed of a given number of bays and the central crossing was in origin a square of two bays each side. The configuration and proportions of the bay were functions of the constructional method. To gain height and introduce light, the Dark Age church stretched upwards. This meant the nave walls had to

29

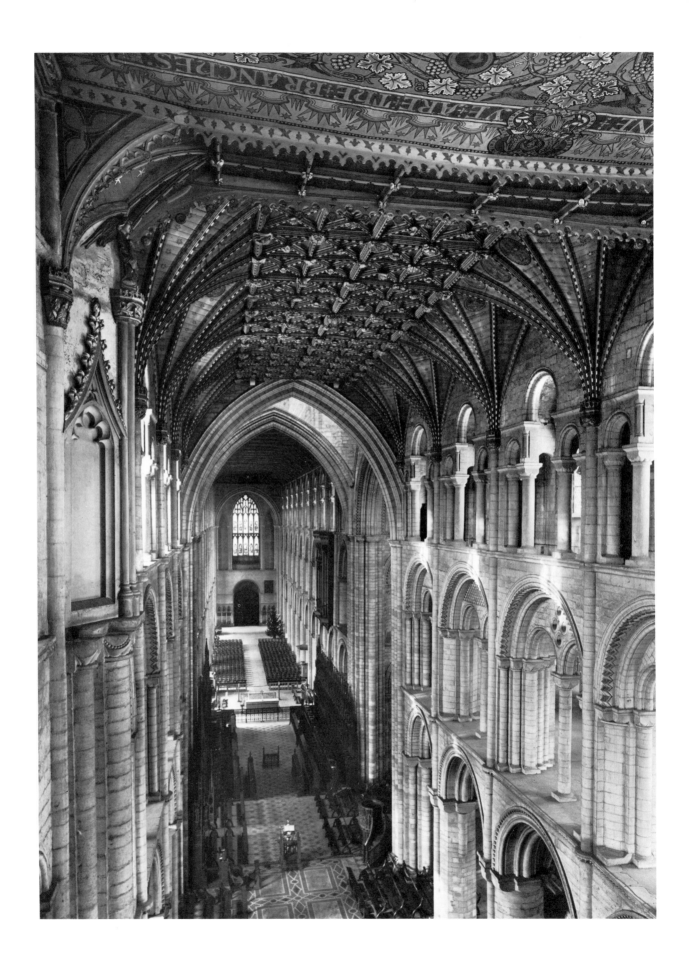

be supported by aisles, to allow a further storey of nave wall, pierced by windows, to be added above. The lean-to roof of the aisles allowed the development of a middle section within, whether as blind arcading or a gallery or, when the pitch of the aisle roof was lowered towards the horizontal, as an additional range of windows. The interior of the bay, rising from the pavement, thus came to consist of three stages: the nave arcade, an intermediate storey (known variously as gallery, tribune or, when blind or a mere passage, triforium), and the top range of clerestory windows.

The art of design, within the limitations of this form, lay in the ordering of the bay: that is, the bay order came to replace the classical orders (in their three Greek and five Roman versions) as the basic grammar of medieval architecture. The cathedral architect had to design this ordering at three levels, instead of just one (in the true classical tradition) or two (at the level of a mere church), and in doing so he had to bear in mind certain structural imperatives.

The development of Romanesque architecture indicates the growing facility – and hence increasing excitement – with which the master-masons tackled this problem, and suggests why the more sophisticated form of ordering we call Gothic, which offered infinitely wider opportunities for invention and display, was bound to happen. The Romanesque ordering at its most basic can be seen in the original nave piers at St Albans, where the additional restrictions of brick and flint, which inhibit carving, mean that the purely functional role of the piers is virtually unadorned; there are no mouldings, merely crude step-backs. The result works on the senses because it is huge and dominant. It has something of what Edmund Burke, in his essay on *The Sublime and Beautiful*, calls the terror of strength, but it does not have grace.

At Peterborough, there is grace abounding, but within essentially the same constructional system. Order, the essence of architecture, has been imposed on brute power. Of course much time has passed; the work began in 1118 and, taking one section at a time, proceeded at the rough medieval average of 10 feet of height a year. The medieval practice was almost invariably to work from east to west, so that the chancel, the operative heart of a church, could be finished and functioning first. The nave thus dates from about 1150 and was finished in the 1170s – a whole century after the basic design of the St Albans orderings – at a time when England was on the verge of the Gothic.

Each bay, then, runs through the whole repertoire of Romanesque decorative language, as expressed in varieties of column, clustered columns, colonettes and piers; in the groupings of columns, single at the arcade level, double at the gallery, triple at the clerestory; in the exploitation of the capital, simple, adorned with scallops or volutes, even animal carvings; and in the multiplicity of mouldings, some plain, some decorated with dog-tooth and chevrons, features which are echoed in the relief diapering in the tympana at the gallery level. Much thought and great skill has gone into the assembling and deployment of this decorative language, into the ratios of the three storeys, and into the proportion of column, arch and space within each. The effect is complex and dense but restful; and lean – here, the quality of the stone helps. Once this masterfully proportioned and ingenious bay design had been conceived, not only the original architect, but one and perhaps two successors had the faith to stick to it throughout the whole gestation period of the church; the variations they perform on it add interest without undermining the integrity of the matrix.

Moreover, and this is what makes Peterborough so rare, the basic Norman

OPPOSITE Peterborough Cathedral, looking west from the east end, showing the fifteenth-century chancel vault.

structure of the church has never been altered, so we still get the same impact as the architect intended in the twelfth century: the pulsing, numbing, almost overwhelming repetition of the bay design, as we move from west to east, through the great trudging length of the church, more than twenty bays in all from West Front to square apse. And over the great ten-bay nave there is another rare survival: the original wooden ceiling, painted about 1220, a little canted and in lozenge patterns, a glowing, subdued sky, inhabited by monsters and saints, musicians and animals, kings, queens and – a poignant and proud touch – an architect with his L-square and dividers.

The transepts also have painted wooden ceilings, and over the chancel there is a fifteenth-century vaulted ceiling, a sort of imitation in wood of a complex stone vault, immensely rich and elaborate, gilded, painted and adorned with splendid bosses. To complete the total effect of decorated wood over stone Romanesque arch, the great crossing tower also has a spectacular vaulted wooden ceiling. Here, it is true, there is an element of deception; the original central tower was taken down in the fourteenth century, being rebuilt in Decorated style, and it was refabricated entirely in the 1880s using the old materials. But the basic scheme remains; in essence, the crossing tower, like the whole church, is directly related to grim old St Albans; but what a range is covered in that relationship, from hoary forbear to elegant scion!

Where the basic scheme of Peterborough has been changed, the beauty and interest of this fine building have been enhanced. One of the last of the medieval abbots, Robert Kirkton (reigned 1496–1528), created a new retrochoir – that is, the back part of the eastern arm which lies behind the high altar – which effectively continues the aisles in the form of an ambulatory, but at the width of the nave. These important spaces were used in the late Middle Ages for church courts and other solemn functions, and great care was taken with their decoration. Abbot Kirkton hired a leading architect (John Harvey suggests it may have been John Wastell, who did the vaulting of King's College, Cambridge) to design a magnificent fan-vault, which floats and writhes above the Perpendicular windows. Of course, the concept of this high and airy stone *salon* is far removed from the Romanesque bulk of the church: but the two are related in that both represent terminations of a style, so that, moving from west to east, one travels through a masterpiece of the refinement of the early Middle Ages, to emerge into a final comment on its last stage – two exercises in sophistication.

What is more, by a combination of accident and inspired improvization, this great cathedral has been provided with an architectural prologue of stunning theatrical power. The English cathedral designers never seem to have reached agreement about what to do with the main entrance of the west front; it is one respect in which they are less successful than the French, or at any rate less consistent. The long English nave could not simply terminate in a mere cross-section. The instinct was to provide a western transept, crowned with towers. Where this instinct was followed with confidence, as at Ely and Wells, it produced (as we shall see) masterpieces. Where there was hesitation, compromise, a change of plan, the result was muddle: an architectural equivalent of the classical military triad – order, counter-order, disorder.

The history of the west end at Peterborough is very complicated. It has four distinct historical stages, which have been elucidated by scholars and set out in the appropriate volume of the *Victoria County History*. Remnants of each stage were left to confuse the next, so that one of an original pair of Norman west

OPPOSITE The fan-vaulting in the retrochoir at Peterborough.

Norwich Cathedral seen
from the east.

towers (with a thirteenth-century top) peeps lopsidedly over the later façade. The
whole is redeemed by the bold decision to impose three giant niches, inspired by a
somewhat earlier experiment at Lincoln, which dominate the front. Unlike
Lincoln, the central niche is narrower than the two lateral ones, and a
superimposed Perpendicular porch at the bottom of it mars the effect.
Nevertheless, the fact that these enormous recesses are a whole bay deep
produces a startling effect of relief and chiaroscuro; the impression is theatrical –
stone scenery which cannot be inspected too closely if it is to retain its credibility,
but whose initial impact is startling. All the more so, since this thundering
operatic set leads one into a church whose keynote is serenity and equipoise.

At Peterborough, the contrast between the general fury and activity at the west
end, and the general placidity of the dull external silhouette (much less noble than
at St Albans, though essentially the same) reminds us that the earlier the
construction, the more the architect conceived the design from the inside and
worked outwards. By this I mean that he had to meet certain liturgical and
ideological requirements on the inside, and since his methods of enclosing in
stone the space thus required were limited, the resulting arrangements appeared
from the outside to be very much a secondary consideration. As his means and
mastery improved, he paid more regard to the desire to create epic scenery in
stone. Hence the features which give drama and excitement to the silhouette are
usually later embellishments of a simple and strictly functional trunk.

The point is well made by Norwich. The shape which now leaps towards us
across the ancient town roofs and under the enormous frame of the East Anglian
sky is without comparison: immensely long, but also tall and graceful. The
fundamental architectural concept of Norwich, a long nave and choir, and a
towering central feature, was ambitious from the start. The Romanesque or
Norman tower, finished in about 1145, was the tallest in England. Originally, of
course, it was equipped with a wooden spire. In 1362 this was blown down in a
storm, carrying with it much of the tower stonework. So much of it had to be

34

replaced that the design was changed, the angle-turrets being decorated with reed-shafts, to enhance the sense of vertical thrust. A century later, in 1490, the present stone spire was added. What we see today, then, is a late-medieval vertical based on a Norman horizontal.

Norwich has strong claims to be ranked among the finest half-dozen of Britain's cathedrals. As a monastic cathedral priory it was a Norman creation and effectively the work of one man, Bishop Herbert Losinga. The old Anglo-Saxon cathedral of East Anglia had been at Elmham. William I adopted the policy that cathedrals must be placed in substantial towns, and in 1075 the see was moved to Thetford. When Herbert Losinga was given the bishopric by William II (by simony, so the canons of Thetford claimed) he moved it to Norwich, turned the establishment into a monastic priory, and began building the new cathedral in 1096. The church was consecrated in 1101, which means the choir must have been finished by then, and by the time of Losinga's death in 1119 the transepts and the eastern bays of the nave had been added.

Norwich, then, is essentially an early twelfth-century church. It emphasizes an important characteristic of the Norman version of Romanesque design. The Norman style, both functionally and in intention, usually stressed brute strength, durability and mass – what one might call the masculine principle – but it was also, on occasion, adapted to stress line, form and dexterity – the feminine principle. While St Albans, and still more Durham, epitomize Norman masculinity, Norwich conveys an impression of feminine grace. It is not easy to discover exactly why this should be so. The nave, with its fourteen bays, is the longest in England, and in many respects is in its original state; the crossing, too, is still lit by the original lantern, a great rarity. However, the first architect, instead of stressing the strength and rotundity of the nave columns (as at Durham), chose instead to point to their height by adorning the surface of the piers with slender attached columns and narrow vaulting-shafts which soar up to the roof. The aisles are low, with primitive Norman groin-vaulting, but the triforium is high, supporting a well-lit clerestory. So, as with the exterior, where long, low nave and high spire contrast, there is an exciting struggle for mastery between the emphatic vertical and horizontal lines.

The architect who worked for Bishop Lyhard in the fifteenth century when the stone spire was added took up the challenge of his Norman predecessor and, without changing the basic interior ordinance of the nave, replaced its wooden roof with one of the most splendid lierne vaults in Christendom, which sits easily on the nave walls and adds dramatically to their upsurge of vertical energy. The light pours in through the clerestory windows set between the cones of the vault; and to bring in yet more light, the fifteenth-century architect punched holes in the external Norman walls of the nave, extending the narrow, Romanesque into elegant Perpendicular glass walls. From the outside, this looks a little disorderly, for of the four storeys of openings, all the third and parts of the fourth are Perpendicular, and the rest are Norman. Inside, however, the Norman ordinance locks impeccably into the fifteenth-century vault and one is only half-conscious of the fact that, for a twelfth-century nave, the light is unusually abundant. It creates the effect of a sunlit forest glade culminating in the light and shade of its vault-canopy, which we normally expect to find only in a fifteenth-century nave (as at Canterbury). Yet, looked at in another way, the immense length of the nave gives a powerful tunnelling effect (especially at twilight) which only the Romanesque can create. Hence, with its paradoxical use of horizontal and

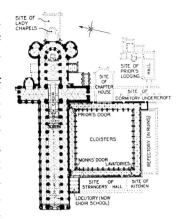

NORWICH

The lierne vault over the nave at Norwich.

vertical stress, Norwich gets the best of both worlds, and this is the key to its interior magic.

In addition, the cathedral has one outstanding architectural virtue, which enables the splendours of the long, well-lit nave to act merely as an extensive prolegomenon to a theatrical choir. The choir at Norwich is one of the very few in England to be crowned with a chevet-apse of three projecting twelfth-century chapels (one of them replaced in the present century). The amount of light admitted within by the windows and arches of the arcade and triforium stages of the apse is itself remarkable for a twelfth-century cathedral. At the end of the fourteenth century, when the wooden spire fell in and smashed part of the chancel roof, the clerestory stage was rebuilt, in a most delicate yet confident fashion, the late-Decorated fretwork silhouette marrying itself smoothly to the generous arches below, with the additional merit of letting in yet more light. This rounded apse, therefore, seen from within, provides an elegant and impressive climax to the church, giving the high altar a noble setting. Seen from without, however, the chevet-apse is still more unusual for an English cathedral because when the wooden roofs of the choir and transepts were replaced by stone vaults in the late fifteenth and early sixteenth centuries, it was necessary to support the stone skeleton below it with flying buttresses. This adds a flavour of Continental spice to its very English external outline, so that the cathedral can be compared to a low, raking stone ship, with its solitary high mast, anchored to its setting by the tethers of its buttresses.

To sum up, Norwich is a Norman cathedral, extensively altered at the end of the fourteenth century and at the very close of the medieval period. The harmony of its parts, and the unity of its impact on the visitor – nothing seems anachronistic or out of place – testify to the skill and tenderness with which late-medieval architects could complement the work of their predecessors even at a distance of three or four hundred years. East Anglia, of course, has a consistently high record of artistic achievement over more than a millenium, and Norwich Cathedral is superbly finished, furnished and embellished throughout, the hundreds of roof bosses being particularly varied and fine, from three distinct periods. It also has one of the largest and best-preserved sets of cloisters in England. The original twelfth-century cloisters were wrecked in a riot by the citizens of Norwich in 1272. They were gradually replaced in three main stages: the east walk (1297–1318), the west walk, over virtually the whole of the second half of the fourteenth century, and the north walk (1410–1430). The square as a whole seems homogenous, but a study of the details reveals a miniature history of English architecture, from the first phase of the Decorated to full-blooded Perpendicular. Here again, the multitude of roof bosses are of superb quality and invention (more than a hundred linked scenes from the Apocalypse) and add to Norwich's reputation for being the most consistently and luxuriously adorned of British cathedrals.

Norwich is a big cathedral: 407 feet long, with the top of its stone spire 315 feet from the ground, but it does not look big. It looks spare and elegant, tall and stylish. Unlike most Romanesque buildings, it does not give the impression of using two stone blocks where one would do – quite the contrary. Like a beautiful woman, it has no spare flesh. This effect is created in part, of course, by the late-medieval work. But in all essentials, and in many of its details, Norwich is a concept of the late-eleventh century: what we see is not so very different from what old Bishop Losinga conjured up in his mind's eye when he first got seisin

OPPOSITE The late fifteenth-century spire of Norwich Cathedral, seen from the cloisters.

37

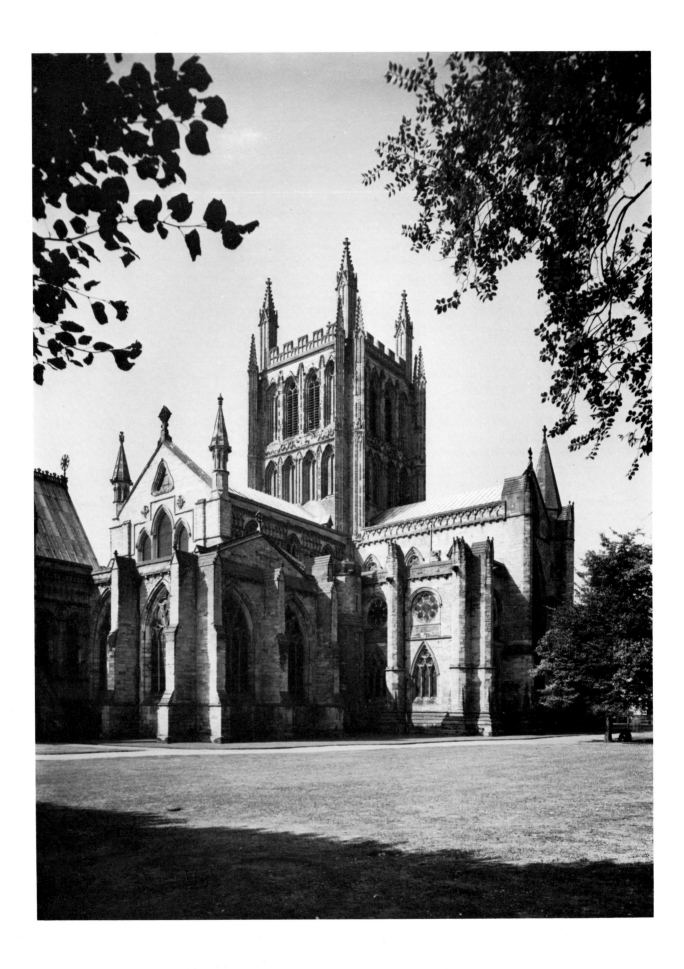

from Rufus, less than thirty years after Hastings. No work conveys to us more surely the ability of English medieval craftsmen to maintain the essence of a style over five centuries.

Hereford Cathedral has an even better Norman pedigree than Norwich, but the building we see today is very different. To put it brutally, there are lucky cathedrals (like Norwich) and there are unlucky ones; Hereford has had a most unfortunate and lamentable history. Herbert Losinga's elder brother, Robert, obtained the see in 1079 from the Conqueror, some years after the Saxon cathedral had been 'utterly burned' by the Welsh. Hereford was a key point in England's most active military frontier and remained a fortress town until the end of the Middle Ages. It was part of one of those 'development zones' which the Cistercian pioneers eagerly exploited in the first half of the twelfth century, and the new cathedral church, built in the early decades of the century, shows marked affinities with the Cistercian foundation of Abbey Dore, not far away. So it is not 'pure' Norman. True, the eastern wall of the south transepts, with its primitive wall-arcading and tiny triforium, suggests the reign of the Conqueror or Rufus; so do the compound piers, which are strikingly bulky in relation to the space enclosed by the nave. But the pillars, crowned with coniferous cappings and equipped with coupled shafts, reflect the colonization by the Cistercians of the English west in the twelfth century. If the cathedral was started by Robert Losinga, Bishop Reynelm, who held the see from 1107 to 1115, is described as the *'fundator'*; Bishop Robert of Bethune completed the work and was buried in the cathedral in 1148. In the later Middle Ages, Hereford had some notable bishops, all of whom made extensive changes or additions to the fabric: William de Vere, credited with the Early English Lady Chapel; Aquablanca, who rebuilt the north transept in the mid-thirteenth century, where he lies in a Geometrical-style canopied tomb; Thomas de Cantilupe, the last Englishman canonized in Rome before the Reformation; his chaplain and successor Richard Swinfield; and Adam of Orleton, who built the central tower from the offerings left at Cantilupe's shrine.

So, although Hereford is rightly classed as a Norman building, a fact made inescapable by the massive piers of the nave, not much Norman work remains in its original form, and it has features from almost every period up to the twentieth century. The most prominent Norman survival is the south transept, with its triple arcading. Acquablanca's north transept, by contrast, is a notable exercise in the Geometrical style of the late thirteenth century (1250–68), a piece of mannerist design which must have looked startling when it was built and is still regarded by some as the best feature of the church. The main arches of the arcade are virtually triangular, as are the triforium arches above, each with three pierced quatrefoils, and above them in the clerestory are circular windows within round arches. This is an intellectual exercise in compass-work, carried by its logic beyond the point of aesthetic tolerance (to my mind) and thus generating unease. On the other hand, the windows, though equally based on a strict Geometrical design, are tall, slender and wholly successful. The transept is an example of both the virtues and the limitations of a style based on the theme of triangles and circles, and repays careful attention if only by showing how risky extreme fashion can be.

By contrast, Orleton's central tower meets with general approval as one of the best towers in England. It is big, but not too big for this smallish cathedral; it is sturdy and strong, yet at the same time graceful. It belongs to the first quarter of

The Geometrical bay design in the north transept at Hereford.

OPPOSITE The north-eastern side of Hereford Cathedral, showing the fourteenth-century central tower.

the fourteenth century and so is covered in ball-flower ornamentation, then very fashionable. Unfortunately, Hereford Cathedral, like others in the West and North-West (Chester, Carlisle, Lichfield, for example) is built of sandstone, which has worn badly. Much of the original fabric has been drastically renewed. Where the ball-flower carving is not crumbling it is new; the pinnacles are modern. The tower is not what it seems.

Nor are other parts of the cathedral. The two-storeyed north porch, a fine example of late Perpendicular, conceals an earlier, crumbling porch. The original Norman east end was pulled down and replaced by a retrochoir, forming an ambulatory two bays deep, and a Lady Chapel, dating from 1220–40, retains most of its original decoration, which is fine though a little over-rich, but the retrochoir was largely rebuilt by Lewis Cottingham in the 1840s.

Originally, Hereford had a tower over its west front. This collapsed in 1786, causing extensive damage to the nave. The Dean and Chapter then took the decision to rebuild the west front completely, and reconstruct all of the nave above the first storey, reducing it by one bay in the process. This calamitous scheme was definitely decided on before James Wyatt was called in to carry it out. He cannot, therefore, be blamed for the demolition involved, more extensive than in any other medieval cathedral. The Early English triforium and clerestory which he placed above the Norman piers are unobtrusive; all the same, the nave is essentially a false superstructure on true foundations. Moreover, the Wyatt campaign was only a prelude to further massive changes and restorations under Cottingham in the 1840s (crossing, chancel, Lady Chapel, retrochoir), Sir George Gilbert Scott in the 1850s and 1860s, and his son J. Oldrid Scott around the turn of the century. The Scotts spent much of their time re-doing Wyatt's work, and the present West Front, unmistakably late Victorian, is entirely the work of the younger Scott. Hereford is thus the ghost of a Norman cathedral, although a fairly substantial ghost.

The process of change continues. George Gilbert Scott adorned the choir with a fine mid-Victorian 'art metalwork' screen, containing 11,200 lbs of iron, 5,000 lbs of copper and brass, 300 semi-precious stones and over 50,000 individual pieces of mosaic. This masterpiece of mid-Victorian applied art aroused growing hatred in the inter-war and post-war period and it was finally removed in 1967, just at the time when such artefacts were beginning to find admirers again. There is clearly a strong case for undoing other aspects of the 'restoration' done between the 1780s and 1920 – and perhaps an even stronger case for letting well alone.

Indeed, the uneasy architectural history of Hereford is, in some respects, as complicated as that of, say, St John Lateran or the Church of the Holy Sepulchre. The documentation is scarce, too. Whereas at Norwich some 3,500 rolls of accounts have survived from the period between the twelfth and sixteenth centuries, allowing us to chart the growth of the cathedral (with some gaps) in minute detail, at Hereford we cannot even be sure in which century the first stone of the present cathedral was laid, and there is heated argument among the architectural historians about the first half-century of its existence.

In a way this adds to the interest of the church; it is a patchwork quilt of stone which positively invites the visitor to engage in historical detective work. I myself calculate that it is composed of a score or more distinct periods, from the eleventh to the seventeenth century – no building in our legacy bears so many different thumb-prints of time. And if Hereford has been unlucky in its fabric, it

OPPOSITE Hereford Cathedral nave.

40

nevertheless contains some fine and unusual things. It has more brasses than any other English cathedral, including a real masterpiece commemorating Bishop Trilleck (died 1360); a fine throne and choirstalls of the fourteenth century; a rare chained library, housed over the eastern aisle of the north transept; the famous *Mappa Mundi* or world map, which dates from 1290 and is the outstanding example of English medieval cosmography; some superb thirteenth-century stained glass in the Lady Chapel; and a notable collection of medieval tomb-monuments.

Moreover, though Hereford Cathedral has no close, properly speaking, and is hemmed in by the town rather like a big parish church (it is 360 feet long with a height of 165 feet), it possesses much of its fifteenth-century Bishop's Cloister; the remains of a Chapter House which probably had the earliest fan-vault in England (earlier even than Gloucester's); a college for the vicars-choral which is full of unusual features and more complete than any other we possess, except those at Wells and Windsor; and a fine Perpendicular gatehouse to the (restored) Bishop's Palace, which itself encases a Great Hall of the late twelfth century. Finally, there are the remains of the original bishop's chapel, built by Robert Losinga himself before 1095 and perhaps the oldest building in the entire precinct. In short, one can spend a great deal of time examining this group of buildings, and probe deeply into the history of the medieval church – an example of the richness which even one of the smaller cathedrals, not favoured by time and chance, can provide.

In fact the smaller cathedrals, especially those of early foundation like Chichester and Rochester, are among the most interesting. Chichester, for instance, although not intrinsically a masterpiece, contrives to look like one. In its exposed setting on the Sussex coast, with the backdrop of the Downs, it is the only significant building for miles around. Its spire tends to dominate its surroundings, as does that of Salisbury, or the spire which it most resembles, Norwich, though it is actually much smaller than either. Indeed, the tower and spire convey a false impression of the church that lies beneath. The original Norman tower, which had a wooden spire, was wrecked by a storm in 1210. The tower we see is a thirteenth century construction, and the spire was added two hundred years later; it telescoped itself in 1861, and was reconstructed, as a replica, by Sir George Gilbert Scott.

Underneath is a sturdy and even primitive Norman building. The old Saxon cathedral was in Selsey, and the see was shifted to Chichester by the Conqueror. Ralph de Luffa, who became bishop in 1091, built the church, though construction continued throughout the twelfth century, interrupted by two fires, one in 1114 and a much more devasting one in 1187. This left only the shell of the Norman church, but the reconstruction stuck to the original design, except at the east end. The eight-bay nave, transepts, crossing and the first three bays of the choir are entirely Norman. The nave is unique, for it has five aisles, rather like some of the later Gothic cathedrals in Spain, or the German *hallekirch* or hallchurch, but these were not part of Luffa's plan, being formed out of discarded side-chapels in the thirteenth century. What was essential to the original design was the heavy, dark solemnity of the main piers, which give the cathedral interior its special cavernous look. If you stand at the west end the nave piers look more like continuous walling than separate constructions; they are, in fact, sections of walling, their ends faced with masonry to form jambs for the arches over them. This brutal and elementary scheme is, however, relieved by two features: the triforium is beautifully designed in pairs of rounded openings within containing

OPPOSITE Chichester Cathedral from the south east.

42

A detail from the twelfth-century sculptured panel at Chichester showing the raising of Lazarus.

arches, and during the reconstruction after the great fire, columns of Purbeck marble were inserted at the corners of the main piers. The result, then, is much less oppressive than it might have been, especially with strong sunlight pouring through the high round arches of the clerestory.

All the same, this is unquestionably a Norman church, and any doubts as to the general flavour of the post-Conquest building are resolved by the presence, in the south aisle of the choir, of two magnificent sculptured panels, carved from Purbeck limestone, which once formed part of the twelfth-century choir-screen (parts of a third panel are in the cathedral library). They depict Christ and his disciples, Martha and Mary, and the raising of Lazarus. They are well preserved apart from the paint and the coloured stones used for the eyes, which are missing; but their primitive stiffness, which goes fittingly with the brutality of the nave piers, led to a much earlier dating until it was conclusively established that they belong to the second quarter of the twelfth century. Evidently the rest of the screen perished in the fire of 1187, and this was one feature of the old church the rebuilders could not reproduce.

They did, however, manage to soften, enhance and beautify the harsh lines of the old structure in many ways. At the west end, an elementary transept-front was turned into two squat towers, which add a powerful dignity to the cathedral without in any way upstaging the central tower and spire. More important, they transformed the east end of the church. Though the first three bays of the choir are, in essentials, the old Norman design, the retrochoir behind the high altar screen was rebuilt to house the feretory of St Richard of Chichester, bishop from 1245–53, whose shrine was now an object of pilgrimage. It is in the Transitional style, that is the point at which Norman, the English version of the Continental Romanesque, began to give way to a form of Gothic. The two bays of the retrochoir have central pillars, with Purbeck shafts at the corners, and Purbeck clustered shafts are also effectively used at the triforium level. The arches are both rounded and pointed, but the incisiveness of the mouldings and the quantity and quality of the foliate carving on the capitals mark the beginnings of the Early English style. An arch at the east end leads directly into the Lady Chapel, which begins with the original Norman design, but then leaps into the Decorated of the 1300s, adding leaf-carvings not much inferior to the famous ones at Southwell, with an elaborate tierceron vault overhead. As for the nave itself, it is further lightened by a splendid perpendicular stone screen. What we have, then, at Chichester, is essentially a grim piece of Norman muscle-architecture, softened and embellished by the cosmetic surgery of the later Middle Ages.

A cathedral has to be seen in its setting, and this is a rule which applies to Chichester more than to most places. There is the outer setting of the landscape, which makes the spire seem so spectacular; and there is the inner setting of the town, one of the most agreeable in England. It is quintessentially a cathedral town, even more so than Salisbury or Lincoln, for the cathedral's own collection of satellite buildings is outstanding. To begin with, it has its detached bell-tower or campanile. These were once common, for they eased the appalling problems of building a central crossing tower by relieving it of the weight of the bells. As architectural skills increased, they lost their function, and when high enough tended to distract the eye from the cathedral itself. So they were pulled down, one of the last being Salisbury's, demolished in the 1790s; Chichester's is the only survivor in a cathedral close.

Actually, to speak of a close is perhaps too pretentious. What Chichester possesses is not a town-within-a-town, as at Salisbury, so much as an informal cluster of ecclesiastical bits and pieces. The most prominent is a fine Perpendicular cloister, set up by a Wykehamist dean around 1400 which, most unusually, has a timber rather than a stone vault. Then there is the Bishop's Palace, a comfortable muddle of medieval flint and eighteen-century brick, but with a business-like fourteenth-century gatehouse, plainly built for defensive purposes. Its thirteenth-century chapel survives, as does another thirteenth-century building which housed the royal chaplains; and the square kitchen has a remarkable Gothic roof, a masterpiece of Sussex carpentry, which some date at the thirteenth century also. The rest of the medieval buildings, including a Vicar's Close, the houses of residential canons, another chapel, a chantry and a gateway, have been constructively restored in the eighteenth and nineteenth centuries. This does not matter, for they fit into the atmosphere of Chichester, which is strongly opposed to the tyrannical purity of period, and favours instead comfort, adaptability and usefulness. The result is remarkably homogenous; nothing in the cathedral or its surroundings jars or is out of place, and it is the sense of aptitude, of belonging, which makes a visit to Chichester so restful.

Rochester is another Norman cathedral of great individual character, though it suffers from handicaps of which Chichester is mercifully free. To begin with, it is overshadowed, and always has been, by the massive outline of the city's stone keep, the largest and strongest of all the great square keeps built in England in the twelfth century. It is a mere shell, but the outer walls are virtually intact and the stunning impression they make on the visitor inevitably pushes the cathedral, which nestles below, into second place. The cathedral site, too, is constricted, and its successive architects have always been frustrated by the shortage of space, and the need to think small. Of course Rochester is a small see, founded immediately after Canterbury in 604, and in some ways is an appendix to it. There were probably two Saxon cathedrals on this site, but in 1077 Lanfranc, the Conqueror's masterful Archbishop of Canterbury, gave one of his leading followers, Gundulf, the job of reorganizing the see, turning the secular chapter into a monastic priory, and building a new cathedral.

Gundulf was described by contemporaries as a great builder, who knew all about architecture, and he certainly designed some of the Conqueror's castles. Not much of his church, however, remains visible, except for the tower, originally a detached belfry, which juts out incongruously at an angle between the two transepts. Much of his nave is encased in later stone, for building work on the church continued throughout the twelfth century, although interrupted by fires. Then, in 1201, the cathedral had a stroke of fortune, when a pious and charitable baker from Perth, on a pilgrimage to the tomb of St Thomas at Canterbury, was robbed and murdered in Rochester. William of Perth was not canonized for another fifty years, but his cult became instantly famous and pilgrims took in the shrine of St William as part of their visit to Canterbury. The proceeds enabled the monks to rebuild all the east end, in a version of Early English style derived from Canterbury, though the shortage of space forced them to confine the choir to a two-storey design.

All the same, Rochester looks Norman, largely because it retains (or perhaps one should say has recovered) its Norman West Front, which is the outstanding feature of the building. True Norman fronts are rare (Norwich and St Davids are other examples), and Rochester has the added distinction of retaining the original sculpture of the main doorway, Christ in Majesty presiding over angels, apostles

and evangelists – a modest English version of the great west door of Chartres. The essence of the Norman-type west front is a combination of sculpture and arcading, with turrets as vertical and lateral punctuation. The original scheme was drastically altered in the fifteenth century, when a vast Perpendicular window was inserted in the centre of the west wall; curiously enough, this does not matter, since the serried verticals of the window echo the endless narrow pilasters of the arcading, and the uninstructed visitor can be forgiven for thinking that the whole front was designed by a single mind. In fact most of the front was cunningly restored by J.L. Pearson in the 1880s, using an engraving of 1655 which gives its medieval appearance. Equally, the low central tower and squat spire, which are in harmony with the cathedral's general low profile and Norman origin, and which do not detract from the West Front, its principal glory, are modern reconstructions (using seventeenth-century prints) by Hodgson Fowler in 1904–5. Much of the stonework throughout the cathedral is the work either of Lewis Cottingham in the 1820s or Sir George Gilbert Scott, in the 1870s.

Yet the extensive restoration is, on the whole, sensitive and unobtrusive, and should not be allowed to spoil our enjoyment of this ancient and honourable church, which is crowded with pleasing detail and hoarded treasure. It has, for instance, a magnificent crypt, one of the best in England. It is only part-Norman, because it was rebuilt and extended at the time of the Early English reconstruction of the east end, and it could be considered to be the only cathedral crypt we possess which is truly Gothic. It has none of the sculptural glories of the Canterbury crypt but it is well lit and the functional beauty of its vaults and columns produces the woodland glade effect which the medieval eye so enjoyed (in marked contrast to a similar, but much earlier and clumsier design at Hereford).

OPPOSITE The Norman West Front of Rochester.

LEFT The Gothic crypt at Rochester.

Another delight at Rochester is provided by the doorway which opens from the south transept into the old Chapter Room. It is a splendid example of what I call English fourteenth-century Baroque. In inspiration it resembles the Prior's Door at Norwich, which opens into the cloisters and has seven figures pinned to the arch, each with its own gable, and alternating ogees and arches. The Norwich door has been dated *c.* 1310; the Rochester door is plainly a little later and its figures, which are much more gracefully carved, go up, one above the other, and include standing representations of the Church and the Synagogue, one of the most popular contrasts of the Middle Ages.

This sculpture, like so much else at Rochester, has traces of strong French influence. Thus the approach to the choir, through the choir screen, is over a French-type *perron*, or stepped platform, and the vault above is a French 'ploughshare', quite rare in England. On the other hand, the nave is deliberately low and very un-French, making a virtue of the lack of vertical space by the wide spacing of the main piers, which opens up vistas into the aisles and creates an effect of horizontal distance. Rochester, in fact, is a difficult cathedral to invest with a salient character, partly because so much has been swept away by time, religious passion and the restorer's hand. Nothing except a marble slab remains of the once spectacular shrine of St William; there are only ghostly fragments of the old monastic buildings, which once housed a community of sixty monks, and the decorative glories of the church have largely perished.

Yet valuable fragments remain. Rochester has a portion of its thirteenth-century choir-stalls, a great rarity; and, more important, extensive traces of its once-magnificent wall-paintings. These are to be found both in the crypt and the choir, where a striking thirteenth-century figure of Fortune stands within her revolving wheel, from which a king is about to be toppled while others climb the spokes. The most significant survival at Rochester, however, is its ancient library of 116 volumes. The library was first formed in 1082 and contains several volumes in Anglo-Saxon. The key to it is the rare and beautiful *Textus Roffensis*, which dates from the episcopate of Enrulf, 1115–24, with some later editions of *c.* 1130, and which is the oldest catalogue of books in England. There is a second catalogue of 1203, and together these manuscripts open important windows into the eleventh and twelfth centuries and, not least, into the study of Anglo-Saxon law. The Rochester library underlines the fact that, until the rise of Oxford in the thirteenth century, the cathedrals, especially those with large monastic chapters, were the principal – indeed, if we include with them the greater abbeys, virtually the only – depositories of learning and centres of culture in the entire country.

The point is brought home strikingly by the preeminence of Durham in the English north-east. Of course, there was nothing unusual or unprecedented in Benedictine monks creating a cultural forcing-house on the very fringe of the known world: they had done so in Iona in the seventh century, and in Northumbria in the eighth. As part of his settlement of the north, the Conqueror decided to create a formidable concentration of civil, ecclesiastical and military power at the monastery of Durham which, turned almost into an island by a great horseshoe bend in the River Wear, is a natural site for a fortress-church. Since 995 it had also been a shrine, enclosing the body of St Cuthbert, the seventh-century saint, the subject of a famous *Life* by Bede. St Cuthbert was the chief object of veneration in the whole of the English north. St Cuthbert's body had been kept in a variety of places until the monks decided that the bend in the Wear was the safest. There, a Saxon 'white church' was built, enclosing the shrine, as the centre

The fourteenth-century doorway at Rochester leading from the south transept into the old Chapter Room.

OPPOSITE The view up into the central tower of St Albans.

PAGES 50–51 Watercolour by William Daniell of Durham Cathedral towering above the river Wear.

48

of a secular convent. What the Conqueror did was to appoint a bishop with orders to turn the convent into a regular Benedictine establishment, liberally endowed, the bishop being, in addition, a great lay and military lord, entrusted with Palatine powers and ample landed resources to hold the northern frontier and enforce feudal discipline across a vast stretch of territory. The bishop-abbot and his prior (effectively the dean of the cathedral) were thus exceptionally wealthy men, with the means to give expression to their faith in man-made stone cliffs.

This was the local situation; but we must also bear in mind the Normans as a Continental force. The years 1093–1133, during which Durham Cathedral, in all essentials, was built, coincided almost exactly with the apogee of Norman power, not only in England but in France and the Mediterranean. During this period, more large-scale buildings were being erected in England than anywhere else in the world; they included a number of Benedictine and Cistercian abbeys, as well as a dozen or more cathedrals, scores of stone castles, and great secular buildings such as Rufus's magnificent Westminster Hall. Continental craftsmen and designers crowded into England, where work was plentiful and the pay high, where new quarries were being opened up, and where a servile multitude was available for heavy, unskilled labour.

In 1088, the Bishop of Durham, William of St Calais, quarrelled with the new king, Rufus, and was sent into exile in France for alleged treason. He spent three years there, and had the opportunity to examine some of the latest abbey-churches and cathedrals in Normandy and the Ile de France. There he seems to have conceived of the idea of a gigantic new cathedral, made possible by the concentration of wealth and resources in the Durham Palatinate. On his return in 1093 he demolished the Saxon church, and the foundation stone of the new cathedral was laid the next year.

Durham was conceived as a whole and built according to the original idea over a period of forty years. Its site overlooking the Wear is without parallel in Western Europe. There is no building to compete with it for attention, and the

OPPOSITE ABOVE Part of the West Front of Peterborough Cathedral, showing the superimposed Perpendicular porch at the bottom of the central niches.

OPPOSITE BELOW A detail of the cloister door at Norwich.

Durham Cathedral from the north.

other medieval structures which surround it – the Bishop's Palace, the castle and the ancient houses of the city – serve merely to draw attention to its majestic supremacy and to complete the architectural composition of which it is the unquestioned centre. Durham, indeed, shows that the Normans, at their most audacious and expansive, were capable of building on a scale never attempted since the Romans.

But of course the Normans did not possess the building technology of the Romans, and in particular they did not have their ability to combine brickwork and concrete to span huge areas; and it is the Norman effort to close this gap in their architectural skills which gives Durham its paradoxical interest. I say paradoxical because it was conceived, first and foremost, as a supreme exercise in the Norman Romanesque style. William of St Calais wanted to use the form with which he and his generation were familiar to create its apotheosis, and it is true that Durham is the finest of all Romanesque churches. But apotheosis implies change, and the designer, in striving to create the Romanesque on an unprecedented scale, found himself moving deeper and deeper into a new technology which was to render the Romanesque method and aesthetic quite archaic. Hence the paradox: Durham is the archetypal Romanesque cathedral on the grandest scale, yet it contains in its bowels the secret of Gothic.

The liturgical demands of the cathedral meant that it had to be designed from the inside outwards. The dynamic force pushing the designer against the frontiers of his technology was the desire for an ever-larger enclosed space in the middle of the church, coupled with a religious and aesthetic urge to let in more light by building the walls higher and higher. To the early medieval man, the great church was an epitome of his cosmology. It was built in stone, symbolizing eternity; the pillars of its walls upheld the firmament above, in which God dwelt and to which he raised his voice and prayers. The act of worship was an upward motion: the higher the ceiling, the closer the liturgical appeals, which filled it with sound, could come to the heavens where God dwelt; and, equally, the higher the roof, the more detached was the worship from the clayey prison of the earth below. One might say that the medieval cathedral sought height as a symbolic escape.

It was not the timber roof itself which raised problems of height and width: it was the desire to conceal it with a stone ceiling, constituting a firmament, and providing the enclosed space with a satisfying unity of material, texture, colour and, increasingly, decoration – a complete stone cosmos, in fact. Such ceilings could be provided by the primitive device of the barrel-vault and its natural development, the groined vault. The barrel-vault was in use even in the backward west throughout the Dark Ages, and the groined vault became fairly common in the eleventh century in smaller Continental churches (especially in France and the Rhineland), and in the side aisles of larger ones.

At Durham the decision was taken to provide a high stone vault throughout, and this forced the architect to devise a new type of vault, in which a skeleton of ribs was first put up, and then the spaces filled in with a much lighter shell. This had the merit both of cutting down the need for expensive scaffolding and centering-equipment, which was required only for the ribs, and of reducing the enormous weight of stone which the main piers had to carry. The designer was inventing as he went along. He put up the vault, as usual, from east to west, and it is clear that some of the more easterly, and therefore earlier, vaulting proved unsafe and had to be replaced in the thirteenth century. The further the vault moved westwards, the more confident and precise the workmanship becomes,

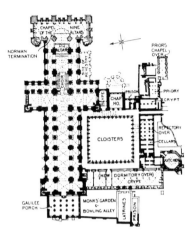

DURHAM

but the designer knew he was moving into unchartered territory. In the barrel vault and its derivatives, the forces created by the weight of the vault move directly downwards and push evenly along the length of the wall. With the rib-vault, the forces move diagonally and outwards, concentrating themselves at the single point where each group of three ribs converges when they meet the wall, and threatening to push it outwards. The designer met this threat by designing a new kind of buttress, a half-arch, built on the outer wall of the aisle, which delivered an inward thrust at the point of the wall where the convergent ribs pushed from the inside. This invention was the flying buttress. It makes its first appearance at Durham, but it was not visible then, nor is it now, because it is covered by the aisle.

The high stone vault involved a further technical innovation. The Romanesque church was essentially a composition of verticals, horizontals and curves. The ribbed vault change this pattern, because the ribs were essential arches, and, although the diagonal ribs were semi-circular, the transverse ribs had to come to a sharp point to reach up to the same height. Thus the pointed arch, in some ways the essence of Gothic, was born of structural necessity.

At Durham then, the engineering was moving decisively in a Gothic direction, and the three innovations – the ribbed vault, the flying buttress and the pointed arch – mark the historic change from an architecture based on sheer strength to one which manipulates rival forces: where the muscle can do no more, the intellect takes over. At the same time, Durham was an exercise in the peculiar conservatism of the English, the desire to conceal change underneath a reassuring habitual skin. The designer, while changing the bones of the cathedral, and giving them a Gothic structure, chose to clothe them in a quite disproportionate amount of Romanesque muscle and flesh.

Inside and out, Durham looks, and was plainly intended to look, more Romanesque than any church based on pure Romanesque engineering. It is by far the most 'Norman' of our cathedrals. In the spectacular nave, what shouts for attention is not the innovatory vault above but the gigantic piers and columns below. They are grouped in twos, each of an alternating pillar and compound pier, which form a 'Great Bay' or duplex bay, of exactly the same strength and width as the supports of the crossing. In other words, the designer adapted the supportive formula used to enclose the space of the crossing to develop the high vault of the nave. By the time he was vaulting the nave, around 1120, he had already designed the concealed flying buttress. Nevertheless he retained the original 1093 design which made the columns and piers enormously powerful, just for the hell of it; or, more likely, because that was how he and his patron wanted them to look.

The pillars are nearly thirty feet high and over seven feet in diameter; their cross-section covers seventeen times the area of the Gothic piers set up at Canterbury in 1175, a generation later, though the weight they carry is roughly the same – an index of the greater efficiency of the Gothic design, pound for pound. They look enormous, bigger than they actually are, and the eye is compelled to return to them again and again, because they are decorated with deep incisions in the four striking patterns: diaper, chevron, flute and spiral. Originally they were even more noticeable, since they were certainly painted and the incisions may even have been filled with gleaming brass.

The high ribbed vault of Durham was not imitated, except at Hereford and Gloucester, as the new technology it unleashed became quickly absorbed in the

OPPOSITE A detail of the north window in the Chapel of the Nine Altars at Durham.

rather different aesthetic aims of the Gothic style. Durham, therefore, can claim to be the only English cathedral which gives complete and detailed expression to all the functioning parts of Romanesque architecture at its best. It is true of course that, seen from afar, Durham, with its enormous and high central tower and its two big western towers, does not look like a Romanesque church. The overwhelming profile which gives it such distinction as a piece of stone landscaping suggests the late Middle Ages. It is also true that, in the twelfth century, the towers would have been lower and equipped with stumpy wooden steeples. The upper reaches of the central tower date from 1460–90; the two western towers are Norman only up to the level of the clerestory in the nave, and all three were equipped with battlements and pinnacles as recently as 1801.

On the other hand, the western towers at least are Norman in conception. They are an integral part of the western transept with which the Norman builders in England often ended their naves – so that the constructional cross-section of the nave and aisles can be faintly seen in the decorative scheme of the West Front. Indeed, the clergy of Durham were so wedded to the Romanesque that when, in the 1170s, it was decided to add a Lady Chapel to the western end, as a kind of narthex, the result – known as the Galilee Chapel – was a superb exercise in late Norman, not early Gothic. Its five aisles of columns are slender (like the columns then being built at the east end of Canterbury) but the arches they support, though richly decorated by chevrons, are firmly rounded and unmistakably in the Romanesque mode.

The windows of this chapel are later insertions, both Decorated and Perpendicular; and, almost inevitably, there are many other later amendments to the Norman structure, especially in the central transept. But only in the east

The late-Norman Galilee Chapel at Durham.

transept is the entire concept post-Norman. The idea of an east transept is rare (it was tried out at Fountains Abbey, and the assumption is that the Durham transept was copied from this Cistercian experiment). Its object was two-fold: to provide east-facing altar-space for the many monks of this rich community – hence its name, the Chapel of the Nine Altars – and to form a sumptuous setting for the shrine of St Cuthbert. Here, the Romanesque unity of the rest of the great church gives place to a dazzling medley of styles. The chapel itself is Early English and dates from the 1240s. Abutting onto it, immediately behind the High Altar, is a magnificent example of late-Decorated sculpture, known as the Neville screen. It was carved in the 1370s, in London, from Caen stone, and brought to Durham by sea, being then equipped with 107 alabaster statues; even without them it is a sensational piece of work. It out-dazzles the meretricious rose-window Wyatt inset underneath the east gable, but not the late fourteenth-century double window of the north wall which, seen at close quarters, is a hair-raising feat of engineering.

What this transept must have looked like at the close of the Middle Ages defies imagination. There is good reason to believe that Durham was the most lavishly decorated of all the great cathedrals, and the Cuthbert shrine was its heart. In 1593 an old man who had been a monk at Durham before the Dissolution wrote an account of life in the monastery called *The Rites of Durham*. He says that the tomb was of gilded green marble, with 'six very fine-sounding bells', and that within the feretory 'were almeries, varnished and finely painted and gilt over with fine little images, for relics belonging to St Cuthbert to lie in; all the costly reliques and jewels that hung about within the said feretory upon the irons being accounted the most sumptuous and rich jewels in all this land.'

All, of course, was swept away in the 1530s. To make matters worse, in Elizabethan times the cathedral fell into the hands not of one but of two successive image-hating deans, who stripped the walls bare. Then, during Cromwell's war against Scotland, the cathedral was filled with 4,000 Scots prisoners who burnt all the furniture and woodwork to keep themselves warm. Durham, too, is built of vulnerable sandstone. The eighteenth-century deans were no better than their Elizabethan predecessors. In 1776 a local architect, George Nicholson, was hired by the chapter to clean up the decaying stonework on the exterior. He scraped no less than four inches off the surface and so removed over 1,000 tons of masonry, including virtually all the original mouldings, at a cost of £30,000. The Dean of the time demolished much of the Chapter House and was barely prevented from destroying the exquisite Gallilee Chapel.

Surprisingly, however, most of the monastic buildings survive and are generally in good condition. They include an enormous monks' dormitory which now houses an excellent collection of the cathedral's treasures. And, although Durham has lost so much, the impact of its twelfth-century grandeur is still overwhelming. No other building erected by the Normans conveys so convincingly the ruthlessness, pride, audacity and burning faith of their race. It is one of the half-dozen greatest artifacts of European Christianity. No photograph or painting can conjure up the ponderous majesty of its presence, which must be seen and experienced by anyone who seeks to understand the truth of monumental architecture. Yet it is, in one sense, a huge anachronism, the end of a long line of architectural development. It is a Romanesque church built with Gothic technology. Gothic was now to escape from under its weighty Romanesque carapace, and emerge as a system of aesthetics in its own right.

3
The Coming of Gothic

o event in architectural history has been more hotly debated than the coming of Gothic. Were its origins utilitarian and structural, or aesthetic? Was its inventor an engineer, or an artist? These questions are related to the problem of defining what Gothic is. Of course we all know it when we see it; but what is its essential characteristic? Is it the ribbed vault, or the pointed arch, or the system of mouldings?

We have seen that Durham embodies the ribbed vault, the pointed arch and the flying buttress, but was still in essence a Romanesque cathedral, and the motive behind its technical innovations was structural, not aesthetic. Certainly, one characteristic of Gothic was its efficiency. For most of the Middle Ages stone was relatively more expensive than labour and at no point more so than in the twelfth century, when the population of Western Europe was expanding fast. The Romanesque compound pier looked stronger than it was, since it had a rubble core. Hence Romanesque towers had a much greater tendency to collapse than later Gothic ones: this happened at Bury (twice), Ely, Beverley, Winchester, Worcester and Hereford. But the Normans learned fast, not least from their ever-growing experience of large-scale military architecture, in England, in France and Spain, the Mediterranean and the Holy Land (where they also came across, of course, the pointed arch in developed form). They discovered that precisely-cut ashlar-blocks, which distributed the weight they had to bear evenly, especially when set in high-grade lime mortar, could safely carry a far greater burden than vast piers of rubble and stone; they also permitted much thinner walls. Thus a building composed entirely of well-cut stone actually used less stone than the massive stone-and-rubble formula. Gothic was, in one sense, merely an accelerated extension of this Norman discovery, which was nothing more than improved craftsmanship.

If this is the answer, then why did not Durham, which was essentially complete by 1133, lead to the rapid development of Gothic in England? In the first quarter of the twelfth century there were more important buildings going up in England than in any other part of Christendom. Then, mysteriously, the technical and artistic lead passed decisively to France, for two generations. Or is it mysterious? In the twenty years after the completion of Durham, England was involved in feudal anarchy, which meant that military architecture took precedence; and even after Henry II established order in the late 1150s, he used the best available designers and craftsmen on a large-scale programme of royal castle-building.

This, however, was not the only explanation. There is strong evidence, not least at Durham, that the English were conservative in taste, albeit innovatory in technique. The French were the reverse. They grasped that the economy of masonry made possible by the Anglo-Norman discoveries could be used to up-end the aesthetic axis of a church. Whereas, in a Romanesque building, one is made almost exultantly conscious of weight, of imponderable downward pressure, in the Gothic one has a distinct sense of upward thrust, of take-off. Sir George Gilbert Scott, who understood its nature better than his detractors allow us to suppose, put it this way: 'Who, while viewing a stately tree in the pride of its growth, ever thinks of its weight or of the pressure of its bows upon the stem? It is with its upwards soaring that the mind is impressed; and just so it is with the Gothic cathedral. The perfection with which all the physical forces are met has to the mind the effect, not merely that they are annihilated, but that they are actually *reversed*'.

OVERLEAF The choir of Canterbury Cathedral, illustrating the 'Canterbury Revolution' and the arrival of Gothic.

Soaring was not the only aesthetic component of Gothic. There was another, related element: the quest for light. If Romanesque cathedrals were dark, this was not a deliberate search for sacred gloom; on the contrary, their designers lit them as well as they could. In the twelfth century, there was much cogitation on the subject of light. The French mystic, Hugh of St Victor, believed there was a special divinity in light. From this it was a short step to seeing a church as a theatre of the numinous. Among Hugh's admirers was Abbot Suger (1081–1151), Abbot of the royal monastery of St Denis from 1122 and virtual ruler of France for two decades. He objected stongly to the view of St Bernard and the early Cistercians that decorative beauty in a church was an offence to God. Though he did not theorize about Gothic he implemented it in his new church at St Denis and, when it was virtually complete, set his reasons down in his *Libellus de consecratione Ecclesiae St Dionysii* (1145). The key to St Denis, the most influential building of its generation, is the eastern arm, where the old Romanesque chevet of separate chapels is merged onto a double ambulatory, so that nothing remains of the chapels save the curved outer wall and window, producing the maximum enlargement of the window surface. Seen from the west, the chancel of the church glows with light from behind an illuminated forest of columns. The rays of light come from all directions and angles and, combined with the new slenderness which pure masonry made possible, make the columns appear to soar, as though weightless. A new kind of aesthetic, the 'Gothic light', had been born.

There was, however, a further element in Gothic: the paramountcy of the moulding. The essence of a classic architecture – that is, one where the needful forms impose their discipline on the individual requirements of a particular building – is the quest for order. The elements of a system of orders have utilitarian origins: a capital to distribute the support of a pillar more widely, a plinth to provide a damp-course, and so forth. But, once evolved, they exert their decorative power with great tenacity.

The Gothic orders evolved from the arch, which is actually built by setting the voussoirs of which it is composed on a temporary wooden centering, which is struck out after the arch has set. As Romanesque developed, the roof of the structure was supported on piers but interior features were carried on the secondary support of columns. This created an inner order of supports, with the arches over them, such as the duplex bay which encloses two smaller ones at Durham. Such features are called 'aedicular', that is 'miniature buildings', and the most common expression of the aedicular is the two-light window or bifora, with its tympanum set back behind the wall-face. The earliest examples in England are the bifora windows in the transepts at Winchester. Once an inner order had been developed, much centering could be saved, as each order acted as centering for the one over it, just as the development of the ribbed vaults saved centering for the shell between them. A perfectly logical development allowed the central baluster of the early two-light windows to develop into the colonette of mature Romanesque, with a quatrefoil in its tympanum, and so into the moulded mullion of Gothic, the quatrefoil expanding into a third light.

At the same time, the system of ordered moulding was developing its own artistic momentum. The moulding was utilitarian in origin but it was quickly adapted to conceal the crude stuctural realities. The basis of every moulding has been defined as the quirk, that is a groove cut into the stonework next to an angle, matched by another parallel quirk, the angle they form then being smoothed into a curve. When the Gothic designer was faced with an aedicular feature in a blank wall, whether window, doorway, blank arch or niche, he immediately began to anchor it into the wall by a system of mouldings, which swept up one side and down the other. Equally, the Romanesque support, whether compound pier or ordered arch, was invaded by the moulding system, which turned the pier into the typical Gothic clustered pillar. The support system and the aedicules were then bound together aesthetically, as they already were structurally, by a single (if enormously complicated) set of mouldings, so that flat surfaces virtually disappeared and each bay was a unified design. In this respect, Gothic was an architectural system of detail, rather than a single constructional or aesthetic principle.

But whatever Gothic was, elements of it had begun to make their appearance in the later Norman churches. They were a factor, albeit a very subordinate one, in the vast building programme launched by the Conqueror in the 1070s and continued under his two reigning sons. At that point the French snatched the architectural leadership from the British, and the arrival of Gothic as a dominant force in England had to await the start of a second great wave of ecclesiastical building which began in the 1170s.

This second wave was driven by two factors. The first was the growing dissatisfaction of the bishops and cathedral clergy with 'their' part of the existing Norman cathedrals. As they had been built from east to west, the choirs had been finished first, often before the year 1100; the naves, used by the congregation, were better built and more modern-looking, and as, in England, they were pushed to great lengths they made the clerical half of the church seem puny and insignificant at a time when clericalism was vigorously asserting its rights. There was, then, a growing urge to rebuild the east ends. The second factor was a new phase in the cult of relics. By the second half of the twelfth century, a period of rationalism and enlightenment, many of the old-style relic-collections had been discredited, and there was fierce competition for the authentic. Great men like Henry II and Frederick Barbarossa engaged in complex diplomatic negotiations for a major relic such as the arm of St James. The papacy became the supreme authenticating mechanism and in particular ruled out the creation of saints, except those who had been officially canonized by Rome. The possession of the undoubted body of a saint, acknowledged as such by the papacy, became an enormously valuable asset to any church, for the growth of population and the taste for travel was turning the pilgrimage into a mass industry.

In England, the new phase of the relic cult began with the canonization of Edward the Confessor (whose remains were owned by Westminster Abbey) in 1161. At Canterbury, the sensational murder of Archbishop Becket in 1170, followed by his canonization a mere two years later, gave the monks the elements of the most successful shrine in Europe, after that of St James at Compostella, and St Peter's in Rome itself. The further accident of a fire at Canterbury in 1174 provided them with the pretext to transform the whole eastern arm into a grandiose approach to and setting for St Thomas's body. Westminster and Hailes Abbeys followed Canterbury in its apse-ambulatory plan as a relic-centre. At Winchester a new retrochoir was built for the relic-collection in 1202. At Worcester the whole of the eastern part of the cathedral was rebuilt from 1224 to accommodate the shrines of its patrons, St Oswald and St Wulfstan, the latter canonized in 1203. Ely followed suit on behalf of St Etheldreda. At Lincoln, its most famous bishop was canonized as St Hugh in 1220. Rochesters's William of

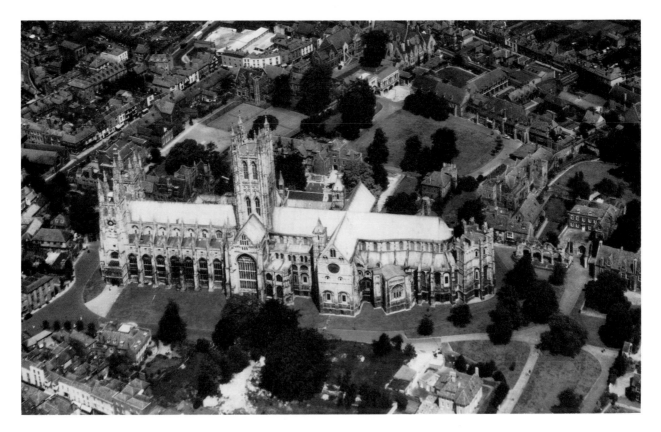

Aerial view of Canterbury from the south.

Perth followed in the 1250s. Desperate efforts were made by the chapter of Salisbury to get their prize possession, St Osmund, canonized. In each of these cases, the relic became the justification for elaborate building or rebuilding.

The Canterbury exercise was the first and, from the viewpoint of architectural history, by far the most important. Canterbury was the ecclesiastical centre of England, with a community of over a hundred monks throughout the twelfth century, as well as having the prestige of being England's oldest see and the seat of the primacy. Kent had tended to have a separate culture history from the rest of south-east England, and certainly Canterbury (along with Rochester) was the most exposed to direct French influence of all the cathedral cities. Lanfranc had pulled down the remains of the gutted Saxon cathedral immediately after his appointment in 1080 and had built what was then probably the largest church in England. In the 1120s it was made even bigger by the replacement of Lanfranc's east end by a more grandiose one, which included an eastern transept and two obliquely-set chapels of St Anselm and St Andrew. The great fire of 1174 did not affect the nave, but it gutted the choir. It seemed natural to the monks to turn to France, now the seat of architectural fashion. St Denis had been completed in 1144, but it had already been superseded by the splendid new cathedral of St Etienne in Sens, the first true Gothic church which had been finished in 1168. So one of its architects, William of Sens, was brought to Canterbury.

This is one of those rare occasions when we have a detailed literary authority to supplement the evidence of mute stones. The chronicler Gervase of Canterbury tells us that the fire started when a spark from a blaze nearby got between the lead covering of the roof and the wood joists. William of Sens he described as 'a man of great abilities, and a most curious workman in wood and stone.' Apparently he had some difficulty in persuading the conservative English

63

monks that the ruined choir must be pulled down completely, and even so they kept much of the wall and the eastern transepts with their Norman towers. Gervase continues: 'The two [chapels] of St Anselm and St Andrew, formerly placed in a circle on each side of the church, prevented the breadth of the choir from proceeding in a straight line. But it was right and proper to place the Chapel of St Thomas [the new Becket chapel] at the head of the church, where was the chapel of the Holy Trinity. The architect, therefore, not willing to lose these towers, but not able to remove them entirely ... yet preserving as much as possible the breadth of that passage which is without the choir [the ambulatory], on account of the processions which were frequently to be made there, narrowed this work at an oblique slant, so as to contract it neatly over against the altar.' William of Sens, in short, was obliged to adapt his scheme to conform to the historical ideas and ceremonial usages of a tenaciously conservative community. Once past the chapels, the building is widened again for the Trinity Chapel and for the so-called Corona, in which part of the crown or skull of St Thomas was kept.

The Frenchman began work in 1175, but at the beginning of his fifth year, while preparing the centering for the choir vault, the scaffolding collapsed under him and he fell fifty feet. He was so badly hurt that he went back to France to die, appointing his English assistant, another William, as his successor. The work was completed in about 1200. The choir at Canterbury is not outstanding as a work of art, but it is of exceptional historical interest, not only as the point at which England embraced the true Gothic style in an aesthetic sense, but as showing two distinct handlings of the new mode. The Frenchman built the choir arcades with a bold and consistent use of Corinthian columns and pointed arches, and with an arcaded triforium again using the pointed arch (though there are round double arches in the gallery). The Englishman, who built the arches between the Trinity Chapel and the Corona, and the windows in the Corona itself, showed an extraordinary ambivalence in his use of rounded and pointed arches, and signalled his reluctance to abandon the Romanesque by a persistent use of archaic decorative motifs, which make a startling contrast to the fine naturalistic leaf-carving on the capitals of the Corinthian pillars designed by his French predecessor.

Canterbury, indeed, is full of surprises for anyone who thinks of cathedrals in terms of typology. Internally, it is no more than the sum of its parts, each of which is strongly individualistic. What gives it a kind of functional unity is its strong sense of theatre. Becket, himself a master of flamboyance and histrionics, was actually killed in the north-west transept, on a spot called the Martyrdom. His body was translated to a shrine immediately behind the high altar, close to a spectacular pavement of Alexandrian mosaic brought back by crusaders, the pilgrimage area being completed by the brilliantly-lit Corona. The shrine was a staggering amalgam of gold, silver and jewels – including a giant ruby presented by St Louis of France – and when Henry VIII broke it up in the 1540s the loot filled twenty-seven carts. What added to the drama of approaching it was the fact that Canterbury, unlike nearly all other cathedrals, is deliberately built upon a series of four levels . The choir is placed sharply above the nave; the presbytery and high altar are above the rest of the choir; and the Trinity Chapel and Corona are higher still. The final act of pilgrimage, then, was an ascent, in which throughout the summer season, the long files of pilgrims shuffled slowly forward, climbing as they went, until they came upon the sudden blazing glory of the sanctum lit by

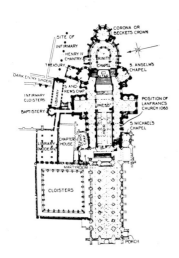

CANTERBURY

OPPOSITE Looking into the Corona at Canterbury.

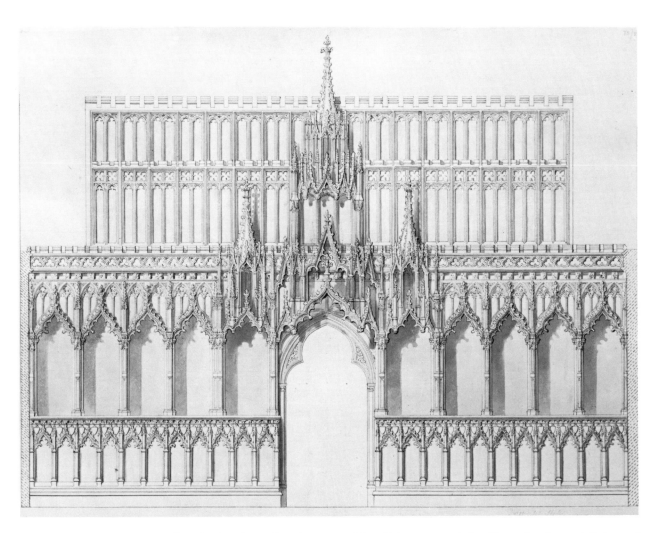

A drawing of the choir-stalls at Canterbury.

hundreds of candles, innumerable oil-lamps, and the filtered coloured lights of the tall Corona windows. Here was liturgical drama to rival Compostella, and when Erasmus visited the shrine in the twilight of the Middle Ages, he was unable to prevent a certain note of wonder from creeping into his generally sceptical account.

Moreover, the rising levels of the eastern arm made possible the largest and most complex series of crypts in any English church: Canterbury has, in fact, a complete lower church, reproducing the outline of the structure above. The earliest and most westerly section has a set of carved Romanesque capitals of great distinction. This merges into an apsidal undercroft built when the choir was enlarged in the 1120s, and opens onto the Black Prince's chantry chapel and the crypt beneath St Anselm's chapel, which has its own painted lower-chapel of St Gabriel. In the middle is the Lady Chapel of the crypt, where some of the most valuable treasures were kept to be shown to privileged visitors. The series ends with the eastern crypt, beneath the Trinity and the Corona, which shows a more confident handling of the Gothic mode and Purbeck marble than the great edifice above it. The crypt-complex, in fact, is a series of miniature churches, or rather an underground cathedral which mirrors the disparate elements, each fascinating in itself, of the great huddle of buildings above it. And of course the crypts, with their smoky torchlight falling on the glowing colours of the wall-paintings, and the dark glitter of the gems, were an important (and expensive) part of the pilgrimage experience, adding to its awe-inspiring mystery like the sumptuous caverns of the Holy Sepulchre Church in Jerusalem.

The wealth that their martyred archbishop continued to bring to the Canterbury monks enabled them to impose an external unity on the church which gives it, especially from afar, a late-medieval appearance, only belied by a surviving Norman tower which pokes its head from beneath the shelter of the south-east transept. At the end of the fourteenth century the Norman nave was demolished and Henry Yevele, the greatest architectural impresario of the English Middle Ages, was called in to provide Canterbury with yet another theatrical *coup de main* – a forest of stone Perpendicular trees of enormous height terminating in the spell-binding canopy of the high vault. Thus the pilgrim walked wonderingly through this high-branching sunlit glade before he began the slow upward trudge through the ascending plateaux of the choir to the Corona summit.

Before, however, he set foot in the cathedral he had seen the pinnacles of Canterbury from the rim of the bowl of green hills in which it is set. If, in the early Middle Ages, architects designed cathedrals from the inside out, in the fourteenth and fifteenth centuries they reversed the process to some extent by assuming a viewpoint from afar and seeing their work in terms of stone scenery. Yevele's nave, a high forest within, is from the outside a dramatic series of upthrusting windows and pinnacles, foreshadowing King's College Chapel, and supplemented by the great apertures of the western transept, the tallest windows in England. In the 1420s the nave was completed by a Perpendicular West Front designed by Thomas Mapilton, whose new south-west tower echoed on a heightened scale the furious thrusting of Yevele's design. As medieval architects, particularly English ones, were usually incapable of carrying a scheme to its logical conclusion, the north-west Norman tower, built in Lanfranc's day, was permitted to remain until it began to fall down from old age in the 1820s and was replaced by a duplicate of Mapilton's south-west tower. Meanwhile, the junction of the two quite distinct – indeed, potentially warring – halves of the cathedral had been brilliantly concealed by a final stroke of petrified theatre, the central or Bell Harry tower, set up by John Wastell in the last decade of the fifteenth century. It was already there to greet Erasmus, and was then surmounted by yet another dramatic device, a giant golden angel which caught the light and proclaimed journey's end to the pilgrim long before he could clearly discern the stone silhouette through the trees. This multi-pinnacled outline grew ever more overwhelming with each step that he advanced, for though the cathedral is over 500 feet in length, the 235 feet of Bell Harry is in proportion, and its enthusiastic groups of verticals make it seem higher still, so that the pilgrim was eventually confronted by a man-made arrangement of Dolomite cliffs, at whose feet he could only wonder.

As artistic taste swung slowly on the great chronological hinge constituted by the 1170s, the cathedral ceased to be a display of brute power, a conquest of enclosed space by sheer mass and volume of effort, the prodigal expenditure of blood, sweat and tears. Instead, it became a network of forces, a cerebral composition which inspired awe precisely because it seemed effortless, indeed impossible. The way in which a Romanesque cathedral held together was obvious even to a dull-witted peasant. It proclaimed loudly: I am here because I am strongly built. The Gothic cathedral was a mystery, and was intended to look like a mystery because it was not immediately obvious why it did not fall down. The medieval layman accepted it as a fact, albeit an inexplicable one, in the same way that we accept nuclear physics.

But Romanesque and Gothic cathedrals – and the majority were both – were alike in that they were prodigies. They were designed to shock, to lift the mortal from the everyday world of low horizons and small enclosed spaces onto the supernal plane of an omnipotent God who suspended at will the laws of nature and whose power was literally terrifying. A cathedral, then, involved an element of showmanship, of conjuring and engineering razzmatazz which was far removed from a rational calculation of ends and means. When, around 1400, the Canons of Seville decided to create the largest Gothic cathedral in the world, they recorded: 'We shall build on such a scale that the world will account us madmen.'

Medieval architects and their patrons did not, therefore, think in terms of suitability but in terms of competitive extravagance. Their enthusiasm constantly broke the disciplines of the forms they (and nature) imposed on themselves, and there is in any great cathedral at least one and usually more elements of excess. Restraint is not usually a virtue in cathedral architecture, and the urge to go too far is part of its creative metaphysic.

Lincoln is an excellent example of the prodigy cathedral. Everything about it is larger than life. In medieval times it was one of the largest and richest dioceses in England, for during the Danish supremacy it had been run from Dorchester-on-Thames, and when the Conqueror restored the see to Lincoln, its boundaries still stretched as far as the Thames Valley. The site of the cathedral on its hill – which also supplies it with the superb pale yellow oolite limestone of which it is built – dominates both the old town immediately below, and the new town at its feet, and Lincoln is the only English cathedral which can be seen broadside on from afar. Unlike Durham, Lincoln Cathedral dominates not only its immediate surroundings but a vast stretch of countryside, for its hill rises from a plain, rather as the great mass of Chartres emerges from the wheatlands of the Beauce. The cathedral is long, 482 feet on the inside, but the prevailing impression is of height, for the masterly central tower was carried up to 271 feet in the early fourteenth century, and this was surmounted, until it fell down in a sixteenth century gale, by an enormous spire, which brought the total height to 524 feet, the tallest in Europe, and enabled the cathedral to be seen from as far away as East Anglia.

Lincoln is stylistically more of a piece than most English cathedrals. The reason is that on 15 April 1185 an earthquake brought the entire church down, with the exception of the West Front. A succession of masterful bishops, including the saintly Hugh of Avalon (1186–1200) and Robert Grosseteste (1235–53), rebuilt the cathedral in the Early English manner, adding a retrochoir, or the Angel Choir as it is called, in the Decorated style in about 1280. Though St Hugh, who inspired the programme, was a Frenchman, and the designer, Geoffrey de Noiers, had a French name, the work is very English throughout and represents the first major native essay in Gothic. The derivativeness and ambivalence which marked Canterbury choir is gone. Bourges, its strict contemporary in France, is totally different. At Lincoln, English Gothic took over, and the architectural primacy, held by France from the 1140s to the 1180s, was wrested back again.

Yet Lincoln begins with a characteristically English-inspired muddle. The earthquake left the Norman West Front standing. It was decided to keep its

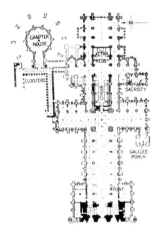

LINCOLN

OPPOSITE Looking up into the crossing tower at Canterbury.

PAGES 70–1 The West Front of Wells Cathedral.

PAGE 71 The West Front and towers of Lincoln Cathedral.

porches and two west towers, but to push the towers high into the sky and to build out in front of the porches a vast screen, 175 feet wide, with a high gable and corner turrets. It is covered in great bands of arcading, but the actual doorways are deeply recessed, as at Peterborough, providing an impressive effect of depth and chiaroscuro. The towers do not grow naturally out of the screen – therein lies the muddle – but the front as a whole is unquestionably sensational, especially as a backdrop for a full-scale processional entry on a great saint's day. It proclaims itself loudly as a curtain-raiser to prodigious events within.

Immediately inside the West Front there is a powerful perspective view of the whole Gothic tunnel of the cathedral, with the spiky shape of the great organ silhouetted against the far-distant, but enormous, east window. When the sun is rising in the east, this is one of the really overwhelming shock-views of English architecture. French critics argue that English cathedral naves are too low, sometimes not much over sixty feet, and that Lincoln, which is eighty feet, looks lower than it actually is, because the piers of the main arcades are widely spaced and the columns from which the vault springs are carried down only to the top of the clustered pillars, thus missing an important vertical opportunity. The answer is that English medieval architects preferred to emphasize the length of the nave, thus suiting the quality of the English light, which is not so much intense as lingering. In the prolonged dawns and sunsets of England, the tunnel effect was the one to aim for, and at Lincoln it succeeds brilliantly. Needless to say, this

The Gothic nave of Lincoln Cathedral, looking east.

OPPOSITE Stained glass in Canterbury Cathedral showing pilgrims at Becket's tomb.

73

tunnel effect could not be obtained by a French-style chevet east end; it is the square English end, with its vast central window, which makes it possible.

At the crossing, there is an exciting contrast to the tunnel, for the vault under the central tower suddenly opens up to a height of 130 feet and one is in a vertical universe. On either side, the eye travels to immense and gorgeous windows: the 'Dean's Eye' to the north, the 'Bishop's Eye' to the south. Then one passes through an elaborate fourteenth-century screen, by thirteenth-century carved doorways to right and left, into the glittering eastern arm of the church. Here, the vault is eight feet lower than in the nave, and the tunnel effect is resumed, but in both directions. One advantage of the tunnel-type vista is that it makes the details of the vaulting and the upper storeys of the bays more comprehensible simply because they are nearer to the eye; and at Lincoln, being Early English Gothic, the details are very important. Stone vaults, which were difficult and expensive to erect, were put into cathedrals for the same primary reason that they were added to castles – they were the best protection against fire. But the collateral reason that they constituted a firmament was also a weighty one, and became predominant as the craft of stone vaulting developed more complex and audacious forms. There is a contemporary description of the vault of the choir in *The Metrical Life of St Hugh*: 'The vault,' the poet says, 'may be compared to a bird stretching out her broad wings to fly – planted on its firm columns, it soars to the clouds.'

The poet also drew attention to the columns of dark-green Purbeck marble clustering around the great piers, which he compares to 'a bevy of maidens gathering for a dance'. The use of Purbeck, which was shipped from Dorset, came in with Gothic and became an important element in prodigy architecture. Its deep brown or sage-green hues contrasted well with the shades of limestone and added a note of solid polychrome to the painted stone. Purbeck was first used in the Canterbury choir, but sparingly; at Lincoln it becomes a salient feature of the decorative scheme. Purbeck is not, strictly speaking, marble but limestone combined with petrified shells of moluscs, which allow it to take polish and bring out its elaborate figuring. It is no good for the outside of a cathedral but makes excellent small columns for inside, its blocks usually lying in beds six to eight feet

The triforium of the Angel Choir at Lincoln.

long. At Lincoln, two or more lengths are used for the main shafts, with annulets to mask the joins. In the choir, Purbeck takes over, for there is a multitude of small shafts, which in the arcading of the aisles are arrayed in double, alternating ranks, the front shafts in Purbeck, the rear ones in Lincoln limestone. Both have elaborate leaf capitals, deeply-incised mouldings, carved figures in the spandrels and interlocking arches. In the choir at Lincoln, indeed, the Gothic carver first begins to flex his muscles and dictate the main lines of the decorative scheme.

Yet the choir at Lincoln is itself only an antechamber to or preparation for the retrochoir (or Angel Choir). This was built 1256–80 to replace the old French-type chevet, when it was decided to provide an appropriate setting for the shrine of St Hugh and the thousands of pilgrims who visited it. Thus, like the Trinity and Corona at Canterbury, it was the climax of the church. The designer, Simon of Thirsk, had somehow to provide an artistic *coup* which did not come as an anticlimax after the successive thrills of the West Front, nave, crossing and choir. He did this by developing to the full the new resources made available by Gothic notions of integrated design: a full range of mouldings, surface polychrome of paint and gilt, the deep polychrome of contrasting Purbeck and limestone, vertical crocket bands between the shafts of the clustered pillars, vertical corbels supporting the vaulting-shafts, foliated hood-moulds for the tribune, much dog-tooth and other devices in the mouldings, trefoils and quatrefoils everywhere with internal cusping, and a systematic, almost frenzied, avoidance of blank spaces and right angles.

A misericord in the choir at Lincoln.

Each level has an eye-catcher: superbly carved trefoils offset from the spandrels of the main arcade; at the top, in the clerestory, a striking new notion of placing veils of open tracery several feet in front of the glazed window – brilliantly copied in Durham's north-east transept – to create an extraordinary depth-effect; and, at the triforium level, where the eye tends to come to rest, sumptuous leaf-carving in the corbels and capitals, and a regiment of angels in the spandrels, some playing instruments, others weighing souls in their scales. All these details are meant to be seen and studied in the strongest possible light. This is provided not only by the large, novel apertures of the clerestory four-light windows but by the enormous window which occupies virtually the whole of the square east end – the first English experiment in bar-tracery, nearly sixty feet high – and provides the key to the lighting-scheme of the whole church. The effect of richness is overwhelming, and it is naked and proud, relying not a whit on the kindness of candlelight and chiaroscuro. The work as a whole is the supreme masterpiece of the English Decorated Gothic; it is not, and it cannot be, to everyone's taste, but it appeals to most people because the sheer profusion of art and artifice is at no point reckless. It has a logical and mathematical underpinning which makes all its parts ordered and disciplined and reveals the presence of a cool, theorizing intelligence, the same type of mind which, during that period, produced the great theological *summae* of Aquinas, Albertus Magnus and Bonaventure.

A great prodigy church like Lincoln could not, of course, be produced without continuous, behind-the-scenes progress in solving the technical problems raised by the constant search for new theatrical effects. If the medieval architect was primarily a showman, he was also, of necessity, a structural engineer. That great east window of Lincoln, introducing bar tracery, marked a revolution in construction. Until then, the aperture in England had been cut out of the masonry; one started with a wall, and made windows in it. At Lincoln, the designer started with an empty space, and filled it in with a stone-bar skeleton, in geometrical patterns (hence the term Geometrical Decorated). The wall containing the window then became a mere afterthought, because there was a drastic lightening in the weight of the stonework and windows could be created mainly of glass, divided by increasingly narrow mullions and supported mainly by frames of wrought iron. This opened the way for the glasshouse churches of later medieval England.

In a much less obvious manner, Lincoln provides a series of startling insights into the constructional underpinning of a great medieval cathedral. It is built on a huge scale. Though the nave is low by French standards, it is very long; there are two large transepts, innumerable side-buildings and chapels, a chapter-house and secular cloister, and three of the tallest towers in Christendom – the two west towers kept their high steeples until 1807 – not to speak of acres of roof. Unknown to the casual visitor, all great medieval churches contain a number of hidden passageways and staircases to render accessible every inch of the fabric for regular inspection and maintenance, for in the lofty recesses of an ancient building fearful damage can accumulate unseen until it proclaims itself by a catastrophe. A minimum circulation system consists of, on the exterior, gutter passageways on the eaves of both the side-aisles and the high roof, and at the top of the side-aisle roofs where they meet the clerestory wall; and, on the interior, passages at the triforium level and within both the side-aisle and the high central roofs, that is, plank walks across the tie-beams and over the stone vaults. These have to be reached by newel staircases within the towers, turrets and pinnacles.

Such a system is the minimum; as a rule, there are passageways within the walls at other levels. At Lincoln, the last, hidden prodigy of this astonishing church is the exceptionally rich and varied system of secret stairs and passages. Some of these newels are beautifully carved and vaulted; others are terrifying. J.C. Buckler, the Victorian architect who restored the towers in the 1860s, and who probably knew the bowels of the cathedral better than any man before or since, noted in 1866 in his book *A description and defence of the restoration of the exterior of Lincoln Cathedral*: 'The galleries in the thickness of the walls, the recesses and the blank passages are so numerous, irregular, and so frequently connected by precipitous steps and narrow links, dark, crooked and fearful to pursue, that no description can be here given of them. Suffice it to say that the builders of the thirteenth century saw good reason to augment the number; and that he of the fourteenth century approved the system ... and assuredly maintained them in the walls with which he interfered. In the way through these singularly connected and circuitous passages, ascending and descending with different degrees of steepness, and at the foot of the archways either open or guarded, the work ... is seen to advantage.' Indeed it is; and, for my part, I find that the awe created by this huge limestone shape, which rises almost organically out of the hill from which its stones were quarried, is intensified by the knowledge that, within it, there is a secret arterial system which, as it were, breathes continual life into its stone limbs.

Lincoln is at one end of the great limestone belt which runs diagonally across England, and Wells is at the other, south-west end. Like Lincoln, Wells enjoyed its own superb quarry, at Doulting. There is another important connection: St Hugh of Lincoln was originally persuaded to come to England as prior of the first Charterhouse there at Witham, by the nearby Bishop of Wells, Reginald de Bohun; and it was the latter, guided by St Hugh, who was the real creator of the present Wells Cathedral. It stands on the site of two predecessors, one Saxon, one late-Norman (1136–48), of which we know virtually nothing. The Norman building was demolished completely in the 1180s, and Wells is thus the first English cathedral to be conceived entirely in the Gothic manner, with pointed arches throughout. Its inspiration, however, is not French, but very English, and it is the product of the great school of West Country stonemason-designers who now became, and remained, a salient element in English art until the end of the Middle Ages.

Wells must come close to the ideal cathedral in the English manner. Seen in its green setting, from the foothills of the nearby Mendips, it is a golden vision of loveliness. At closer quarters, as townscape, it is a resounding climax to one of Englands's prettiest village-cities, for its position on the outskirts has enabled it to preserve from encroachment its medieval bishop's castle-palace, with its gardens and encircling, swan-decked moat. Finally, examined in detail, it is a brimming treasure-house of marvels. Wells was not in itself a leading pilgrimage-church, for its candidate for sanctity, its former bishop and Edward I's treasurer, William of March, failed to obtain canonization at Rome; on the other hand, it was closely linked to neighbouring Glastonbury, England's oldest Christian foundation, which continued to draw pilgrims until the Reformation; so Wells shared in this valuable trade. Certainly, there was (and is) enough in Wells to astonish even a case-hardened collector of cathedral prodigies.

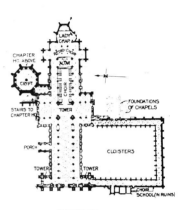

WELLS

The first shock is the West Front itself, where for the first time English designers were able to pull off a masterpiece. Adam Lock (died 1229) and his continuator (Thomas Norreys) were not handicapped, as at Peterborough and Lincoln, by Norman survivals, and so were not driven to the risky expedient of slamming on a wide screen to conceal the bases of the towers. Despite the width of the front (147 feet), the towers were part of the integral design from the start, being locked into it by a system of six enormous buttresses which give a radical effect of depth of the type that, at Peterborough and Lincoln, is created by the giant niches. These strident verticals are echoed in the tall and narrow lancets of the great west window, and a new Gothic device of 'extended mullions' in the upper storeys of the towers. The intention, clearly, was to complete the towers with spires or, failing that, corner-pinnacles, for the width of the front presupposes great height. But the towers remain incomplete, perhaps because the central tower over the crossing, which is very fine in itself, is too low to keep its necessary paramountcy against two noble monsters to its west. At all events, the west towers lack their crowns, and therein lies the only weakness of this splendid church.

The purpose of the West Front was clear: to provide a large-scale gallery for a permanent exhibition of virtuoso sculpture. This was a challenge to the architect to produce a first-class piece of elevational design, and he responded with a ground floor of serried aedicules, an expansive *piano nobile* twice its height, with room for two rows of superimposed statues, and a third sculpture-storey in the gable of the west window. Driven by the Gothic urge to excess, he extended the sculpture-gallery round the sides and backs of the towers. This fact, plus the stress on the storeys, provides a strong horizontal counterpoint to the verticals; the two planes fight for mastery and give the front a feeling of fierce tension for, without the spires, the conflict is unresolved.

The Front originally provided places for 340 sculptured figures, of which 150 were at least life-size. On the bottom storey were prophets and apostles; on the *piano nobile* martyred kings, virgins and bishops and abbots representing confessor-saints; and in the centre gable apostles, angels and Christ in Majesty. It took the craftsmen two centuries to produce these sculptures, and about half of them were smashed by the puritan rabble. Some, lacking heads or arms, are now being attended to in a vast programme of restoration which reflects the importance of Wells as the greatest single repository of English medieval sculpture. The quality of the original work varies. It lacks the unforgettable stylistic panache of Chartres; but it includes a score or so of excellent naturalistic pieces, most of them on the rear side of the north-west tower.

Moreover, the West Front, spectacular though it may seem, is intended merely as an introduction to the wealth of sculpture of the nave within. Wells, for the first time, exposes the rich potentialities of the Gothic nave as a homogenous design system. Lock, as the West Front shows, had a strong sense of the integrated elevation design. This is confirmed by his nave-bay elevations which are immensely satisfying and rhythmical. He had to work to a low total height (only 67 feet), and he met this by reducing the triforium to a set of three small aedicules, like the ground-floor of his West Front. But the clerestory lancets are very tall indeed, and merge with the springing of the vault to echo the arches of the ground-floor arcades. This is designed to force the eye downwards onto the arcades, which are indeed the key to the composition. The Wells nave marks the point at which the old Romanesque compound pier is strikingly transformed into a new art-form of unrivalled potential – the Gothic clustered pillar. What, in effect, Lock did was to apply the principles of the Gothic arch-mouldings, already well-developed, down into the orders of the pillar so that each moulding becomes the counterpart of the shaft and appears to grow out of it, an illustration of the principle that an organic flow nearly always produces good architecture by making it seem 'natural'. In the process, the flattish arch-soffit became wedge-shaped, and the architect therefore took the opportunity to swing the ground-plan of the cluster through an angle of forty-five degrees, so conforming to the central Gothic dictate, which is a hatred of flat surfaces.

The flow of the arch-mould into the clustered shafts in theory made capitals unnecessary. In practice, however, no Gothic designer was going to forego such a splendid opportunity for divine madness and only poverty was ever allowed to deprive the mature Gothic nave of capitals. At Wells they are, beyond argument, the finest set in any English cathedral, the collective masterpiece of a whole *atelier* of skilful naturalistic sculptors. There are eight capitals to a pier, well over 200 altogether, and each has a fine piece of carving, all taken from life and nature. The leaf-work is superb, but it is the occasional figures which arrest the eye. On the West Front the carvers were bound by all the rules of liturgical symbolism; on the capitals (not counting the corbel-heads and the bosses) they had free rein for their fancy. We see peasants at work; boys stealing fruit; a cobbler making shoes. Medieval man looked long and carefully at such spontaneous flourishes and thought about them, so that often enough they acquired divine overtones. Near one of the capitals, which depicts a toothache-sufferer with painful realism, lies the later tomb of Bishop Bytton, who died in 1274, and who thereafter, by a process of transference, acquired an unsubstantiated reputation for curing toothache.

In the thirteenth century there was nothing else in the nave to distract the attention of the goggling peasant from the capitals. But from the mid-fourteenth century there was fierce competition. The crossing-tower, which was set up in the years 1315–22, began to give trouble in the next decade, and at a meeting of the chapter on 29 May 1338 the church was described as *enormiter confracta* and *confracta et enormiter deformata*. A brilliant master-mason called William Joy was brought in, and during the next ten years he provided the nave-crossing complex with monumental strainer-arches, like stone scissors. There is nothing like them anywhere else, and they have been variously described as saltires, St Andrew's Crosses, intersected ogee curves and arches standing on their heads over normal arches. They are deliberately sensational, and give to the very centre of the church a futuristic look. Rarely if ever in English medieval architecture has a designer so plainly intruded his own personality on a major collective work. Some experts hate them; most ordinary visitors, as I have discovered, think they were part of the original design. This is powerful testimony to Joy's brilliance in using the system of mouldings, the notion of the rib, the ogee arch and the circle-eye to absorb a brutal piece of pure engineering into the design of the whole interior. It indicates the sheer resourcefulness of the Gothic style, its protean capabilities which, in its revived form, were to embrace cast-iron bridges and railway stations. It suggests, too, how many tricks the exponents of twentieth century concrete architecture are missing – for these great strainers treat stone like moulded ferro-concrete – and adumbrates, to my mind, a third Gothic age which we may live to see.

Hence Wells became a prodigy-church almost by accident. The great strainers clamour to be looked at. They complete the nave like a tremendous drum-roll, and they then, at the entrance to the choir, perform a further function of concealing the manifest poverty of the choir-stalls (Victorian, except for the fourteenth-century misericords), and the re-working of the choir screen and the arcades by Anthony Salvin, a brilliant castle-restorer but a heavy hand with thirteenth-century Gothic. Instead, the eye leaps directly from the bold lines of the strainers to the majestic delicacy of the choir vault, which has a pattern of cusped lierne ribs, serving a decorative rather than a structural purpose, and marking the emergence of the English lacework vault, which was to culminate in the gossamer fan-vaults of the early Tudors.

When the eye falls from the vault, it is almost irresistibly attracted, especially in strong daylight, by the deliberately-created vista behind the high altar, a glimpse into a low-level glade of stone trees. This was created when Joy, having saved the crossing tower with his strainers, went on to restructure the last three bays of the choir and the whole of the east end. The typical English east end, externally, is square, but of two types: the straightforward cliff, as at Lincoln, or the square steps. The cliff has the advantage that it accommodates a bigger window, and so provides the spectacular tunnel effect, as at Lincoln. Square steps, on the other hand, can be used to produce some striking stone scenery on the outside, and within allow the designer to experiment with some of the light effects used in the French chevet-type east end.

At Wells, the step system gives the designer room for both a retrochoir and, at the very end, a Lady Chapel, connected by spaces. The six clustered pillars of the retrochoir, splaying out into a marvellous canopy of vaulting, give an intriguing glade-effect when seen over the high altar, because they are silhouetted against the big windows of the Lady Chapel and retrochoir aisles. The windows are of great interest in themselves, for they provide a historical progression through the late Geometrical-Decorated to the flowing art nouveau curves which superseded it. However, if one descends into the retrochoir – intended, of course, for the

feretory of St William of the March, if only he had been canonized – and so the final *coup* of the whole cathedral, one gets an even more thrilling perspective due west. Now one is actually in the forest glade, softly lit from the painted glass behind, the low foliage of the vault pressing down and producing a panorama of shadowed curves and verticals of almost infinite complexity.

The prodigies of Wells do not end, however, with this climactic east end. If, instead of progressing from the crossing into the choir, one turns left into the north transept, a door opens on new wonders. The door itself, which leads to the Chapter House, crypt and treasury, is worth study because it shows that the thirteenth-century naturalistic sculptors of the nave capitals had their counterpart among the ironsmiths, for the great iron hinges are spread out over virtually the whole wooden surface of the door, in a spidery pattern of branches, twigs and Baroque curves.

The door leads to a double or bifurcated stairway, itself a noble piece of masonry. One arm leads to a bridge, which passes over the narrow street outside into the Vicar's Close. The other takes us into the first-floor polygonal Chapter House. The splendid series of chapter houses are among the glories of English cathedral art and this one, which was finished by 1319, at the culmination of the Decorated style, is perhaps the finest. Even more than the blank space and the right angle, the Gothic hated the dome, so the design of the Chapter House, where the canons sat as theoretical equals, was not a circle, as was natural, but an octagon. It was roofed, not by building up supports from the sides, but by planting a stone tree in the middle, which meant that the windows could be huge and pointed. The art of the polygonal chapter house lay in the number of ribs or branches springing from the clustered column which formed the trunk of the tree. In the chapter house at Westminster there are 16, at Lincoln 20, at Exeter 24; Wells has 32 which meet at the top, the ribs springing from the corners in a maze of carved bosses, the whole producing the effect of an umbrageous palm-tree which, since the rib-projections are not deep, seems to shimmer and shiver in a breeze. Under the windows there are 51 canopied stalls, and these swarm with sculptured dignitaries, mainly kings and bishops, who smile and laugh, in sardonic comment on the high-powered canonical debates below.

The cathedral at Wells is the focus of the most agreeable and harmonious collection of ecclesiastical buildings in England, Salisbury excepted, which includes a superlative medieval palace. This essentially dates from the late thirteenth century, which was when the elegant three-bay chapel and the magnificent great hall, 115 feet long and 60 wide, were built. But bishops tended to become objects of popular hatred in the fourteenth century, and it was then that the palace was moated and a license obtained to crenelate the walls. One enters therefore through a fourteenth century gatehouse, like any other castle. However, generations of sedentary tranquillity, from the sixteenth to the nineteenth centuries, have romanticized the interiors and turfed the open stretches, so that this bastion of ecclesiastical privilege now appears as unwarlike as the magnificent church over which it once stood guard.

Wells is the first wholly Gothic cathedral; but it does not have the unity of a single composition. This is the unique claim of Salisbury, the only one of our medieval cathedrals to be built in a single campaign, according to the master-plan of one directing intelligence. It had a further, in some respects more important, advantage: it was built on a virgin site, so there were none of the practical pressures, as for instance at Wells, to force the ground-plan to conform to the

The roof of the Chapter House at Wells; the clustered column comprises 32 branches.

OPPOSITE The strainer arches at Wells; looking into the north transept from the south.

81

outlines of its old Norman predecessor. This was on high ground at Old Sarum, two miles away; but lack of water and the affronting presence of a royal castle nearby led Bishop Poore in 1219 to request papal permission to transfer the cathedral to the valley below. It was granted and, as a result, the cathedral was laid out not only with an enormous green surround, but with an ideal close for the secular canons, who were able to choose the plots of ground for their houses even before the foundation stone of the cathedral was laid in 1220. This explains why Salisbury has such a large, magnificent and uncluttered collection of episcopal and canonical buildings, by far the best of any English cathedral, almost rivalling the great church itself. When Trollope conceived his Barchester, he modelled his old cathedral largely on Exeter; but his notion of a cathedral society came to him, as he says, while meditating in Salisbury Close.

The Trinity Chapel at the east end of Salisbury was finished five years after the foundation-stone; the east transepts and choir by 1237, and the main transepts and nave by 1258. So the main construction took only thirty-eight years, compared with the thirty-six years of new St Paul's, the only other English cathedral built in one campaign. Whether there was a presiding, solitary genius, like Wren, is more doubtful; there is still a dispute as to whether the designer was

Salisbury Cathedral from the south west.

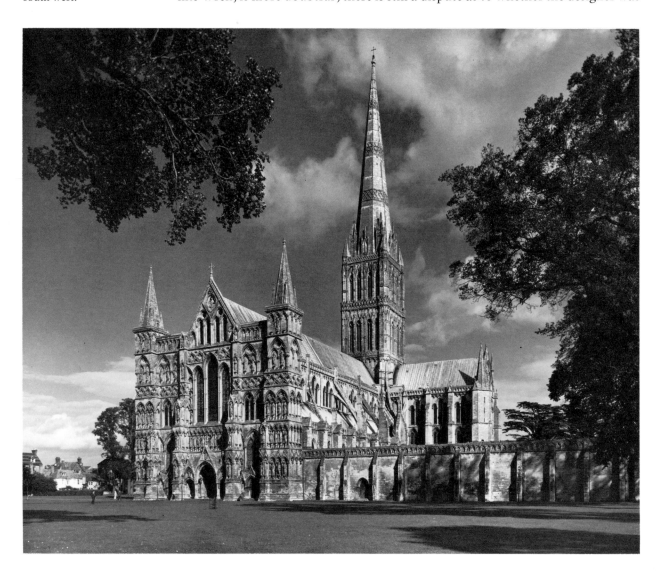

an ecclesiastic, Elias of Dereham, or a master-mason, Nicholas of Ely, or – as I am inclined to think – both of them working together. The West Front, cloister and Chapter House, finished after 1238, were part of the original design. The only change introduced was a miraculous improvement. The Elias-Nicholas Salisbury called for a low tower, scarcely more than a roof-abutment, with a squat pyramid-spire above it. In about 1330 two very high storeys were added to the tower and topped with an eight-sided stone steeple, designed by Richard of Farleigh, which is 100 feet higher than any other in England, and the second highest in Europe. It is, curiously enough, this radical change in the design which seems to complete and perfect it.

Might this not be because we have been conditioned to see Salisbury, which has been painted more often than any other English cathedral, as the archetype or divine image of a great cathedral with a single spire? All cathedrals in medieval times were, it is true, built from the inside out, and this is true even of Salisbury. But by 1220 the enormous technical advantages brought by the use of solid-stone Gothic design were giving architects a growing feeling of confidence in their structures, and new ambitions to plan them not only from the point of view of stability and enclosure of space, but as totalities, to be seen from all angles. Gothic encouraged their interest in elevational design, and not just of three-storey bays seen from within, but of whole facades, seen from without. At Salisbury, the unprecedented opportunity was given to the designer to develop a huge and unencumbered site, and so to design the surrounds as well as the church itself. For the first time he had some control of how it would be seen from the outside, and was able to think of it, *ab initio*, in terms of stone scenery as well as space-enclosure. He not only conceived a church, but placed it in a landscape.

This is why we automatically judge Salisbury, as a work of art, primarily in scenic frames. There is no one view of Salisbury; there are dozens, and they can be savoured either by approaching it from afar in a series of diminishing concentric circles or, in reverse, by leaving the north porch and backing away, allowing the enormous mass gradually to assume its scenic functions. Thanks to the change in the design brought about by the great spire, the radius of approach can be as far away as fifteen miles: it was from this distance that Constable, ascending the tower at Fonthill on 29 August 1823, saw Salisbury spire 'suddenly dart into the sky like a needle'. From five miles away it is seen as a townscape-dominator. Within the radius of a mile it enters into a configuration with the water-meadows of the Avon, and there can be no doubt that the designer conceived it as being seen not only by, but across, water. We cannot know what allowance he made for the natural framework of trees, for the relationship of trees and buildings in man-made scenery was not consciously studied until the seventeenth century. For Constable it was the key conjunction, for he exulted in the fact that, when the cathedral is seen through foliage, the 'solitary grey' of the spire is 'made to sparkle'.

From within the perimeter of the Close, it becomes obvious that the designer conceived the church, externally, as a series of spiky triangles, which constantly change their relationships as one circles round. But the angle of vision must always be oblique. Seen from a point dead-centre of the West Front, the design looks wrong; it has an offensive symmetry, in which the spire is not seen at all or, further back, peers incongruously over the great gable. Equally, seen from a point dead centre of the east end (as Turner once painted it), the design coalesces into a striking but monstrous pyramid of triangles.

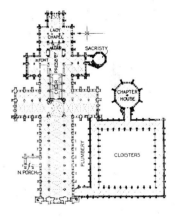

SALISBURY

In fact, had the original scheme of squat tower and pyramid spire remained, the design might have toppled over into mathematical mannerism, as happened to a number of thirteenth-century experiments with square and compasses when Geometrical Decorated was the rage. As it is, the spire turns the triangle concept into a masterpiece, especially in the great series of oblique angles within the close, for it creates new kinds of triangles of its own, in the angles formed by the nave and great-transept roofs. The series begins with the view from the south-west of the close, moves through 180 degrees to the north-east, and terminates in the south view from within the cloisters, which Turner painted in a masterly water-colour, now in the Victoria and Albert Museum, using a shattered cloister-window as a frame. The cloisters, I should add, are an important part of the scenic design. Their sheer size (they are England's biggest in area), and the complex black caverns created by their bay elevations, more like formidable doorways than windows, constitute a series of frames which seem to double the height of the spire, and turn the staircase of the east end into an Alpine range.

The visitor should try to see the church not only from all possible angles, but in every sort of weather, for Salisbury is the most protean of English buildings. This is because the stone, a Jurassian Portland oolitic limestone, quarried at Chilmark, ten miles away, while almost white in its natural state, matures to a fine light grey, which virtually mirrors light. So the colour changes with the weather, from a pewter-grey to a kind of lime-green, or a dusty yellow flecked with rust and gold; and sometimes, as Constable was aware, the enormous amount of moisture in the air invests the cathedral with a humid halo, which makes the shadows exceptionally deep blue. The big rainy skies, constantly marching in from the south-west, give the cathedral surface no peace: it changes constantly. That is why Constable, who painted Salisbury in all seasons, and at all times of day, often had to work at Impressionist speed.

Certainly, one visit is not enough. Ruskin, when he first saw the cathedral, his eyes fresh from Italian skies, dismissed it as 'profound and gloomy ... the savageness of the Northern Gothic'. He did not realize that it can glow like white gold in the sun, even in December. He thought the West Front, with its grass plinth, rose 'like dark and barren rocks out of a green lake'. Others, such as Nikolaus Pevsner, have subjected the West Front to ferocious and detailed criticism. Certainly, it is less enterprising than the front at Wells – conservatively English, in fact, for it is essentially a Gothic veneer over a Norman front, like that at Rochester. It has preserved far fewer of its original statues, of which only nine remain in 120 niches; and also much of the decoration is restored. Yet it seems to me to be a judicious balancing of horizontals and verticals, which works extraordinarily well (and unobtrusively) once it is accepted that the designer was thinking in terms of a total concept of stone scenery, and manipulating angles as well as surfaces.

The interior is another matter. It has been described as too cold and cerebral, and there is some justice in the charge, as the cathedral is now seen. There is very little carving of any kind, so the shapes and mouldings of the Early English style have to make their point by sheer purity of line and logical progression; any effect of richness is left to the Purbeck shaftings, indeed marble is used in prodigious quantities, which further lowers the temperature. Originally these shafts were blackened, and a liberal use of paint and gilding everywhere gave the interior quite a different colour-scheme and atmosphere. As it is, a series of nineteenth-century restorations swept all the clutter hygienically away, and though the

OPPOSITE The choir at Salisbury, looking west.

circular vault-paintings have now been recovered from beneath Wyatt's whitewash, the interior is still under-decorated.

There is, too, a weakness in the basic bay-design. The arcade level, though wide-spaced, is excellent of its kind. The clerestory with its two-dimensional triple lancets complements it perfectly. But the vault is a mere eighty feet in height, and this means that the triforium level, where the designer had tried to cram in two biforas supporting a huge and complex pierced tympanum, looks crowded – and it is, unfortunately, this level which attracts the eye. The church, too, is exceptionally well lit, for virtually all the ancient coloured glass has gone, so that any design-faults proclaim themselves vociferously. Entering the cathedral for the first time, after a prolonged enjoyment of the external perspectives, is therefore an aesthetic let-down.

There are, however, merits in the internal design, and these slowly emerge. If we go to the back of the Trinity Chapel, at the far east end, where it was planned to place the feretory of St Osmund (finally canonized in 1457), we can see that the designer had thought in terms of one tremendous tunnel-vista, after the pilgrim had enjoyed the glories of the shrine, and then turned to look back westward through the entire church; though it is true this idea may have been obscured by screens. The vista is nearly 450 feet long – the height of the spire and more – and it is framed not only in the slender stone columns which flank the high altar but in the two etiolated marble clusters, as exiguously slender as palm-trunks or giant flower-stems, which hold up the chapel vault as if by magic. The vista is now interrupted by a pretentious giant cross, suspended from the high vault, but even with this obstacle the effect is magnetic and leads me to think that the cathedral should first be entered at the east end.

Moreover, the tower and steeple, which transformed the external design from a work of great merit to an unparalleled masterpiece, also came to the rescue of the interior. The addition of the high tower and stone spire raised the total weight to be carried by the four crossing piers to 6,400 tons. The builders hoped to meet this strain by vaulting the crossing below the tower, placing internal buttresses within the clerestory walls, and adding flying buttresses outside. But during the next century the crossing piers bent inwards – as one can see by looking up them – so double inverted arches were added in the choir transepts, and flat-topped girder arches in the main transepts between the crossing piers. The inverted arches are not as sensational as those at Wells, but they are striking enough, while the Perpendicular girder arches are things of beauty.

Together, these structural additions turn the two crossings into complex arenas of angles and shadows, a point on which Turner, whose masterly Salisbury interiors complement the Constable landscapes, seized with enthusiasm. He seems to have done these water-colours in the early morning and late afternoon, noting that the excess of light from which Salisbury (not being a Perpendicular church) appears to suffer does not apply if the sun is low, when its angle of entry produces dramatic bands of light and darkness and creates mysterious areas of chiaroscuro. The same principle applies to Salisbury's palm-tree Chapter House and its superb (though heavily-restored) double entry. Except for its fascinating series of Biblical low reliefs over its stalls, it has less intrinsic beauty than the Chapter House at Wells, being simpler, higher, lighter and sparer; but at the right time of day it produces some mesmeric light-effects, as Turner showed in his two drawings of it.

But everything at Salisbury returns to the spire; within or without, it pulls the whole composition together. It is more than a structure; no one who has visited Salisbury often, or better still lives in its close, can doubt that the spire has a metaphysical quality. From his house there, Sir Arthur Bryant has written: 'Every time I look out of my windows or stand in my garden, I am confronted with the amazing spectacle of the most beautiful spire in the world. Its relation to the tower which supports it and to the thirteenth-century cathedral it completes and adorns is faultless and, from whatever angle and in whatever light it is seen – a light that is ever changing with the hours – it satisfies the eye and mind of the beholder as the quintessence of perfection.'

The maturing of the Early English style as a distinctive arm of Gothic led to the creation not only of masterpieces on the largest scale, as at Wells and Salisbury, but to the reconstruction of the eastern arms of many smaller (though still important) churches. Southwark has ranked as a cathedral since 1905, when the see of South London was carved out of Winchester. Originally it was an Augustinian canonry, and an appendage to the Bishop of Winchester's London palace. After a fire in 1206, the site was cleared and reconstruction began, in the same year as the foundation-stone of Salisbury was laid down, with an ambitious eastern arm. The five-bay choir is itself impressive, because it has a multi-arch triforium, a French touch in an English design, and was squared off to the east by Bishop Fox of Winchester in 1520 by a sumptuous late-Perpendicular screen (its statues are Victorian). But what gives the church real distinction is the four-aisle Early English retrochoir, an echo of the forest-thicket hall at Wells, which was used in fact as the grandiose and menacing setting for the diocesian consistory court. Hence, under Lord Chancellor-Bishop Gardiner during the Marian persecutions, it was the theatre of some of the most pitiless heresy trials. The nave is an exercise, and a good one, in thirteenth-century Gothic by Sir Arthur Blomfield in 1890; but the hand which really brought this fine collegiate church back to life again, after centuries as a neglected parish church, was that of Sir Ninian Comper, who restored the dramatic tombs of John Gower (1408) and Lancelot Andrewes (1626), and cleared the retrochoir of its mess and clutter.

The late-Perpendicular screen in the choir at Southwark Cathedral.

Five years after Southwark began its new east end, in 1220, Carlisle followed suit with the foundations of a splendid seven-bay choir. It too was an Augustinian foundation, but it acquired its cathedral status as early as 1133. However, it was a poor see, a border town which, as capital of the West March, experienced repeated vicissitudes in the fierce raiding which continued from the reign of Edward II till Elizabeth I's time. The Norman nave was narrower than the choir, and much neglected, as is testified by the agonizing depressed arches where the nave aisles enter the transepts. The nave was partly-ruinous at the beginning of the Civil War and wholly so by the end of it. In the 1850s, Ewan Christian reduced it to two bays and rebuilt the ruins as a West Front, the two bays serving as a military chapel for the Border Regiment, so Carlisle is the only one of England's cathedrals to have virtually no nave at all.

The giant east window at Carlisle, inserted in 1340.

Yet it has some marvellous things. After a serious fire in 1292, the choir was slowly reconstructed. Each of its fourteen piers acquired a new, superbly-carved capital, the whole series surviving intact; and, even more important, a giant east window was inserted in 1340, at almost exactly the same time as the great west windows of Durham and York. Carlisle's is the finest of the three; a triumph of English-style curvilinear tracery, 51 feet by 26 feet, and evolving from a virtuoso display of drawing-board skill, in which the designer had to strike his tracery from 263 different centres. The window alone justifies the journey to Carlisle, for it is a work of mesmerising beauty, not at all the kind of vulnerable masterpiece you would expect to find in an active garrison-town. More predictable is the carving of a kilted Scotchman being swallowed by a dragon, which figures on a misericord in the fifteenth-century choir stalls. Carlisle is full of fine wood-carving: the early Renaissance Salkeld Screen, erected when the last prior became the first dean in 1541; a magnificent pulpit of about 1560, from Antwerp; and, in particular, a bishop's throne by G.E. Street, whose pinnacled canopy echoes the stalls of the choir. There is spirited incidental carving from the thirteenth and fourteenth centuries all over the choir, and the gossamer wood screen in St Catherine's Chapel off the south transept. Carlisle is rewarding for a careful and observant visitor; and a visit must include the magnificent fifteenth-century fratry, well restored by Street, which serves as the Chapter House and library, and which is built over a striking arched undercroft.

The Early English vernacular spread much further than Carlisle. During the thirteenth century, the Celtic periphery was drawn into the English architectural system. English military and ecclesiastical penetration of Wales continued, despite Celtic risings, so that churches in the North echoed Chester, and in the south St Davids reflected Wells, Glastonbury and Bristol. In Scotland, the nobility was Anglo-Scottish and many religious houses were daughters of English abbeys. Glasgow Cathedral acquired its lower church and choir in 1233–58 under English influence, and the penumbra of English Gothic even covered parts of Norway. Thus, it affected Stavanger Cathedral (c. 1272); and at Trondheim there is a type of cusping in the clustered shafts which can be found nowhere else except in two piers at Lincoln. In 1137–52, the Norman cathedral of Kirkwall in the Orkneys, which then belonged to Norway, had its old apse knocked down and a new great square-ended presbytery was built in the English fashion.

St Davids, Kirkwall and Glasgow are each of considerable intrinsic interest. St Davids was an important pilgrimage centre, whose patron St Dewi or David (died c. 600), though not officially canonized till 1311, was famous enough to attract visits from William the Conqueror, Henry II and Edward I. Its inaccessibility, like Compostella, was a challenge, and on the indulgence scale it rated half the values of Rome. The cathedral is deliberately hidden in a hollow, out of the wind (and invisible to sea-pirates); you descend thirty-nine steps to enter it, and the slope continues throughout its length. The precincts include a bishop's palace, a college and other buildings which form a small ecclesiastical town enclosed within a fortified wall, all of rugged Caerbydy stone from the cliffs a mile away. The contrast with the calm of Salisbury Close, especially on a wild day, is pointed. Yet the links with England are everywhere. The West Front of 1180–98 – that is, very late Norman, with four turrets – is manifestly of the same family which bred those of Norwich and Rochester, and later Salisbury itself. The bay-design of the nave, from the same campaign, echoes that at Worcester – that is, an uncertain acceptance of the 'Canterbury Revolution', with pointed arches only in the triforium floor, while arcade and clerestory remain obstinately Romanesque. The thirteenth-century rebuilding of the bishop's church, which made the cathedral essentially what it is, conforms to those we have examined elsewhere. The tower, built in two campaigns, 1328–47 and 1509–22, though spare and austere, is closely related to other western towers at Worcester, Hereford and elsewhere. It has some special glories though: a superb Decorative rood-screen of the fourteenth century; and a chapel, built by Bishop Gower, 1509–22, with a Tudor vault whose delicate shapes are touching in this grim place. The low-slung

OPPOSITE The monument to Lancelot Andrewes in Southwark Cathedral, restored by Sir Ninian Comper.

PAGES 90–1 Salisbury Cathedral painted by John Constable.

PAGE 91 South view of Salisbury Cathedral from the cloisters by Turner.

form of the church as a whole, with its giant buttresses on the north side, is in excellent proportion, as anyone who draws it will have the satisfaction to discover. In short, St Davids is a church which conserves its evident cathedral status and dignity even when the design is stripped to essentials.

Kirkwall's cathedral of St Magnus is something more: a small-scale masterwork of severe and massive Romanesque. It is chiefly built of grey flagstone, but brilliant use is made all through the church of red-and-yellow sandstone contrasts. The transepts (the oldest part) were built by masons from Durham. The three Early English bays, added to the choir in *c.* 1250 and which relate it to the English Gothic mainstream, are the real *clou* of the church, for their massive central piers enclose, in a pinewood chest, the skeletons of the founder of the church, St Rognald, and its patron, St Magnus – the latter with his skull smashed in martyrdom, as it was discovered in 1926. Kirkwall is the only cathedral, in fact, which definitely houses the remains of both patron and founder. Nearby are the ruined palaces of the bishop and the earl. This last is among the finest examples of Renaissance domestic architecture in Scotland. The 133-foot cathedral tower, though squat, is no mean feature, and the building as a whole is not merely dignified but resolutely self-possessed, even proud.

Glasgow is still more distinctive; a church which was conceived, it it true, in the mould of thirteenth-century Early English Gothic, but which is a dramatic

ABOVE The crypt, or lower church, of Glasgow Cathedral.

OPPOSITE The choir of St Davids Cathedral.

BELOW St Davids from the north east.

The interior of St Magnus Cathedral, Kirkwall.

OPPOSITE Glasgow Cathedral from the south west.

piece of architecture in its own historic right. It is, indeed, the only unmutilated survivor of the great Gothic churches of southern Scotland. Nearly 320 feet long, and 63 feet wide, it is almost exactly the same size as Southwell. But there all real resemblance ends. The church was begun in 1197, but in all essentials is mid-thirteenth century (the stone spire is fifteenth century, by which time English influence had diminished). The slope, however, is so steep that the nave, which ends in a superb fifteenth-century choir screen, is really only a prolegomenon to a double church, and the choir, three feet above the nave, is merely the roof to the magnificent crypt, or rather lower church, where the cathedral's patron St Mungo (d. 603) lies, along with other great Glaswegians. This is St Mungo's glory: plain and substantial early Gothic, without a trace of English Perpendicular or French Flamboyant; or, as Walter Scott put it in *Rob Roy*: 'A brave kirk, none of yere whigmaleeries and curliewurlies and open-steek hems about it – a' solid, weel-jointed masonwark, that will stand as lang as the warld – keep hands and gunpowther aff it.'

The nave, I should add, was re-processed in the fourteenth and fifteenth centuries, and is less spartan; and there were successive waves of thorough restoration in the nineteenth century. Yet the puritan atmosphere, which is pre-Reformation, remains, and the feeling that the church was essentially built for sermons is intensified by the elaborate arrangements for accommodating the

94

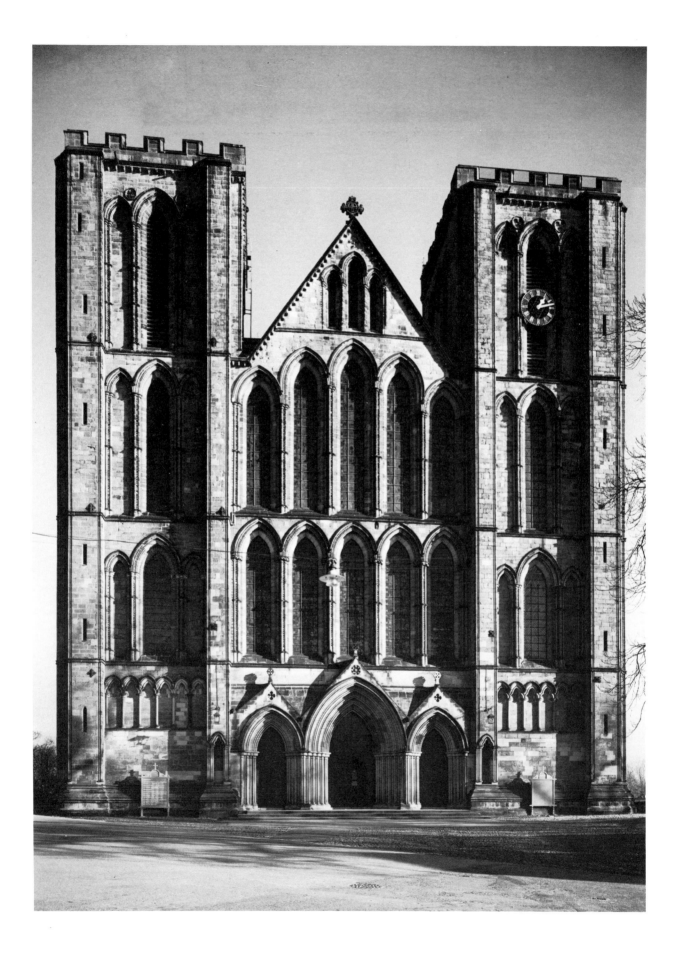

Ripon Cathedral choir.

various business groups of the city in particular pews. In 1650 Oliver Cromwell sat patiently in the nave while he was systematically denounced from the pulpit; there he heaped coals of fire on the surprised cleric, Zachary Bond, by inviting him to dinner, and took a well-judged revenge by terminating the meal with a three-hour extempore prayer. This is a strong, black-boned, deep-browed, muscular church, built for rugged and obstinate spirits.

Ripon Cathedral, in south Yorkshire, the last of what I term the Early English group, has a complicated history. It was a cathedral briefly under the auspices of St Wilfred in the seventh century, and part of Wilfred's crypt is preserved beneath the present church. The church was collegiate throughout the Middle Ages, acting as a pro-cathedral for York; the college was broken up by Edward VI, then re-established by James I; Ripon was finally raised to the rank of a full cathedral for south Yorkshire in 1836. Ripon, then, has many of the aspects of a cathedral, not least a pilgrimage shrine in the *c.* 670 crypt, which is only partly preserved but gives one some idea of how a pilgrimage reached its climax before the building of the great prodigy-churches. It is not immediately obvious, from the inside, why Ripon should be included in the Early English group, for the nave is very late Perpendicular, 1502–22, by Christopher Scune, a famous master-mason from Durham. Yet the core of the church, the chancel, and indeed part of the nave, are very early English Gothic, strictly contemporary with William of Sens's work at

OPPOSITE The West Front of Ripon Cathedral.

97

A carving of the elephant and castle on one of the choir stalls at Ripon.

Canterbury, but derived from Cistercian importation rather than directly from Sens itself. Drastic nineteenth-century restoration has blurred the historical evidence, yet it is clear that Gothic was reaching up into Europe, by 1175, quite independently of the 'Canterbury Revolution'.

By the time the West Front was built, around 1220, French influence had tapered off and the Early English manner was maturing. At Ripon, the designer contrived to produce a definite, if restrained, masterpiece, which even Pevsner, so critical of the west fronts of Salisbury and Wells, acknowledges as noble. Unlike Salisbury, it has two definite towers (intended to carry steeples, which were taken down at the Restoration) rather than four turrets; and as a collapsed Norman crossing tower was replaced by a weak fourteenth-century successor (as at Winchester), the front remains the chief feature of the church, and has the power to carry the role. Unlike Wells, it is not a display-cabinet for sculpture. What it does, in effect, is to replace the old Norman arcading, endlessly repeated, with the new and salient feature of the Early English style, the lancet window. This ingenious and novel idea makes it, as it were, a symphony of lancets, which are repeated with variations on the three upper floors of the towers and both levels of the gable between them. Four corner-turrets of the towers act as buttresses to provide depth, and the lancets themselves are deep-set so that the whole front is full of shadows and is seen to live as one marches across it from north to south. The design is very English, but in no way provincial; on the contrary, it testifies to the pervasiveness of the first distinctive style of national architecture to establish itself in Britain.

4
Splendours of the Decorated Style

The Gothic system, which was an empirical rather than a theoretical mode of architecture, proved extremely popular. The reason is simple: it achieved spectacular effects at comparatively low cost. In the twelfth century the population of Western Europe was growing fast and labour was cheap. Gothic added marginally to the labour bill in that it required the services of more expert stonemasons and carpenters; but it reduced the bill for unskilled labour and cut the cost in stone (and timber) quite dramatically. To medieval patrons, Gothic was excellent value for money; hence its adoption everywhere where Latin Christianity held sway. It did not exist in AD 1100; fifty years later it was definitely superseding Romanesque for new buildings in the leading centres of culture, the Île de France and south-east England. By 1250 it had become virtually the only mode, and had spread throughout France and England, the Rhineland and West Germany, Ireland, Scotland, Norway, the north of Spain, most of Italy, Sicily, Cyprus and parts of the eastern Mediterranean. For the next century and a half, 1250–1400, it was dominant in the Latin West, and it remained the prevailing system throughout the fifteenth century, except in Italy; indeed, it was still spreading even in the early sixteenth century, since the Spaniards took it to the New World – the first American cathedral, Santo Domingo, 1521–7, was essentially Gothic.

In England, there was a half-century of transition, 1150–1200, during which Gothic became the norm and Romanesque slowly disappeared. Thereafter it is possible to distinguish certain successive national phases in the evolution of the mode, a form of classification first introduced by the architect Thomas Rickman in his momentous study, *An Attempt to Discriminate the Styles of English Architecture from the Conquest to the Reformation* (1817). The subject has generated more heat than understanding, and I do not propose to enter into the controversy. A good rough guide is to date the Early English style from about 1175–1250 (later in the more remote areas); to date English Decorated 1250–1350; and to date English Perpendicular from its introduction in the years 1330–50; after this, Perpendicular was the prevailing style until the Reformation of the 1530s, when ecclesiastical building virtually ceased. In secular building however, a distinctive style which it is convenient to call Tudor began to emerge in about 1450.

The Decorated style is itself divided into two periods: Geometrical before 1290, when the ogee curve makes its appearance, and after 1290 Curvilinear. This is, of course, a very arbitrary classification but it reflects an undoubted tendency in the second half of the thirteenth century of designers to rely simply on circles and arcs, and then, during the next fifty years, to develop them into a rich and complex system of flowing curves. The period as a whole sees an abundance of naturalistic carving, and is rich in gilt, paint, marble, alabaster, brass, bronze and Purbeck stone. At the same time, the introduction everywhere of bar-tracery and the use of iron in window construction accelerated the lightening of windows and wall-surfaces, with glass and stone webbing increasingly replacing solid masonry.

Exeter is the supreme example of the English Decorated cathedral, but this is far from obvious at first sight. It is built on a constricted site at the top of a steep slope, and all the views one gets of it are angular, oblique and spiky. The whole design seems, and in truth is, curiously muddled. What in fact happened was this: a large and apparently splendid Norman cathedral was built on the site and

OVERLEAF Stone carvings in the Chapter House at Southwell Minster.

100

finished in the 1130s. Exeter ignored the movement in the rest of England to replace the eastern arm until as late as 1275 when it was decided to rebuild the entire church, except for its twin Norman towers. These were kept, not as a westwork but as transepts, the new choir and nave being built between them. Why did they do this? We do not know; presumably because they were much loved. The arrangement is unique, at any rate in England, and it provides some fascinating vistas in the 180-degree arc running from the cathedral green to the north, through the garden of the bishop's palace to the south-east, to the garden of the deanery, almost due south. These are not broad and sensational views, as at Salisbury, but domestic, intimate and unexpected; Exeter is hugged closely by the town and precinct, as if sheltering from the terrific winds which sweep up the Exe Valley from the west.

Of course the key external view ought to be from the green to the West Front, with the towers behind. The West Front was built in 1346–75, right at the end of the rebuilding period, and it seems to have been an attempt to reproduce, at the west end, the staircase design used so successfully at a number of English cathedrals, including Exeter, at the east end. It is built in three receding planes. The bottom story is an immense stone screen, used as a sculpture-gallery, as at Wells. The sculpture is worn but it is original, and there is no argument that this part of the design succeeds admirably. The second storey is the main west gable consisting of an enormous late-Decorated window, with sloping gable-ends

The West Front of Exeter Cathedral.

101

which also contained sculpture once. The actual top of the gable is reserved for the third storey, which is deeply recessed, and contains another large window. The bottom of each window is masked by the storey below, and it is difficult to discover what the ideal viewpoint was that the designer had in mind – if, indeed, a single designer was responsible, which I find hard to believe. It says a lot for the protean nature of Gothic that this weird arrangement, a kind of anti-design, is not a total disaster; indeed, some people find it compelling, and certainly on the afternoon of a sunny day, with the light coming from the south, the shadow-patterns are sensational.

Exeter has a complete set of fabric rolls, running without a break from 1279 to 1514. Such documents provide a mass of detailed information but they do not necessarily tell you who designed anything. The original designer seems to have been Master Roger, succeeded by William Love in 1310; and the actual work was carried out by John of Glaston (stalls), Thomas of Winton (bishop's throne and nave), William de Schoverville, William Joy and Richard Farleigh (western screen and nave vaulting), and Robert Lesingham (cloister, east window and north-west porch). In short, many major artists were involved, over an extended period, and the West Front may reflect successive changes in plan.

The first-time visitor who has paused to study and puzzle over the West Front will not, therefore, be prepared for the overwhelming beauty of the interior once he enters through the north porch. It is, in fact, the contrast of Salisbury but in reverse. For Exeter is the only English cathedral (except Salisbury) whose interior is designed as a whole, from the west end right through to the Lady Chapel beneath the great east end window. Moreover, it has a perspective advantage which Salisbury lacks. Since the Norman towers were retained as transepts, by the simple expedient of knocking down the bottom halves of their inside walls, arching the aperture and punching through big late-Decorated windows on the outside, there was no need for a crossing as such. Since the nave and choir are well lit, there is no call for the central lantern either. Thus the functional interruption of the crossing is dispensed with. In one sense this is a drawback, for in the greatest cathedrals the crossing provides opportunities for stupendous space effects. But its absence, in this case, gave the designer the chance to visualize a nave and choir, 300 feet long in all, as one continuous flow of bays under a single roof. As the bays and vaults were designed and constructed as a single operation, the result is the longest Gothic perspective in the world.

If the designer created this unique opportunity for himself by dispensing with the normal transept and the crossing, he certainly made the most of it. We have noted that the basic bay design at Wells is very fine. At Exeter, which absorbed the Wells model, it is even better. The arcade of clustered columns and arch mark the perfection of pure Gothic. They are big and rangy, but they are matched and balanced by the huge Decorated windows of the clerestory, from which the light pours in abundantly, through the integrated frame of the vaulting. Since the vault as a whole is low, the risk of the design was that the middle, triforium storey would seem crowded. Master Roger avoided the trap by introducing the French device of a low arcade, topped by a brilliant fringe of decorative quatrefoils – a device which permits miniaturization and eventually enabled Perpendicular designers to eliminate the middle storey entirely by extending the great clerestory windows downwards.

Since the vault was designed at the same time as the bay, it appears to spring from it naturally, from inverted-triangle corbels which offer a rich field for

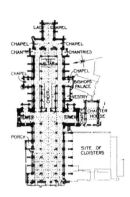

EXETER

sculpture, and which link the main arches directly with the actual spring-point at the clerestory level. The effect, then, is to suggest that organic growth which nearly always distinguishes great architecture, especially in Gothic. The vault-ribs are thus anchored firmly at one end; at the other a single line of ribs and bosses runs, straight as an arrow, the whole 300-foot length of the roof, from the giant Decorated window at the west end to its Perpendicular sister over the choir.

We have, then, at Exeter the best-designed interior of any English cathedral; indeed, I know of nothing to compare it with in mainland Europe. But it is more than just good design: it has an enveloping warmth which enormously intensifies the contrast with glacial Salisbury. This is achieved by a highly sophisticated use of materials. I strongly suspect that the designer, having been given the chance to produce an integrated design for the whole length of the church, was determined to avoid the mistake made at Salisbury of using too much polished Purbeck. At Exeter, the basic material is limestone from the chapter's own quarry at Beer, twenty miles away. Purbeck is used to strengthen the piers, but it is left unpolished, and today is a mellow mid-grey; in addition, the designer used two distinctive local sandstones, red and yellowish in colour. So four different stones are used, and enormous trouble has been taken to get the bandings regular and symmetrical, especially on the clustered pillars, producing a marvellous series of horizontal eye-lines. The concept, then, is philosophical, as good Gothic must be; but, as with Dr Johnson's philosophical friend, 'cheerfulness keeps breaking in'

The vault of the south nave aisle at Exeter.

as the warm stonework makes the vast interior glow even on the chilliest winter day. Indeed, the cathedral is seen at its best under a winter blue sky with snow on the ground, when the reflected sunlight pours in through the great windows and the interior almost bursts into flames.

The designer, having picked on a gallery arcade to solve his bay-design problems, added a stroke of pure genius, by turning one of the galleries over the fifth arch in the north arcade into a musical display of sculpture, where fourteen angels play the bagpipe, citole, recorder, viol, harp, Jew's harp, trumpet, hand-organ, gittern, shawm, timbrel and cimbels. This enchanting piece of work was meticulously restored and re-painted in the 1930s by the leading authority on English medieval painting, Professor E. W. Tristram, who also dealt with the murals and splendid monuments with which this church is crowded, and the superb sculptured corbels of the choir. Part of the choir, indeed, is painted as it was in the Middle Ages, and the cathedral as a whole is in an excellent state. It abounds with the sharp observation and the riotous fancy of the medieval mind at its most exuberant. There is an early fourteenth century bishop's throne of Devon oak, which is over sixty feet high; a choir screen (or pulpitum) of the same period, made of Purbeck carved in the Curvilinear Decorated at its most Baroque, and adorned with a fascinating series of seventeenth-century painted panels; and above all, everywhere in the church, a mass of fine carving in wood and stone, including a brilliant reconstruction of the Becket murder on one of the nave bosses, a portrait head of a master-mason on a corbel and a misericord of an elephant. It is thus possible, at Exeter, to study the age of English Decorated, from say 1275–1350, not only at its best, but in virtually all of its aspects.

Nevertheless, Bristol must also be examined, in conjunction with Exeter, for there the same school of designers added some unique and exciting features. Bristol, of course, was not a cathedral in medieval times, but an Augustinian canonry founded by Robert Fitzharding, the first of the great Berkeley lords; it was, therefore, a late-Norman building. Very late in the thirteenth century, perhaps a few years after the Exeter rebuilding began, Abbot Knowle commissioned a new eastern arm. What he got for his money was something entirely novel: a hallchurch, in which the aisles swept up to the same height as the main span, and the bay system, as a structural feature, was virtually abandoned, with no blind storey and no clerestory.

In effect, the chancel is a vast room resting on a forest of pillars; but in the aisles, to provide additional strength, a new (and, except at Gloucester, unique) system of vaulting was introduced. Here, the side of each pillar, which is more a set of mouldings than a cluster of shafts, is joined to the aisle buttresses by a strainer-arch, or flying shore, with a horizontal king-post set on top of the arch to prevent it from buckling upwards, and each spandrel set with a fierce eye for extra strength. Thus the thrust of the main vault is transferred across the aisles to the buttresses on the outside of the church, and at the same time upwards to meet and counter the downward thrust of the aisle vault, which forms a cone resting on the centre of the king-post, thus dividing each vaulting bay of the aisle into two. It sounds complicated and indeed in a sense it is, though the engineering concept behind it is obvious once it has been formulated. Therein lay the genius of the idea, for what no one could really have known, until the structure was aloft and finished, was what a masterly composition would result, in terms of mass and shape, light and shade. These aisles are marvels; they mark the beginning of a new epoch of mastery in the architectural enclosure of high space, and they

OPPOSITE Fourteenth-century aisle vaulting and strainer arches at Bristol.

produce the metaphysical consequence of pulling the eye irresistibly upwards. There was nothing else like it on the Continent at the time, which indicates the technical superiority of the English masters, especially in the West Country.

These master-craftsmen seem, indeed, to have taken a virtuoso delight in their ingenuity. At Bristol they added a coda to the great stone symphony of the chancel-vaulting in the antechamber of the chapel they designed for the Berkeley tombs. Here, a flat stone ceiling is supported, not by an opaque vault, but by a complete system of flying ribs, springing from side-shafts and pinned along the centre-axis by a series of giant floral bosses, but without any stone shell in the gaps, as though the designer was anxious to show the layman, gawping at his creation from below, exactly how a medieval vault worked. Like the massive saltires of Wells, but on a far more delicate scale, it treats stonework as though it were poured ferro-concrete, and contains a wealth of advice for modern designers.

The great vaulting cones of the choir burgeon into a magnificent set of arches at the crossing, supporting a huge and complex canopy of vaults which were not completed until the 1470s, but afford some startling vistas at the junction of crossing, transepts and choir-aisles, all of them high up – Bristol is a place where the neck soon begins to ache. There are some deep and tremendous shadows, for the system of natural lighting is complex and elusive. Above the crossing, on its four massive piers, the canons placed a powerful two-storey tower, but they did not have time to build a new nave before they were nationalized by Henry VIII, and the church was turned into a cathedral (1542). Indeed, the nave was not built until 1868 when G.E. Street was called in and supplied one which is neat, elegant and broadly in character with the Decorated inspiration of the chancel (as well as two west towers finished after his death).

What comes as a delightful surprise to the unsuspecting visitor is that Bristol, generally regarded (and rightly) as a later medieval work, has preserved its original Norman chapter house. This is 1150–70, just before the 'Canterbury Revolution', but deep Romanesque still. The vestibule or entrance has a series of large and powerful arches, masking a simple stone vault; and the chapter house itself is square, with a gigantic but elementary vault, the ribs fiercely dog-toothed, and a system of arcaded patterning on the walls which demonstrates the rich sources of Romanesque decorative schemes, but makes Gothic – already rearing its head 200 miles away in Kent – seem many light-years off.

Chester Cathedral has a similar history to Bristol, that is, it was a regular foundation (Benedictine) turned into a secular cathedral by Henry VIII in the 1540s. Like Bristol again, it is basically a Norman structure subjected to a grandiose rebuilding programme starting in the late thirteenth century. In Chester's case, however, the programme was so leisurely that it stretched throughout the fourteenth century and for most of the fifteenth. Chester was not a big city like Bristol but a garrison town forced to contain itself within the restrictive perimeter of the old Roman fortifications. This may help to explain why the cathedral is such an odd shape, with a large choir, a small nave, virtually no transept on the north side but a gigantic one – the biggest in England – on the south side, where it was probably used as a self-contained parish church. The stone is softish pink sandstone, and most of the external detail has disappeared, or been replaced in a self-confident series of nineteenth-century restorations, mainly by Scott.

It is fashionable to dismiss Chester Cathedral as undistinguished in the first

OPPOSITE Norman blind arcading in Bristol chapter house.

The choir at Chester facing west, showing the late fourteenth-century choir stalls.

OPPOSITE The sixteenth-century fan vault of Henry VII's chapel in Westminster Abbey.

PAGES 110–1 The nave of Exeter Cathedral, looking east.

PAGE 111 The west front of Ely.

place, and over-restored in the second. In fact it has a number of minor virtues, and one of great importance. The minor virtues centre mainly on the Chapter House, the only early thirteenth-century rectangular chapter house to survive in anything like its original state, with a superb set of lancet windows, a vaulted vestibule of singular grace and simplicity, and internal vaulting of great energy. It is not something to be expected in a small and poor Benedictine house like Chester, and one is very glad to have it. There are other monastic buildings of interest, especially the thirteenth-century frater or refectory, which has a rare (perhaps unique) stone pulpit, its elegant stairs set into the thickness of the wall, from which it projects menacingly on a corbel.

However, what makes Chester worth a visit is the most exotic and complex set of choir stalls in the British Isles. They date from the 1380s or 1390s, which puts them a little later than the series at Lincoln, and they clearly formed the centrepiece of the entire decorative scheme worked out so patiently from its beginnings in the 1290s, to its Perpendicular culmination in the late fifteenth century. The benches have a perfect set of forty-eight misericords, which are worth examining individually. They include a crafty fox, and one pretending to be dead; a man beating his wife, and a woman beating her husband; a tiger hunt and a stag-hunt, a man with a captive lion and a sow with her litter; men wrestling and racing; and a whole range of mythical and religious scenes. What makes the ensemble such a prodigy of design, however, is the profile-line of

the high canopies of the stalls, which leaps from one summit to the next like a fierce upward flame, casting fantastic shadows when lit from below by candles fixed to the pews. The stalls culminate in a gigantic entrance canopy like a spiky tiara, which provides a breathtaking view when seen from in front of the high altar, silhouetted against the high and well-lit Perpendicular nave to the west. No one who has enjoyed this cunning vista, so spectacularly characteristic of the late-Gothic ethos, can dismiss Chester as unrewarding.

Lichfield, another worn sandstone cathedral, is much more obviously a prodigy-church in the English Decorated manner, though what we now see is a bruised and battered masterpiece. Both its ecclesiastical and its architectural history are complex. Lichfield, of course, was the capital of an expanding Mercia until the ninth century, and an early see with a big Saxon cathedral on the present site. The see was moved to Chester in 1075 and to Coventry in 1102 (a joint see). Nothing has been found of the pre-Conquest church, and little of the Norman one, *c.* 1090–1150; and as a result of Civil War looting the cathedral's history is virtually undocumented. Nevertheless, patient research has made possible a reconstruction. Work went on throughout the whole of the thirteenth century and the first third of the fourteenth. The last three bays of the choir were completed about 1200. The Early English transepts and the Chapter House, by Thomas the Elder, took shape in the 1230s and 1240s. But the *clou* of the interior, a masterpiece of Early Decorated, was the nave designed by William's son, William Fitz-Thomas, around 1250, but not completed until 1330. In the period *c.* 1265–80, that is, the height of the Early Decorated, Thomas Wallace, a Welshman, designed the West Front and the three-tower system.

Lichfield, then, was a very ambitious exercise in English Decorated, inside and out. Two Irishmen from Dublin, Simeon Simon and Hugh the Illustrator, visited it on their way to the Holy Land in 1323, when the massive building scheme was almost finished, and described it as 'a church of most gracious and wondrous beauty, with very high stone steeples or belfries, paintings and carving, well enriched and adorned with other church furnishings'. So it remained, for over 300 years, though the weather progressively eroded its external mouldings and sculptures, and the great shrine of St Chad, erected at enormous cost by Edward I's treasurer, Walter Langton, was despoiled in the 1530s. Then, in 1643, the royalists occupied its walled and battlemented close against a besieging army led by Lord Brooke. The Parliamentary commander was shot dead by a deaf-mute from the parapet of the central steeple, and in consequence Brooke's artillery bombarded the outside of the building for the next three days, and his infantry ransacked the interior after the surrender. The central steeple was smashed, and was rebuilt at the Restoration on more or less the old lines; and in the late eighteenth and nineteenth centuries, a host of thorough-going restorers came and left in waves, beginning with Wyatt and progressing through the usual nineteenth-century pattern. It is customary to condemn their work as insensitive, out of period, 'Victorian' and offensive to good taste. Certainly, the plates in Britton's great cathedral series of 1822 show a different system of decoration to the one we now have on the West Front; but much of this was itself composed of seventeenth- and eighteenth-century repairs to the stonework. We do not really know what the church looked like in detail before the Civil War disaster.

Let us, therefore, take what good things remain and be grateful. From afar, there is no question that Lichfield is a stunning sight. The spire triad, which might have erupted so magnificently at Wells, say, or Ripon, is here seen in its reality.

OPPOSITE The tomb of Henry VII and his queen, Elizabeth of York, in Westminster Abbey, by Pietro Torrigiano.

Moreover, it is combined with a West Front which resembles the type of virtuoso display of statuary we find so often in France, and notably at Amiens and Rheims. It is said that the doors are too small; that the statues are all Victorian; that the great Geometrical Decorated west window, under its matching gable, is a fake; and, with more justice, that the two corner turrets of the front merge awkwardly into the pinnacle-structure at the base of the two west steeples.

Nevertheless, the front has an unforgettable impact when seen at a distance of between 100 and 200 feet. It can be taken head-on, with the central steeple making a ghostly and sinister appearance between its two lower sisters; or, to the north-west and south-west, there are magnificent stonescapes formed by the spiky trio and the abundant flying buttresses of the nave. The north-east approach is also of great interest; for here, in the foreground, is the best-designed of all Lichfield's features, the Lady Chapel, which has the same internal height as the choir and forms an apsidal end to the whole eastern arm. With its massive buttresses, and its very narrow, trefoil-headed windows, it pulls the eye decisively upwards to the pinnacle of the crossing-spire and its two shadows peering over the roof of the north transept. There are many permutations of these vistas.

The north side of Lichfield nave, showing the bay design.

As for the interior, it benefits from two salient features. The first is an exceptionally well-designed bay, which has all the confidence of the early Decorated clustered pillars – well carved and spaced, and not much inferior to those of Wells or Exeter – plus an ingenious cinquefoil motif in the spandrels, divided by the vault-shafting, which relates neatly to the triple trefoils in the triangular clerestory windows. These light up the nave adequately, but leave ample space for a full-scale Decorated triforium level, reminiscent of Lincoln. Thus the bay is well-balanced, and the lowish nave is adequately heightened by the springing shafts which are carried right down to the pavement.

The second feature is the unusual length of the eastern arm, made possible by an unbroken choir built as one vast room, and extended, indeed, into the Lady Chapel, which is effectively part of it. Hence, from the east end of the lady Chapel, well lit by its tall and elegant windows, a long and leisurely vista opens, taking one through the crossing and into the nave, where it loses itself in the blazing tracery of the west window, fake or not. The crossing arches, which cannot be later than about 1200, are particularly fine, and the transepts are good Early English too, though one ends in modern lancets and the other in a Perpendicular window. Never mind – at Lichfield, chronological puritanism and logic should be firmly thrust aside, and the cathedral enjoyed for the pleasure it gives to the eye and the confidence with which it has surmounted adversity. On close examination, there is a sound case to be made for most of Scott's work, and even some of Wyatt's; and nothing can detract from the delight of its three golden spires seen from afar, as endearing today as when they were first glimpsed by Hugh the Illustrator, who probably drew them, as I have on many occasions.

The approach to Ely, of course, is much more spectacular, especially on certain mornings in autumn and early summer, with a low-lying mist. The lowlands around seem to stretch to eternity, and the immensely long silhouette – it has twenty-seven bays in all – conceals the size of the mass at first sight; but as one draws nearer, the sheer magnitude of the thing becomes apparent, underlining the uniqueness of this man-made escarpment thrusting up out of the marshy plain. The town is still mercifully small, and nothing distracts the eye from the minster: it has an unsurpassed natural stage on which to display its prodigious existence.

Ely was the quintessential pilgrim-cathedral. Its seventh-century founder, the

OPPOSITE Lichfield Cathedral from the north west.

A roof boss in the choir of Ely Cathedral showing its founder, St Etheldreda.

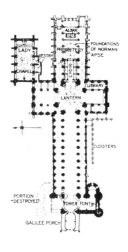

ELY

Princess Etheldreda, had been revered as a saint from the time of her death, and throughout the Middle Ages she was by far and away the most popular woman saint in the British Isles. The Benedictine Abbey was always rich, in lands as well as offerings, and from 1107 the Abbot was made, in addition, bishop of a see carved out of the giant Lincoln diocese. The two Saxon minsters on the site have disappeared, but thereafter Ely can display examples, usually superlative, of every phase of English architecture over 600 years: Norman West Front and nave (1081–1150); transitional north transept (completed 1174); Early English merging into early Decorated eastern arm (1234–52); late Decorated and early Perpendicular central octagon and lantern (1322–40); late-Perpendicular west tower lantern (1390s); and the beginnings of English Renaissance in the east chantries (1488, 1533).

There is, therefore, no unifying plan in strict academic terms. But all the architects involved – and Ely seems invariably to have employed the best it could get – were united in their aim to shock and inspire the pilgrim, and therefore cleverly used their predecessor's work to build up the effects. In that sense Ely is homogenous, so that the chronology becomes less important than the sequence of vistas.

The approach over the marshes was designed to emphasize length rather than height, up to the point when the approaching pilgrim became aware of the great mass of the building; at that stage his attention was abruptly and cunningly switched to the height of the West Front. English Romanesque architects had great difficulty with west fronts, as we have observed, because they thought in terms of bay-units rather than complete elevations. They tended, therefore, either to continue the elevation of nave and aisles into a façade, as at Durham, or to build a west transept. This, indeed, is what is done at Ely, but a transept turned into a miniature cathedral in itself. In its original form, it had not two towers, but five (one at each corner), and an enormous six-storey belfry over the main west entrance. Moreover, these towers, and especially the central tower, do not simply emerge from the transept – and thus reveal their false pretensions – but were built from the ground up, and thus confirm the old architectural maxim that a tower looks taller (and aesthetically secure) when the eye can follow it from the ground up. The huge extra belfry, with its corner staircase turrets, which was added in the 1390s makes it taller still, thus piling Pelion on Ossa. It has been attacked by the purists, to my mind quite wrongly. For what they forget is that the west tower was balanced, in the original scheme, by a high stone lantern over the crossing. When this fell in 1322, and was replaced by the much larger octagon-lantern, the west tower had to be raised to get back to the original balance. Of course, adding this huge storey caused structural problems below, which worry the surveyor even today, but that is another matter.

The west front scheme was further adorned in two ways: the use of round, or rather polygonal surfaces, at the corners throughout, which delights the eye today as much as it obviously did in the twelfth century; and a virtuoso display of Romanesque arcading and window-arching. This west wall was built up over seventy or eighty years, and the mason-architects did their best according to the lights of their generation. Thus the five-storey scheme becomes more sophisticated at each level; and the great display-wall which once, naturally, contained a mass of sculpture, is a historical lesson in the evolution of a style, made logical by the fact that the eye travels upwards.

Of course the northern third of the front has gone – collapsed, like the Norman

The central lantern at Ely,
seen from the west tower.

crossing-tower. This is a tragedy, and I think a strong case could be made for building a replica, if the money could be raised. After all, who seriously worries about the fact that the north-west tower at Canterbury is an early nineteenth-century replica? Indeed, ninety per cent of the visitors assume it is genuine; and to put it there a perfectly good Norman tower was actually demolished. It is not logical to allow our predecessors useful liberties which we now deny to ourselves on doctrinaire grounds. The plain truth is that Ely would be vastly improved if the north-west transept were restored.

Objections are also made to the Early English Galilee porch, which juts out from the West Front and (it is said) destroys its purity. In fact it blends remarkably well: its three lancets are deliberately archaic in the Transitional style, so that their family resemblance to the late-Norman arches on the upper storeys of the west tower is very striking. The arcading, too, blends naturally, continuing the history lesson begun in the front before the Galilee was even thought of.

More important still, the Galilee, with its exquisite double arch of about 1215, forms a matchless frame – the proportions were deliberately designed to correspond – for the visitor's first glimpse of the interior. The vista is incomparable: one sees all twenty-seven bays at once, actually from outside the church (a privilege proffered by no other cathedral, I think), and the exceptionally high and narrow proportions are repeated throughout, from Galilee, to crossing,

117

to the lancets at the far east end. Rarely do we find such a vivid demonstration of medieval architects working in harmony with each other over the centuries.

The nave is Norman arcading at its very best. The main stress, of course, is on length, to provide the silhouette from afar, and the tunnel-vista from outside. But a striking effect of height is also achieved, by narrowing the nave. The bay-design is perfect: Norman arcade-architecture at its most serene. The proportion of arcade, triforium and clerestory is classically correct – six, five, four – and with each stage the arch miniaturizes itself, so we get two above the arcade and three in the clerestory. But the designer not only produced a classic statement of Romanesque form; he was clearly moving on to something finer yet. In the nave the mouldings, springing from the multiple columns of the first and second storeys, have acquired a degree of sophistication and interdependent logic which clearly prefigures the Gothic moulding-system. They are, indeed, Gothic without the arch. When we turn the corner, however, and advance into the north transepts, we get a further surprise, another architectural history lesson, in fact. For while the ground storey is blank wall, and the middle storey richly-decorated arcades, the pointed arch supersedes the round one in the top storey, and the arch mould descends into clustered shafts. What this seems to indicate is that, quite independently of the 'Canterbury Revolution', English designers moved from the late Norman forms into a transitional phase which adumbrated Gothic.

In the thirteenth century, the great nave and transepts, with their double aisles, having been completed, it was decided to rebuild the eastern arm to provide a more magnificent setting for the high altar and a retrochoir for St Etheldreda's shrine. The scheme followed is one of the best of its kind; it draws all the lessons from the Early English work in the Lincoln nave, and proceeds on lines which foreshadow the Angel Choir at Lincoln (though it has no figure-statues as an integral part of the decoration). Hence it may well be that the same team of designers and craftsmen moved from one cathedral to the other – the dates of the Ely east end (1235–52) fit this assumption. Certainly, the six bays of this presbytery (the first three bays of the east end are fourteenth-century reconstruction) display a highly-successful combination of the boldness of Early English with the richness of Decorative, the triforium being a classic example of design on these principles. It includes an impressive amount of detail – side-shafts interlaid with bands of trefoils, arches trefoiled, quatrefoils in the side-spandrels matched by a quatrefoil and leaf-sprays in the centre one – yet it is uncrowded and the proportions are exactly right. What we have here, in these eastern bays, is a very cleverly thought-out and integrated architectural setting for a notable shrine. The three fourteenth-century bays nearest the crossing (the arcade now covered by the choirstalls) make an instructive contrast, for they indicate what happens when the controlled English Decorative topples over into mannerism.

At the beginning of the fourteenth century then, Ely had followed the characteristic building pattern of most English cathedrals: a Norman nave, with a spectacularly rebuilt east end for its shrine. Then, in 1322, came the catastrophe which turned Ely into a unique masterpiece. The crossing-piers collapsed, and the great central tower, like the west towers but bigger and heavier, came crashing down, bringing with it much of the transepts and the first three bays of the choir. There was thus a huge hole in the middle of the church. How to fill it?.

Ely's sacrist, who was in charge of the fabric, was Alan of Walsingham, who seems to have been familiar with the capabilities of both stonemasons and carpenters. Like many thoughtful clerics, he must have been puzzled by the evolution of the crossing-space. In a Byzantine church, the crossing would have been covered by a dome, and used by the congregation, but English cathedrals had a nave for that. The nave terminated in a rood-screen. The bishop's church, or east end, began with the choir-screen. The space in between was simply an ambulatory or no man's land.

Alan conceived the idea of making the crossing the climax of the church. He would not fill the hole; he would roof it. The roof would not be a dome, since Gothic rejected the dome completely. It would not be a vault, since stone could not be used to cover so wide a space. Indeed, at Ely only the six surviving bays of the choir were covered in painted wood. There was a further factor. As the transepts were double-aisled, the basic supports for an octagonal structure already existed. What this suggested, therefore, was an enormous piece of carpentry, providing a roof-cover of the same basic type as the polygonal chapter house, of which several already existed, but without a central clustered pillar. And, to provide light, this octagonal roof-cover would be punched through by a tall lantern, with a matching lantern on the west tower.

C.A. Hewett, the leading expert on English cathedral carpentry, suggests that the eight enormous piers which provided ground support were completed up to the upper string courses by 1328. Then the carpenters took over the stonemasons' scaffolds and centering. Three head carpenters were involved: Master Thomas, Master William de Houk and William Hurley, the king's master-carpenter. It looks as though a detailed plan of the stone-and-timber structure as a whole must have been made, since the masons had worked into the stone the vital sill-hooks and squinting-pockets the carpenters needed. Indeed, it is very likely that a large scale-model was set up, to determine the complicated and vital order of procedure.

Hewett argues that the need to effect repairs to the octagon and lantern over the centuries, notably by James Essex in the 1750s, now makes it impossible to determine exactly how the original structure was set up. The structural evidence, when closely examined, appears to conflict with the documentary evidence. What the carpenters seem to have done is to erect a perforated foundation-platform on timbers resting on the eight stone piers. On top of this were the eight giant timbers of the lantern, shored up by sixteen timbers resting on the piers. The greatest timbers came from Chikissand in Bedfordshire, where Alan and master Thomas bought twenty enormous oaks for £9. Such trees do not exist today. It is usually said that the eight great lantern-posts are sixty-three feet long and in one piece. In fact one post is scarfed throughout most of its height, and others have extensions scarfed on the top. As the wooden lantern was covered in lead, the weight was enormous; and the timber support-structure has become so complicated over the centuries that an effective isometric drawing has to omit a great many of the pieces. What is clear is that the wonderfully gifted carpenters were working at the very frontiers of their technology and doing something which had never even been attempted before. (The feat was repeated at Windsor, where Hurley built a similar roof for Edward III's round table banqueting-hall for the newly-created Order of the Garter – a structure long since demolished.)

Alan of Walsingham's head is carved on the splendid octagon he designed, and deservedly so. He transferred the choir into the centre of the crossing, thus giving it a new function, and leaving all the eastern arm for 'St Audrey'. This arrangement has since been reversed, though the crossing still has a plain modern altar in it. But the real function of the crossing, at any rate as we see it today, is not

liturgical but emotional and metaphysical. We move up the long, twelve-bay nave, which is narrow and therefore, seemingly high, and pass under the great end-of-nave arch into what seems almost infinite space. The light streams in diagonally from four different sides, and it also pours in from the lantern at the top; we have, in effect a circular vaulting structure with an airy hole in the middle, and a brilliant display of eight enormously high clustered pillars. The effect is so unusual for an eye trained to take in Gothic formulae, and the sense of unleashed space so hard to fit in with one's notions of 'normal' Gothic, that one experiences a certain disorientation. The lantern, soaring above the darkness of the vault that supports it, looks even higher than it actually is. Not even the high vaults of the Île de France, not even the monstrous Beauvais, contrive this stratospheric effect. The light impact varies radically according to the time of day and the sky-quality, but I have never known it fail to be striking because of the variety of angles of the vaulting and the different levels of perception. Moreover, it changes as one advances or retreats along the four axes of approach – nave, choir and transepts – where the four principal arches provide stupendous framing. From the back of the transepts, for instance, several distinct systems of light-and-shade are visible, and one marvels at the complexity of the problems which confronted Turner when he was painting this astonishing enclosure of space in the fugitive medium of water-colour. Here is a case and there are many others in Gothic architecture, where our understanding of the structure, and our appreciation of its ingenuity and success, is fundamentally improved by the effort to draw it.

Ely must have swarmed with able artists and craftsmen in the second quarter of the fourteenth century. Most were working on the Octagon-Lantern; others were in the mannerist section of the choir; yet others were building and decorating the spectacular Lady Chapel, which is a kind of huge annexe to the north transept. Work there began in 1321, just before the tower collapsed, and the decorating went on till the 1370s. I suspect that the master-mason in charge, having watched the carpenters carry off all the glory of the Lantern, vowed to produce a stone prodigy, no doubt encouraged by the masterful Alan. At all events the vault, forty-six feet across, is the widest in England. The interior scheme, which is late Decorative at its most ambitious, has been ravaged by the bigots, for Ely lay deep in puritan territory, and the Virgin was particularly objectionable to them. So the glass and statuary have gone, but the great rectangular hall, as big as a parish church, is by no means bare. The stalls, as in a chapter house, have superb canopies, which here take the form of what are called 'nodding ogees', part of the swirling, swaying, rippling spirit which made up fourteenth-century English Baroque, and which is echoed in the fine tracery of the windows. Above is a sensational star-lierne vault, with endless bosses. What this great chamber must have looked like at the end of the fourteenth century, with the stalls painted and gilded, the niches brimming with painted statues, the altar glittering in gold, silver and semi-precious stones, and the vast windows filtering the light through blue, green, orange and red glass, is almost beyond our capacity to conceive. St Etheldreda, by the middle of the fourteenth century, effectively occupied the whole of the east end – the only woman saint to achieve this distinction – and it is characteristic of the monkish sense of proprieties that the Virgin should receive at least comparable treatment. So this rectangular palace was erected and adorned; the iconoclasts raked it, and the ravaged beauty is left to exercise our imaginations.

Ely is rich in decorative schemes of all periods, which have in common the

OPPOSITE Ely: the view from the choir to the lantern and nave.

enviable self-confidence of the first-rate artist. In the south aisle of the nave, the Prior's Door which opens onto the cloister has magnificent late-Norman carved pillars and arch, with a tympanum of a majestic Christ, using the hard-setting local limestone which looks as though it was carved yesterday. At the other end of the Middle Ages and the church, that is in the corner-niches of Etheldreda's retrochoir, two episcopal chantries herald a new era. Bishop Alcock's dates from the early years of Henry VII and is still essentially medieval, though a squaring off of the design-patterns, especially over the doorway, denotes the coming of the Renaissance. In Bishop West's chantry (1533) it has triumphantly arrived, with its straight lines, right angles and ornamental devices, especially in the infillings of the vault, though the fundamental concept is still medieval. What, indeed, gives Ely its tremendous fascination of detail, as well as its obvious sweeping effects, is the fact that its designers were repeatedly, over the centuries, poised between the two systems of beauty, caught as it were in the act of relinquishing one style and embracing another. The whole cathedral is a gorgeous experiment, an architectural laboratory in which new ideas and concepts were tested; one is always conscious in admiring it of the restless intelligences, the probing, questing, adventurous – even reckless – minds which went into its making.

Piecing together the cathedral architecture of thirteenth- and fourteenth-century England, one is uneasily conscious of the great gap left by the disappearance of Old St Paul's. This was the biggest and richest of all English cathedrals, and in many respects the most consistently innovatory, reflecting the pride of one of the wealthiest cities in northern Europe and its determination to be first. Literary evidence and pre-1655 drawings tell us a great deal but they do not justify the confident assertions which are often made about the influence of Old St Paul's on other buildings. With Westminster Abbey it is a different matter. It is still there, though greatly changed, and although only a cathedral during the years 1540–50, it has always been the ceremonial church of royalty (it was, and is, a 'Royal Peculiar' in terms of ecclesiastical structure). Until the reign of Henry VIII, the main royal palace was at Westminster and the abbey was called upon to perform many cathedral functions. Indeed, it seems to have been the only church in England whose whole fabric had actual liturgical purpose, for even the gallery, which elsewhere was decorative, was used at coronations (and still is).

Understandably, then, Westminster was an important pace-setter in English cathedral architecture from the 1150s, when Edward the Confessor began building the first Norman great church in England, to the reign of Henry VII, when William Vertue replaced the central apse-chapel with the great pendant-vaulted chapel which houses Henry's body (1503–13). Essentially, however, the Abbey is the creation of the second half of the thirteenth century. It thus fits into the historical pattern in which English cathedrals demolished their eastern arms to provide prodigy-shrines, but in the case of Westminster the change came late and was markedly different. The Confessor was canonized in 1161; but it was not until 1245 that Henry III, the greatest English art-patron of the Middle Ages, felt wealthy enough to begin a grand scheme of renewal. By 1245 a number of things had happened which made him unwilling to follow the aesthetic route traced by Wells, Lincoln and others. France had recaptured the architectural leadership by her stupendous high-vaulted cathedrals of the Île de France – notably Rheims, which like the Abbey was a coronation church as well as a shrine-church. Henry admired Rheims, and his designer, Henry of Reyns, almost certainly came from there.

Westminster, then, was rebuilt from the east end mainly, though not entirely,

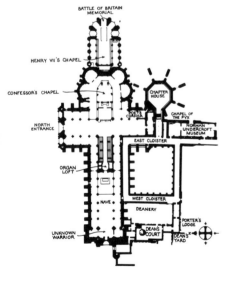

WESTMINSTER ABBEY

on the French model. It has a chevet-type apse. It adopted French theoretical notions as to the height and proportions of the nave. Thus, the arcade is half the total height; the triforium (or tribune, or gallery) is one-sixth; and the clerestory is one-third – the figures being 51, 17 and 34 feet, making 102 feet in all, easily the highest vault in England. Where French theory was abandoned was in the length of the nave, which kept exactly to the Confessor's plan and is thus of traditional English length – six double bays.

The Abbey, therefore, is an Anglo-French exercise in various modes of the Decorated style, built over a prolonged period. By the time of Henry III's death in 1272, the eastern arm, the transepts, the choir (which again followed the plan of the Confessor's church) and the first two bays west of the choir screen had been finished. The structure is Francophile, and the main cluster-columns, to carry the height and weight of the vault, are of solid Purbeck; but most of the decoration is obstinately English, relating to the similar scheme at Ely – though on a much bigger scale – and preceding the Lincoln Angel Choir.

Where the Abbey is quite exceptional is in the opportunities it gave to individual craftsmen of the highest calibre. The feretory of St Edward in the retrochoir, completed in 1269, drew on the resources of all Europe. Porphyry, jasper and marble for its pavement came from Rome, and so did the designer of the shrine itself, Peter the Roman. The shrine vanished at some time in the Reformation, and what we have, on its Italian base, is a wooden superstructure from the time of Mary I. On the other hand, the Confessor's body, like a magnet, attracted the tombs of Henry III and many of his successors, which lie at two levels around it; many have effigies, which include the strikingly realistic figure of Philippa of Hainault, wife of Edward III, by the Paris sculptor Hennequin de Liège, and the superb flowing idealization of Richard II, by Nicholas Broker.

Historically more important are the tombs of some lesser folk which lie nearby. The work available at Westminster was copious enough to attract the settlement of several entire families of craftsmen, such as Michael of Canterbury and his sons, and the Ramsays of Norwich. Edward I and his family gave sculptors ample employment, the king through the great series of crosses he put up to mark the resting-places of the body of his wife, Eleanor of Castile, on the way to its tomb in the Confessor's Chapel at Westminster. The same decade (the 1290s) saw the construction of three tombs in the Westminster sanctuary: that of Edward's brother, Edmund Crouchback, Earl of Lancaster; that of the King's cousin, Aymer de Valence, Earl of Pembroke; and that of Aveline, Crouchback's wife. As on most of the royal tombs, the occupants appear in effigy, but these three are surmounted by spectacular canopies, flaunting the ogee curve and marking the climax of the distinctive English school of Curvilinear Decorative. Aymer de Valence's tomb, by Michael of Canterbury, is the best of this group and shows the extent to which the riotous profusion and exotic curves of this brilliant decade could be given discipline and dynamism by a noble and simple frame-structure. These London-style canopy-tombs are, of course, only a step or two away from the independent chantry, with the tomb inside an extended canopy. One can see every stage in the development at Westminster, to the enormous church-chapel of Henry VII, with its inner chantry, and supplementary chapels at the apse end, to the resumption of the canopy-tomb for Queen Elizabeth I and Mary Queen of Scots.

The finest sculpture at Westminster, however, dates from the years 1245–59, and is in the transepts – often, alas, invisible from ground level. In the south

Tombs in the north side of the presbytery, Westminster Abbey. Aymer de Valence, Earl of Pembroke, and Aveline, wife of Edmund Crouchback, Earl of Lancaster.

The chapel of Henry VII at Westminster Abbey.

Thirteenth-century sculpture of a censing angel in the south transept, Westminster Abbey.

transept, in the south wall of its 'nave' at the triforium level, there are two large figures of censing angels which reveal the existence in England at this time of a master-sculptor capable of work of the most ambitious complexity. In an important article in the *Journal of the British Archaeological Association* (1972), David Carpenter has shown that this master and his *atelier* are responsible for most of the surviving sculpture, including some marvellous bosses to be found in the south transept, eastern chapels and apse. There is also a mass of high-quality sculpture in the north transept, the bosses, spandrels, sides of windows and in the soffits of window arches, particularly in the north wall of the transept, where a whole regiment of spirits, framed in medallions, are engaged in decorous angelic activities. In other portions of the church, notably in the nave but scattered also in the chapels with which Westminster abounds, are other fine pieces of sculpture, often difficult to examine except by means of photographic enlargements, but collectively constituting an unrivalled gallery of high medieval art.

The Abbey was never, strictly speaking, completed. The nave was hardly begun at Henry III's death. Edward I was too busy building his incomparable castles. Edward III chose, rather, to adorn Windsor. Right at the end of his reign, in 1375, the great Henry Yevele began to work on the nave again. Conscientiously and with remarkable self-effacement – for he designed the greatest naves in Europe – he proceeded to carry out the scheme of the original architect. Some of the West Front, which was still being built when the Abbey was secularized in the

sixteenth century, is part of Yevele's design. But the towers were left to Nicholas Hawksmoor (1735–40), and are genteel rather than Gothic. The front as a whole cannot do justice to the great Anglo-French church within, or its museum of treasures.

To the casual visitor, the principle elevational feature of Westminster appears to be the façade of the north transept, which was the main entrance, with three porches, reflecting the 'nave' and double-aisles within, and fully visible from the street. Here, however, we come to the locational weakness of the Abbey. Like so many metropolitan Gothic churches, it is awkwardly placed. Now that it is being cleaned, we are learning to enjoy its exterior, albeit that much of the detail is the work of Scott, but there are no great vistas until we go into the cloisters. These are magnificent in themselves, illustrating varied modes of Decorated open-window tracery at its most imaginative and ethereal. From the south-west corner there is an arresting vista of the western portion of the great church, soaring above, which brings out the spiky elegance of its buttress rib-cage, and makes those gentlemanly towers seem almost as though they belonged to the Middle Ages.

Westminster drew many of the best provincial masons to the capital, and royal patronage kept them there, but during the period of English Decorated there were probably more expert and gifted stonemasons in the country than at any other time, before or since; and many of them worked not from patterns but from life.

The south wall of the nave at Westminster, showing the three-tier flying buttresses.

Busts of angels on the soffit of a window in the north transept.

Stall-canopies in the chapter house at Southwell.

As we have seen, there was an important group in the West Country. There were others at York, Lincoln and in East Anglia. Southwell is only twenty-three miles from Lincoln, and within its artistic orbit. Ecclesiastically, however, it is the centre of the Nottingham Archdeaconry of the huge diocese of York, and like Beverley and Ripon had served as a pro-cathedral, until in 1884 it was finally raised to cathedral status. It always had a chapter of canons; but no dean or provost, so the Archbishop of York acted as overseer and if necessary bullied the canons into contributing to the fabric fund. The canons dominated the town which was (and is) somnolent and clerical, a minor Barchester. Most of their houses still exist, and communal lodgings for the vicar-choral; but the centre of gaiety, the Archbishop's Palace, was blown up in the Civil War, and its vast deer-park despoiled.

The Minster looks like a small Norman cathedral, and 'looks like' is apt, for its stone-pyramid steeples on its plain west towers, though actually rebuilt in the nineteenth century, are closer to the original Norman wooden steeples than anything else to be seen in England. The nave is emphatically Norman, with vast aisle pillars and broad arches, culminating in two cavernous crossing arches, which rest on semi-circular piers of vast strength and height. In 1234, however, the Archbishop of York, Walter Grey, had all the eastern arm pulled down, added four bays, east transepts and a Lady Chapel, and built them all in classic Early English, with emphatic verticals and masses of long, narrow lancet windows.

All this is as one might expect from a collegiate church hovering uneasily between parish and cathedral status – indeed, the chancel is humble enough to drop the intermediate storey. What makes Southwell special is its chapter house, which dates from the great naturalistic phase of English medieval culture, the last quarter of the thirteenth century, and especially from that miraculous decade, the 1290s. The wonders proclaim themselves from the entrance, a sumptuous double doorway with two trefoil arches and a quatrefoil tympanum, the serried moulding-arch carrying a broad band of delicate leaf sculpture, echoed in the capitals of the columns.

The hall within is unique. Like Wells or Salisbury, it is octagonal, with a high conical roof; but being only thirty-one feet across (compared with fifty-eight at Salisbury) it has no central pier; so instead of a palm-tree effect it aims to maximize the space and light and tops it all with a celestial star-vault, peppered with brilliantly carved bosses. These, in turn, lead the eye down again to the fine multi-trefoil windows, which mark the point at which the rigours of Geometrical Decorated begin to yield to the caresses of the curve; and the windows guide the eye to the thirty-six carved stone prebendal stalls, with their trefoil arch and gable, decked with leaves, the corbels for the arch-springs being usually adorned with heads as well.

The Southwell carvings, which compare in variety and quality with anything else produced at the time in Europe, are not exclusively based on foliage. Occasionally figures and animals lurk amid the greenery; thus, in one gable, the tails of two marvellously slithering lizards not only interlink but sprout maple-leaves. But leaves dominate: oak, hawthorn, maple, bryony, apple, hop, rose, buttercup and many other wildflowers. The undercutting is ferociously deep and impressive, but virtuosity is always kept under restraint and many blank spaces are left to act as foils to the rioting foliage. It is worthwhile spending a good half-hour examining the gables, capitals and mouldings, with their thematic unity,

OPPOSITE The west front of Southwell.

significant variations and wonderfully confident style, because they exhibit an important principle of decorative art in general, and the English Decorative in particular. The naturalism is intense, but the sculptor is rigorously faithful to his material; these are not real leaves but stone leaves, smooth, strong, firm, virile, leaves carved for eternity, of which stone is symbolic. They give me the impression, nonetheless, that they were carved easily and swiftly, by a master-sculptor (and his team) at the very height of his powers, full of the professional joy of his work.

So triumphantly successful was the chapter house that, I surmise, it made the Early English rood screen (or pulpitum) seem homely; so in about 1320 the canons took it down and replaced it with a vaulted, twin-façade affair, in elaborate ogee-work, with endless cusping and crocketing. The virtuosity is stunning – like the work in the chapter house it owes something to the quality of the fine-grained magnesian limestone from Mansfield, fifteen miles away – but the taste is another matter. I enjoy it; but I recognize that it can be argued that Decorated had gone 'over the top' by 1320, and was not so much mannered as overloaded. It is, however, possible to like both, especially if they are taken in chronological order and the screen is ignored until after the chapter house has been thoroughly examined.

The craftsmen who made this screen may have come from East Anglia, one of many travelling teams to be found in thirteenth- and fourteenth-century England. But the Midlands, both east and west, were rich in their own resources of skilled men, as dozens of churches survive to testify, not least the principal cathedral of the West Midlands, Worcester. Worcester ranks with Durham, Ely, Salisbury and Chichester, in being superbly sited; in this case it is seen across the majestic River Severn, not on a great cliff like Durham but high enough to stand out from its surroundings, while low enough to have its majestic reflection printed on the placid waters of England's greatest river. The profile of this great church is superb, for the extended eastern arm is almost equal to the long nave, so that the church's total length of 425 feet is exactly bisected by the high central tower, built by John Clyve in 1374, the first of the great Perpendicular towers, created when the new style was fresh and stretching its muscles. It then had a timber spire, and may have looked stupendous; but even today, despite Victorian re-facing, its perfect proportions, virile corner-buttresses and thrusting pinnacles make it a tower to remember, especially for those who have seen a new Australian touring team play their first cricket match against its peerless backdrop.

Worcester was always an important see, with its great tenth-century saint, St Oswald, and in the time of the Danelaw it over-saw most of the archdiocese of York. Its second great bishop, Wulfstan, was the only member of the Saxon hierarchy who approved of the Norman church reforms, on the lines of the Hildebrandine programme of Rome, and therefore kept his see, and embellished it from 1084 with a fine new Norman church. He is said to have remarked at the time: 'We pull down the work of our predecessors in order to add lustre to our own names.' His name survives, for he was canonized in 1203, giving Worcester the rare distinction of two saintly bishops, both safely housed in the church; but of his work little remains. That little, however, is important: a fine, if early and rude, crypt, running under the big eastern arm; the two western bays of the nave, the last to be built, which show the arcades already pointed (if only just); and a fascinating if eccentric blend of Romanesque and Gothic in the triforium – perhaps the first essay in Gothic in all England, and another indication of the

OPPOSITE Worcester Cathedral seen from the south west, across the river Severn.

move into the new style independent of the Canterbury Revolution.

By the time these bays were built, in the early 1170s, another phase had opened with the resounding collapse of the crossing-tower in 1175. This event, combined with the need for a suitably imposing setting for the double shrine – not to mention the body of King John, which the church was very glad to have and adorned with a majestic effigy of Purbeck marble (1230) – led to a leisurely programme of extension and renewal which lasted until the new nave was vaulted in 1377, and left the church interior virtually as we find it today.

The result is unquestionably one of the most impressive and unified interiors in England; not so warm as Exeter, not so graceful and appealing as Wells, but assured, rhythmical, well-proportioned, sophisticated and ingenious. The eastern arm (begun in 1224) has four bays of choir, plus a three-bay retrochoir, plus a Lady Chapel. It is distinguished by a brilliantly-designed triforium level, with triple plain Early English arches fronted by a double arch with Purbeck shafts, to produce a two-dimensional effect heightened by multiple mouldings, a carved central tympanum and foliage capitals. The nave, rebuilt from the end of the two Norman bays, dates from 1320 and after; but the style conforms to the Early English of the east end, except in one important respect. The high vaultings

Prince Arthur's chantry at Worcester, from the retrochoir.

OPPOSITE The nave of Worcester Cathedral, facing east.

131

rise directly from the pavement, with tall half-shafts forming part of the pillars. This was a valuable innovation, one of the elements of the Perpendicular system, for it anchored the vault firmly into the elevational design of the whole bay, and thus made possible the wonderfully unified scheme of the great Perpendicular vaulted naves. At Worcester we see this ingenious device in its infancy, but already working well and, in addition, heightening the nave-effect.

The Norman parts of Worcester are oolite limestone plus local sandstone; in the later additions sandstone predominates. This is a pity; like other western cathedrals – Carlisle, Lichfield, Chester – Worcester has worn badly on the outside. This necessitated a very thorough nineteenth-century resurfacing and redecoration, so that the Norman West Front, for instance, is basically Victorian, quite apart from the obvious west window of 1865. In my view it is well done; and I do not accept that the quality of the exterior, so promising when seen from afar, deteriorates and dissolves into pastiche as one gets nearer. Nor, I think, should we censure A.E. Perkins for replacing Perpendicular windows with what he conceived to be the original Early English ones. After all, if the fourteenth-century nave conformed to the basic Early English scheme, why should not an antiquarian architect correct the ruthless (or lazy) work of fifteenth-century routine designers? The Middle Ages had no monopoly of taste or judgment. As we get the nineteenth century more into historical perspective, the solid virtues of its restorers begin deservedly to stand out and overshadow their admitted errors; but more of that later. Worcester is a fine and very English cathedral, which convincingly displays the manner in which the Early English and Decorated forms of the English Gothic vernacular could be made to work together in a unified scheme; at the same time, it subtly hints at the Perpendicular to come. By the 1320s, when the new bays of the Worcester nave were going up, English architects were poised to embark on a truly distinctive national style, which was to carry the country up to and over the threshold of the Renaissance.

5
The True Native Style - Perpendicular

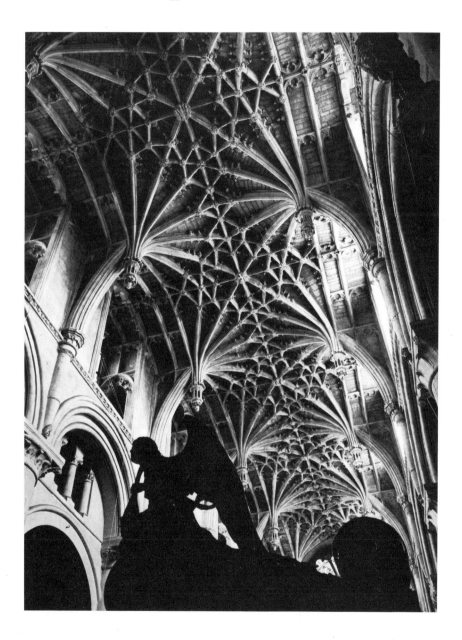

I n 1327 King Edward II was brutally murdered in Berkeley Castle by agents of his wife, Isabella, and her paramour Earl Mortimer. The chronicler of Gloucester Abbey tells us that, a few years before, King Edward had dined at the Abbey, noticed portraits of earlier English kings on the walls, and asked if his would join them. The chronicle continues:

The abbot, John Thoky, replied rather in the spirit of prophecy than jest, that he hoped he would have King Edward II in a more honourable place than this; as indeed came to pass. For after the King's death, his venerable body was refused by certain monasteries hard by . . . for fear of Roger de Mortimer and Queen Isabella and their accomplices. Yet Abbot Thoky fetched him from Berkeley Castle in his own chariot, sumptuously adorned and painted with the arms of our monastery, and brought him to Gloucester, where the abbot and all the convent received him honourably in their solemn robes with a procession of the whole city, and buried him in our church in the north aisle, hard by the same altar.

So Edward came to Gloucester; and a few years later his son, Edward III, had the tomb (which is still there) embellished with a touching alabaster effigy, and covered with a gossamer stone canopy, like the great tombs at Westminster. The episode had an important bearing on the history of art in England. In those days, an anointed king, murdered in mysterious circumstances, was bound to receive the popular accolade of martyrdom. The tomb became a shrine, 'so that,' says the chronicler, 'within a few years so great was the concourse of people to our city that it could scarcely contain the multitudes who flocked there from . . . throughout the kingdom.'

Hence the abbott's charitable gesture was bountifully rewarded. The chronicler says the offerings of the faithful were so munificent that the whole church could have been rebuilt from top to bottom; and he does not even mention the valuable financial privileges which Edward III gave the house in memory of his father. Thoky's successor, John Wigmore, 'took much delight in divers arts, so that he himself very often wrought in them and surpassed many different workmen in divers arts, not only in mechanical work but in designing.' Under Wigmore (1329–37) a building-programme was launched which was to last 150 years, introduce the English Perpendicular style and make almost inevitable Henry VIII's decision, when he dissolved the abbeys, to turn Gloucester into a cathedral.

Until the second quarter of the fourteenth century, the Benedictine abbey of Gloucester, though large and important (it had 100 monks in the twelfth century), had been unusually conservative in updating its buildings. It had been built from 1089–1120, in the severest possible Norman, so that visitors to the abbey who know nothing of its history receive a shock when they enter. Seen from afar, it looks like a building from the late Middle Ages. The West Front is light and airy. Once inside the nave, however, the page of history rolls back 300 years, and we are in a Norman tunnel-nave. It is true that, in 1242, the monks had been scared by the fire-risk into replacing their wooden ceiling with a stone vault, and in doing so they cleared away the Norman clerestory and put in Early English windows. True, also, that when the new West Front was built in the early fifteenth century, the two most westerly bays were recast in the Perpendicular style and given a lierne vault. But the dominating feature of the nave is the seven-bay Norman section, with its gigantic round columns, thirty-one feet high, capped by little more than a narrow and primitive triforium level, from which the Early English vault springs. The effect is heavy, daunting and inhibiting: we are

OVERLEAF The pendant lierne chancel vault at Oxford Cathedral.

OPPOSITE The tomb of Edward II at Gloucester.

back in the world of the early Middle Ages, where enormous mass and effort is required to hold a building aloft, and horizons are low and lowering.

Then, in a few brief steps, we march out of the vault into the crossing, and receive another shock. In a few seconds we have travelled centuries; it is a Perpendicular church after all. There is no more exhilarating sensation in the whole of English architecture than the sudden emergence from the Gloucester nave-tunnel into late-medieval space and light. At Ely, the shock is vertical – the new space soars irresistibly aloft. At Gloucester it is on all sides, like walking into a gigantic green-house, the direct ancestor of the Crystal Palace. Even at night-time the sense of space remains, as though in a vast observatory with a star-canopy. In full sunlight the airiness is almost palpable; one feels the sunbeams on the cheek and smells hot dust and warm stone; the eyes blink and are disorientated; it takes a few seconds to adjust the focus on definite objects in this blinding world of glass and wafery stone.

The Perpendicular style is England's greatest single contribution to the art (and science) of architecture. It is a national mode. It is not found elsewhere, except in places where English influence was direct. It sprang into existence in the 1330s, the decade which marks the historic bifurcation of English and French culture. It spread rapidly with the rising nationalism of the middle decades of the fourteenth century – the first and violent phase of the Hundred Years' War – when English displaced French as the language of the court, parliament and the law, and the rapid development of a vernacular literature became possible. For the first time, English artists and designers were working within a mode which was wholly English in inspiration, and not merely an English domestication of a foreign importation. As such, when once established it proved exceptionally pervasive and tenacious. Indeed, it is hard to point to any other comprehensive architectural mode which enjoyed so long an ascendancy. Between 1337 and 1537, about ninety per cent of all major buildings erected in England were in Perpendicular; and in Oxford and Cambridge it was still in use right up to the Civil War.

What, then, was Perpendicular? In one respect it was an extension of the fundamental Gothic tendency to conserve stone by enlarging the window space and lightening the walls, a tendency which had operated through Transitional, Early English, Geometrical Decorated, Curvilinear and Late-Decorated. Windows had been growing bigger and walls thinner all the time. In another sense it reinforced the equally important Gothic tendency – which marks all great architectural systems – towards unification of style, so that all elements in a building are directly and visibly related to each other stylistically.

Perpendicular pushed these tendencies very much further, but it did so by a definite and marked change of line: the return to verticals and horizontals. If there is one vital characteristic it is the compulsion of the vertical line, whether a window mullion or panel-division, to rush straight up to the arch or top, crossing laterals at right angles. An architecture of curves (within the upright framework dictated by gravity and nature) becomes an architecture of rectangles. The utilitarian advantage is obvious: curves 'waste' stone, rectangles use the minimum. The aesthetic advantage is obvious too: it is much easier to unify separate forms based on rectangles than those based on curves. A further advantage was both utilitarian and aesthetic. Gothic architecture, like its predecessor Romanesque, was essentially based on the bay unit; and the bay unit was composed of tiers or storeys (three for a cathedral). Perpendicular

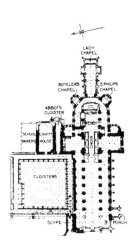

GLOUCESTER

architecture, being immensely more efficient than anything which preceded it, abolished the structural tyranny of the bay and the tier. Where the bay was retained, it was purely for purposes of aesthetic punctuation. The three-storey form merged into two as the giant clerestory windows swallowed up the old triforium; and into one for display purposes. Indeed it became possible to conceive of monumental buildings – the great chapels at Eton, Windsor, King's, for instance – which had only one storey throughout. The old aisle system, at any rate for structural ends, was thrown out with the rest of the lumber.

The English return to the rectangle was, from a purely aesthetic viewpoint, a classicist revulsion from the curvacious excess of the early decades of the fourteenth century. Yet Gothic, being a metaphysical system as well as an aesthetic, had an inherent tendency to excess all the time. The Christian refrain 'All to Jesus' does not mean some, or an appropriate amount, or the right amount, but *all*; Christianity is not about reticence or moderation or restraint but whole-hearted and total surrender to God. The principle applied to the artist as it applied to everyone; the response tended, therefore, to be an endless proliferation of virtuoso forms, a form of aesthetic inflation which corresponded to the spiritual inflation of the system of indulgences. An inflated art is ostentatious; hence we call French Gothic in the fourteenth and fifteenth centuries 'Flamboyant'. Spanish Flamboyant of the same phase is termed Plateresque, that is the employment by the stonemasons of the elaborate three- and two-dimensional designs of the silversmiths.

English Perpendicular is a sounder and cleaner aesthetic than either, which helps to explain why England was so slow and reluctant to receive the Renaissance, but it has excessive tendencies of its own, notably to copy the panelwork designs of the carpenters, and so to engage in endless repetition. Perpendicular was put up in enormous quantities and inevitably at times reveals a poverty of ideas, not concealed by ornamental reiteration – 'Businessmen's Gothic', as it has been termed. This was the 'excess' against which the English Gothic theoreticians of the nineteenth century were revolting when they insisted on a return to an earlier, 'purer' phase, just as painters rejected Raphaelesque perfection. The origins of Perpendicular lie in just such a revolt against excess, a surfeit of curves; and it is well to bear in mind that its first protagonists saw it as cleaner, simpler and purer than the conventional art of their fathers' age.

This, then, was the background to the 'Gloucester Revolution'. Of course it is possible, as always in such cases, to trace its origins further back. The claims of French precursors are advanced. It is also argued that John Ramsay, before he moved his family to London, designed a rectilinear-type window in a chapel at Norwich Cathedral. In 1332 his son William Ramsay designed windows in the new Chapter House at Old St Paul's which, to judge by a pre-fire drawing, are effectively Perpendicular. It is argued, therefore, that what we see in Gloucester is an importation of the 'London Court Style', itself reflecting Continental importations. Certainly the younger Ramsay was involved in the Gloucester operations, for he came down to design, among other things, the canopy of Edward II's tomb. But the West Country had such a strong artistic tradition of its own – particularly in stonemasonry and innovatory design – that it is probable the influence worked both ways. For what happened at Gloucester was that a number of new design-elements, some local, some metropolitan and some latent in existing practice, were assembled together into a striking new system, whose impact was enormous and whose appeal was immediate and ubiquitous. The

137

master-mind behind the system, in my view, must have been Abbot Wigmore, playing the role that Alan of Walsingham played at Ely. Ramsay the Younger was important too, but so also was Thomas of Gloucester, who went to London immediately after he had finished his main work at the Abbey, and emerged three years later as Edward III's master-mason.

Of what did the Gloucester Revolution consist? It seems to have begun even before Edward II's death and the bounty brought with his body, for work begun in the South Transept around 1318 shows a curious mixture of Curvilinear and Perpendicular forms. Perhaps it was the success of this experiment, as well as the sudden access of wealth, which led the monks to take the great plunge of recasting the whole eastern part of their church in a new style. Even so, they retained some conservative instincts. They kept not only the Norman crypt, but virtually the whole groundplan and elements of the walls, especially the aisles. What the designer did was to take off the whole of the main east roof, demolish the apse and part of the chancel walls, and slip in a new wall-casing, composed of thin walling and glass, which carried the height up to over ninety feet. The old east-end aisles remained, but the effect of the casing was to extend the chancel by two bays and to add an extra twenty feet of window-space on both sides. This new Perpendicular chamber or presbytery, arising out of the old choir, was completed by adding a high lierne vault and turning the huge open space at the east end itself into a gigantic window.

The window is thirty-eight feet wide and seventy-two feet high, with the two main vertical mullions carried virtually up to the top, and rectangular panelling throughout. The window is actually bigger than the wall-space it had to fill, for it is canted outwards at the sides, an engineering device which gives it added stability in high winds. It was built soon after the spectacular English victory at Crécy and contains a large element of heraldic and nationalist propaganda in its glass. The window is by far the biggest ever set up in England, and certainly had no rival in Europe at the time. Even today its effect is dazzling, even on those who have visited the church time and again, and know what to expect. What, then, must have been its impact on fourteenth-century men who had never seen, and could not conceive of, anything remotely like it, and who had to take in not only its size and splendour but its vainglorious heraldic codes which were to them an open book? No wonder the noble lines of its tracery became the matrix of a thousand other windows, and set the stamp of Perpendicular indelibly on English church-building.

The great Crécy Window was finished by 1350, the choir vaulting seven years later; but as money still flowed in, the work of turning the old Abbey into a Perpendicular prodigy-church went on steadily. By 1370 the north transept had been transformed. At the same time work proceeded on the east range of the cloisters, which ultimately turned the entire cloister-square into the finest example of this noble and challenging art-form in Europe. The cloisters are particularly interesting in their arrangement, and include a lavatorium where the monks washed before eating in the north walk, and, on the opposite side, a scriptorium of twenty recessed niches which were fitted with desks. Also surviving is the original Norman Chapter House from which, in 1085, the Conqueror decreed the making of Domesday Book.

What gives the cloisters special distinction, however, is not just the fenestration, which is still glassed, but the revolutionary new type of vaulting. The great choir-vault had virtually exhausted the possibilities of the tierceron

OPPOSITE The choir of Gloucester Cathedral, showing the east window.

vault even with lierne modifications, which allowed more varied patterns; and the most ingenious masons were becoming sated with the endless carved bosses which concealed the joins. The tierceron design, in fact, was in danger of degenerating into a muddle. At Gloucester this is cleared up in one sweeping but logical change, the introduction of a half-conoid, inverted, which spreads out like a fan. The ribs all have the same profile curve and are equidistant from each other, so a kind of standardization is introduced; and each set is carved from a solid block of stone, which the abbey got from the oolite limestone of the Cotswolds. So the new fan-vault was really part of the Perpendicular revolution, in that it was another step in the ordering of the wild forms of late Decorated.

Nor was this the end of the new wonders at Gloucester. The lierne vault over the choir was adorned by boss-carvings too large and noble – though eighty feet above the pavement – to be called anything less than pieces of sculpture. They include sixteen angels playing musical instruments, finer even than those at Exeter. It was decided, too, to carry the vault across the space to the far side of the crossing. In order to do this, the ingenious West-Country masons invented a support in the form of an ogee arch, suspended in mid-air across the lateral crossing arches, and soaring up into the vaulting cones. It is both a virtuoso conceit and a cunning piece of structural engineering, illustrative of the fine tolerance with which the masons were now designing their force-structures.

The cloisters were finished in about 1415; the West Front went up in the next two decades, together with the first two bays of the nave; the august and substantial central tower, demonstrably related to the Worcester tower, and a prominent member of the great fifteenth-century family of Perpendicular towers, was finished around 1450. Immediately afterwards, the monks turned to the last element in their programme. This is the Lady Chapel, which projects from the old apse, enlarging itself into a dramatic glass-and-stone room, with a huge east window and a lierne vault of its own. So it consciously echoes the choir behind, but in the manner of a new age, for it was finished in 1499, almost 150 years after the Crécy Window. As a final, astonishing coup, the monks made use of the Old Norman feature of the apse-passageway, which runs between choir and Lady Chapel, to turn it into a glass-and-stone Venetian bridge, over the entrance to the Chapel. From it the visitor can look down into the Chapel's wonders, and inspect the vaulting from close quarters; and from the east window of the Chapel one looks across and through the bridge, through the vast Crécy window, and sees faintly the wonders of the choir. It is a dazzling perspective, virtually impossible to draw or paint except in impressionistic terms, for the various systems of forms are too complicated to analyse clearly in this baffling juxtaposition, and the light-systems, especially in late afternoon, defy description. At this point the monks decided that their church was complete, as if in acknowledgement that it was impossible to draw fresh sensations from this particular line of aesthetic enquiry. The Perpendicular style had exhausted itself.

By this time, however, it had transformed the face of English architecture, and most notably in some of the ancient strongholds of the Romanesque. Perhaps the place where it had the first and biggest impact, soon after the completion of the Gloucester choir, was at Winchester. This ancient cathedral-abbey was even more conservative than Gloucester, and when it embraced Perpendicular it did so in a conservative fashion, as we shall see. It had never been a seat of an archbishop, but it was one of the most ancient religious foundations in the country, the capital of Wessex and Saxon England, and an administrative rival to

OPPOSITE The fan-vaulted cloisters of Gloucester Cathedral.

London throughout the Norman period. It was sanctified by the bones of its great ninth-century bishop, St Swithun, and throughout the Middle Ages the diocese, which stretched upto the London south bank and encompassed much of the most densely populated part of the south, was by far the richest in England. The princely prelates who ruled it in the later Middle Ages built and endowed some of England's noblest foundations, including Winchester College, and New College and Magdalen College in Oxford.

Winchester itself is an archaeological and historical site of unrivalled interest, for in the 1960s an intensive campaign uncovered most of the secrets of the two successive Saxon minsters, which lay alongside the present Norman foundation. Yet visitors are often disappointed with the cathedral itself. It lies in a hollow, and there are no dramatic views from afar. Its tower, a late-Norman replacement after the original tower fell in 1100 (in outrage, the monks claimed at having to shelter the body of that scourge of the church, William Rufus) is low and undistinguished. The building is immensely long, at 556 feet the second longest in Europe (St Peter's in Rome is 694 feet); but its size fails to register on the exterior, and there is no striking feature, no special angle or vista or striking perspective to jolt and arrest the eye. The interior, however, is a different matter.

There are two ways to investigate this church. The first, and to my mind the more logical and rewarding, is to start with the transepts. These constitute the most important remaining element of the vast Norman church which was built between 1097 and 1098. It carries us straight back to the early Norman period, for it is possible to distinguish between the masonry used in the repairs carried out immediately after the 1100 collapse, which is well-jointed and sophisticated, and earlier, rougher stone hewn when the Conqueror was still on the throne. There are some very early Norman bifora, and the triforium double arches exhibit, for the first time, the emergence of a primitive inner order, the initial step on the long road to Gothic. Much of the wall-surface is exactly as it was when first built, and no part of any English cathedral gives one such a tangible sensation of being in a grand and august, but primitive, Romanesque cathedral.

Even before 1100 Winchester had attained much of its present size, and this included, by Norman standards, a large eastern arm. The incentive to rebuild in Gothic, therefore, was lacking; and when, between 1189 and 1238, two successive bishops, Godfrey de Lucy and Peter des Roches, created a new setting for the shrine of St Swithun and the cathedral's enormous relic-collection, all they did was to add on a single-storey extension, with three equal aisles, and a Lady Chapel. The latter was later remodelled (1486–92), but the retrochoir is one of those splendid Early English vaulted chambers which make one thank God for the twelfth-century relic-cult. They rarely receive adequate attention from the visitor, and at Winchester the room is so cluttered with tomb-furniture (admirable in itself), that the strong, logical lines of clustered pillar and simple quadripartite vault find it hard, as it were, to make their voices heard over the necrological din – but they are worth listening to.

Winchester then seems to have slumbered through the rest of the thirteenth century and the early decades of the fourteenth. It was awoken by the Gloucester Revolution, and two magnifico-bishops, William of Eddington (1345–66) and the incomparable William of Wykeham (1367–1404), proceeded to modernize the vast twelve-bay nave. At this point, the visitor should leave the church and approach it again from the west. Eddington began at the West Front, which is his, plus the first two nave bays. The front illustrates the continuing difficulty English

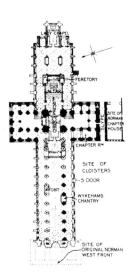

WINCHESTER

The West Front of
Winchester Cathedral.

architects found in designing elevations. As we have seen, the most primitive type of English Romanesque front was a mere cross-section of the nave and aisles. They had worked hard to get away from this feeble pseudo-solution by experimenting with arcades, towers, sculpture-galleries and the *piano nobile*, and in the thirteenth century had largely succeeded. But now, Eddington's architect, equipped by the Gloucester discoveries with a revolutionary new vernacular, fell at the first fence and produced a mere cross-section again. It is true that one weakness of Perpendicular is that its great windows look dull from the outside; and the enormous west window here takes away from the designer, in one stroke, the whole centre of his operating area. He might have balanced it with two tall towers, as at York; but that would have meant transforming the whole exterior, and building a new crossing-tower. It is evident that he had no such wide mandate and was limited by his patron to designing a minor feature in harmony with the cathedral's conservative exterior. So he resorted to an obvious pinnacle-plus-buttress formula.

Inside the western end of the church, however, the great building comes to magisterial artistic life. We are now effectively in the hands of Wykeham's favourite architect, William of Wynford. Wykeham knew what he was doing; he was the most experienced and successful English organizer of building-schemes

143

in the whole of the Middle Ages, and as Prior of Wells he had become thoroughly familiar with West Country developments, even though he was about the King's business most of the time. Wynford was a great architect; some maintain that his claims are higher even than those of Henry Yevele himself; but he, too, had a limited mandate. Wykeham may have been inhibited by the fact that the nave-rebuilding scheme was already under way by the time he took over; or by the sheer weight of tradition which invests this venerable church. At all events he must have told Wynford not to tear down and rebuild the Norman nave, but to give it a Perpendicular face-lift. In a sense, then, the work at Winchester was similar to that at Gloucester two or three decades before. Wynford began by taking off the nave roof and dismantling the main walling down to the aisle roof. His next step was to cut back the masonry of the Norman compound-piers and whittle them down into Perpendicular clustered pillars. Although they still retain a certain stockiness, which reminds us of their origin, the vertical Perpendicular effect is cunningly created by a new system of mouldings and by carrying the vaulting shafts right up from the pavement. Meanwhile, the clerestory windows were carried right down into a two-storey scheme, the triforium level becoming a mere railing, and the whole was capped by a tremendous new vault. The effect from the west entrance is sensational because the great length of the nave makes itself felt despite the strong, repeated vertical lines of the vaulting-posts; one becomes dramatically aware, for the first time, of the huge scale of the cathedral, and the sheer distance of the great east window from the point at which one stands.

Distance, indeed, is the great advantage which Winchester possesses over Canterbury. It must be conceded that, in absolute terms, the somewhat later Perpendicular nave at Canterbury, by Wynford's arch-rival, Yevele, is finer. He had, of course, an open mandate and demolished the old nave completely. His marvellous clustered pillars and high vault are incomparable – to my mind Perpendicular at its purest and most successful – but he lacked the *gravitas* of length, which adds an extra and important dimension to the total vista at Winchester, and fits well with the indelible inner character of this cathedral, which clings so grimly to its long past. There is no need for controversy; both naves are works of high art, and we can enjoy their distinctive features as well as their common grasp of the Perpendicular aesthetic system.

Winchester Cathedral is full of beautiful objects, and it has an exceptionally large number of chapels, chantries and distinguished tombs – one or two of them designed to look very gruesome. There are exquisite wall-paintings, both in the Chapel of the Holy Sepulchre (*c.* 1230) and in the Chapel of the Guardian Angels (*c.* 1240), and there is some sixteenth-century work on the walls of the re-decorated Lady Chapel. Fox, who was Bishop here from 1500 to 1528, installed the magnificent stone reredos, not unlike the one he provided at Southwark, but the still intact canopies are finer, and the Victorian statuary replacements are much better done. The aisle screens also went up in Fox's day (*c.* 1525) and carry the chests which contain the bones of many Saxon kings and bishops.

The cathedral is a great cemetery of its bishops, though some of the earlier tombs cannot be identified by name. Of the later bishops, however, no less than seven have sumptuous chantries. Bishop Eddington's is the earliest and simplest (*c.* 1366), though it has a fine effigy of him in alabaster; Wykeham's (*c.* 1404) is, as one would expect, more splendid, even if the effigy is realistically unflattering; Cardinal Beaufort's (*c.* 1447) is the grandest, as befits an ecclesiastical prince who

OPPOSITE The Perpendicular nave at Winchester, facing east.

was also of the royal blood (and exceptionally rich, too); Wayneflete's (*c.* 1486) is in excellent taste, so it is no surprise that he built that dearest of all Perpendicular towers at Magdalen; Langton's (*c.* 1500) has some fine wood-carving. Fox's chantry (*c.* 1528) is to my mind the most sublime of the group and, surprisingly, still Perpendicular throughout, in contrast to Bishop Gardiner's (*c.* 1555), which is a mixture of Perpendicular and two distinct layers of Renaissance. Taken together, this series of little prayer-chapels is a tour through 200 years of English architectural history, conducted by powerful ecclesiastics who played a major role in shaping it. Indeed, one of the delights in exploring English cathedrals is to discover how often, and in such unexpected places, the movements of taste can be traced in minor artefacts. In the choir at Winchester is a magnificent carved-wood pulpit, donated by one of the last priors of the Abbey, just before the Reformation; his name was Silkstede, and skeins of silk are carved on the panelling. More significant, however, is that in this light and elegant exposition of late-Gothic form, which has the effortless bravura of thoroughbred art, the knobs on the hand-rail are Renaissance – the shape of things to come. In general, however, Winchester clung to the last enchantments of the Middle Ages long before anyone was threatening to whisk them away: its nave is in the fifteenth century but its heart is in the twelfth (if not the eleventh).

For a cathedral whose spirit is wholly attuned to the later Middle Ages, we must turn to York. Here is a church built upon the very largest and grandest scale – by most systems of measurement it is the biggest of our medieval cathedrals – and which consciously strove for size throughout medieval times. The first cathedral, when the see was founded in 627 by Paulinus, was of wood. A stone church was later built by St Wilfred, but not on the site of the present cathedral, as was shown by an archaeological survey carried out during the recent £2 million stabilization programme. The Saxon cathedral burnt down in 1069, and was replaced by a very large Norman building. As happened elsewhere, its eastern arm was replaced, 1154–81, by a larger and more splendid one, no doubt in the Transitional style. But the men of York were still not content, and between 1227 and the early 1470s the entire vast cathedral was rebuilt again.

York is big and, unlike Winchester, it always looks big. It is often said that it looks French, and in one respect it does. There is nothing rural about York; it is part of a very distinctive urban landscape, as are most of the French cathedrals. The great Vale of York, an area of rich agriculture since long before Roman times, makes a natural long-distance setting. So, at an intermediate distance, it is best seen by walking along the surviving stretches of the city walls, where its grandeur heaves itself high above the roofscape. Closer to, one catches glimpses of it from the narrow streets of the Old City, grey, benevolent, vast, unchanging, an enormous, brooding and ubiquitous presence. In York, more than anywhere else in England, one feels the sheer weight of ecclesiastical dignity, pressing down upon the townsfolk.

It is often said that York has size and splendour without beauty, magnificence without charm. I do not agree. Some of its finer points have only recently become obvious, as a result of the largest restoration programme ever carried out on an English cathedral; but it has always seemed to me to have a powerful masculine beauty, muscular and confident, thoroughbred, sinewy and bold. Its charm lies in its combination of fine limestone from Tadcaster and oak (York has more exposed wood than any other great English church), lit by ancient painted glass and grisaille – for a large proportion of our total surviving medieval glass is to be found at York, most of it in the cathedral, which has more than a hundred windows with their original glazing.

Another, very important, factor is the homogeneity of York's architectural structure and decorative schemes. All that is visible is mature Gothic. It is true that the church we see took nearly 250 years to build: transepts (*c.* 1225), Chapter House (late thirteenth century), nave (1291–1350), presbytery (1361–*c.* 1370), choir (1380–1400), crossing tower (early fifteenth century) and west towers (1433–75). But the nave adumbrates Perpendicular, and the later designers worked in aesthetic sympathy with the church as they found it. After Salisbury and (internally) Exeter, York was the most successful in harmonizing its various parts, though it shows examples of every Gothic style and sub-style, and an architectural history of English Gothic would be written on its windows alone.

For this reason there is no need to approach York in anything but the most obvious manner, beginning with the West Front. There are conflicting views about this Front, and some say it is 'too French'. But, closely examined, it is not French at all; every element in it is distinctively English. In my view it is the most successful of English west fronts on the grand scale; less imaginative than Wells, perhaps, but then Wells is incomplete; less unusual than Ely certainly, but then one third of Ely is missing. The centrepiece, as at Winchester, is the enormous west window, in flowing Decorated – the finest in Britain, with the possible exception of the big Carlisle east window. But it seems in proportion because of the sheer size of the Front, and the prominence of the two Perpendicular towers. The decorative scheme is linked together by the window-canopies, in the central window and in the second and fourth storeys of both towers, and over the main west door. The gable-parapet is carried right across the Front, echoing the tower parapets and providing the necessary horizontal binding; and for vertical binding there are four massive canopied buttresses, recessing in four stages until they reach the pinnacle-level of the towers. It lacks statuary, but then which west front does not?

The West Front, though very big, nevertheless deceives one about the proportions of the interior which are on a huge scale. The Norman church was very wide throughout. The Gothic church follows its ground-plan, making the nave nearly fifty feet broad. Hence, though the height is over ninety-eight feet – the highest in England, after Westminster – it takes a few minutes for the size of the enormous pillared chamber to sink in. The clustered columns are vast, and the tiny foliate capitals which crown them add to their size. The style cannot be called Perpendicular as such, for it was conceived before the turn of the fourteenth century, a good thirty years before the Gloucester choir. But the springing columns of the vault are carried right down to the pavement, providing a strong vertical rhythm as the arches march to the east; and the huge clerestory windows, though manifestly Decorated, have absorbed the triforium in all but name, a salient characteristic of the Perpendicular bay-scheme. The vaulting is wood, for stone would have been too heavy for so wide a span, and there is a certain severity in the decorative detail, such as it is. There can be no doubt that the 'forest glade effect' is achieved in grand style, even though the canopy-line is lower than at Canterbury, thanks partly to a blinding explosion of light at the crossing.

The crossing, which came into existence about 1400, is the outstanding internal feature of the cathedral. At this point the ample ground-plan becomes a marked advantage, for the unusual width brings a sense of amphitheatre, of vast

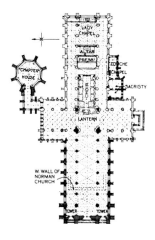

YORK

spaces floating above one, into which the huge crossing-piers surge with breath-taking power. The crossing-tower looks enormous even from outside, when it has to impose its majesty on the cathedral's dimensions as a whole; but inside it is a firmament indeed, for the vaults go up to 185 feet, and provide a sensation of release from gravity second only to the Ely Lantern. Here we have one of those vast, stone-enclosed spaces which later Gothic architect-engineers strove to create. The views up into the Lantern Tower seem to stretch into infinity, the angle-conjunctions are thrillingly monumental, and we are at the junction of five different lighting-systems, so that one longs for the organizing genius of a Piranesi or a Muirhead Bone to set it down on one plane.

The transepts are an important element in this triumph, though they were conceived a hundred years before. Indeed, York suggests to me that there is something to be said for beginning a cathedral with the transepts, for it makes the designer think in terms of lateral vistas and lighting, and not only the tunnel or glade. These transepts are interesting on their own account, also, for the triforium level (as if to compensate for its near-disappearance in the nave) is the chief feature of the bay, a four-arch display in high-pointed Geometrical-Decorated, under an immense Romanesque arch – the last twitch of the dying system. I am not quite sure whether the design succeeds, but it certainly catches the eye, especially in the south transept where there is less competition. In the north one, however, one is drawn to the gentle and solemn beauty of the Five Sisters lancets, only five feet wide but fifty-three feet high, the tallest in England, whose original grisaille glass diffuses a modest sunlight at the middle of the day. Lancets can so easily become chilly and discouraging, especially when much-repeated; but these ones are rightly loved, for they fit the frame of the crossing-arches perfectly – an ingenious stroke of architectural style-linkage.

The east end was built inwards, in the last forty years of the fourteenth century, and is unmistakably Perpendicular throughout, though clever and conscientious efforts have been made to echo the earlier nave, even in quite small details (small ogees, for instance in the aisle windows). The enormous east window, which was the largest in England after the Crécy window at Gloucester, and which makes the centrepiece of the great cliff-like east front, signals across nearly 490 feet to its colleague in the west. The fenestration throughout this massive east end (eight very wide bays, four each for choir and presbytery) is startling, in the high-risk Perpendicular manner, and there is some brilliantly-engineered trick buttressing on the exterior of the last four bays. But the finest feature is the east transept, which conceals in its modest proportions two immensely tall and narrow Perpendicular windows, which provide a sudden and unexpected shock both inside and out.

Engineering is a prominent feature of this vast cathedral, for everything is on a big and weighty scale, and the Gothic system is throughout seeking to break records for load-carrying. The Lantern Tower, with its burly frame and high vaults, had kept its piers in groaning agony for centuries; that is why it has never been given great pinnacles, a sad loss. Now that the soft underbelly of the cathedral's foundations has been hardened with hundreds of tons of concrete, and steel pinnings have been inserted at various stress-points, perhaps the pinnacles will at last be added. But we need not be sorry that York has so much wooden vaulting. England is generously endowed with late-medieval vaults of all types, and wooden varieties (not to be confused with the wooden roof-systems) are of great interest. At York there is in addition the rarity of the late thirteenth-

OPPOSITE The crossing at York Minster.

century polygonal Chapter House which has no centre-pillar but a superb tierceron wooden vault, over a clear span of fifty-eight feet, much wider than Southwell's. There is nothing to compare with Southwell's stone foliage, but the roof is an enormously complicated masterpiece of carpentry, built around a sixty-four-foot spire-mast (itself a miracle of scarfing). The way in which the weight is transmitted between the central mast and the base square, which passes it on to the brackets and the buttresses, is an insight into the stress-problems of large-scale medieval carpentry, a science now largely lost to us. Lost too is the skill and sequence with which the assembly of these vast timbers took place, especially the pinching together of the longest supports around the spire-mast. Even Mr Hewett has been unable to discover quite how this structure, which is too complicated to be fully described by any isometric diagram, was assembled.

There are close ecclesiastical and architectural links between York and the collegiate church of Beverley, which is not technically a cathedral but otherwise has as much right to a place in this book as Ripon and Southwell. It was, in fact, the chapel-of-ease cathedral for the East Riding and would have eventually become a cathedral in name had it not been so close to York itself. It is a cathedral in size, over 330 feet long, with double transepts, and when the college was suppressed in 1547 it had a cathedral-size staff: nine canons and a provost, seven parsons, nine vicars-choral, fifteen chantry priests, seventeen clerks, sextons, acolytes, choristers and minor officials, making a total of seventy-seven.

As at York, the Norman buildings have vanished and the present Minster is entirely Gothic. Documentation is sparse, but building seems to have begun about 1230. So the east end is Early English, with plentiful lancets (though the big east window is Perpendicular, about 1410). The scale is about two-thirds that of York, the arcade plain, the triforium of four colonnetted arches in two planes, with quatrefoils in the spandrels and lancet arches above in the clerestory. What catches the eye is a fascinating double staircase from the north choir aisle to the Chapter House (now gone). The design is very simple, really nothing more than a transference to this feature of the blank arcading with Purbeck shafts; but the confident dexterity with which the thing is done, and the audacity of the designer in framing the stair-head with tall thin columns from the aisle-vaulting supports, illustrates the sheer professionalism with which the Gothic system was wielded by about 1260. The nave was continued, after a pause, about 1308, in an updated version of the east end scheme which preserves continuity with skill and tenderness. Thus on the south side we get the same pointed trefoiled wall arcade of the choir and the staircase, though on the north side the arches are ogee and crocketed. The shape of the main piers and arches remains the same throughout though the nave capitals are elaborately carved in nobbly leaf.

What gives the east end a tremendous lift is the presence, just north of the high altar, of the sumptuous tomb of Lady Idoine, wife of Earl Percy (d. 1365), which seems to have been erected about 1360. There is no effigy but the structure of the tomb-canopy is bewilderingly rich and elaborate, with buttress-shafts, a maze of pinnacles, and nodding ogee-arches sprouting fruit, greenery and even angels. At the top of the arch Christ holds Lady Idoine's soul, and the supporting angels on either side are miracles of small-scale carvings. The canopy is vaulted and even its bosses have angle-carvings, some quite elaborate; there must be a hundred or more angels, or heads of angels, on this enchanting tomb, which is saved from garishness or mannerism by the purity of its workmanship. The choir stalls nearby are c. 1525 and with their canopied tabernacles almost as fine in their own

OPPOSITE The tierceron wooden vault of the Chapter House at York.

Beverley Minster seen from the north west.

way; just as the Percy Tomb ignores the Perpendicular, so they betray no touch of Renaissance – this is the Conservative North. The misericords are a sumptuous medieval bestiary; hawks, eagles, lions, bears, foxes and deer, cat and mouse, cranes and hares, elephants, unicorns, dragons, boars, cocks, geese, and a platoon of rustics brawling and raising riot.

The size of the crossing-piers makes it clear that the canons intended to build a massive crossing-tower, on the York model. But they never did so. That leaves the West Front as the main feature of the church, a role it carries with aplomb. Indeed, there are those, not in the City of York needless to say, who prefer it to the York West Front. It is somewhat later (1400–50) and was built all in one campaign, a big advantage. The main west window and the lantern windows of the towers fit perfectly, the panelling is in tune throughout, and the marvellous corner-buttresses sweep up the towers, through six storeys, in one tremendous

152

Steps leading to the Chapter House at Beverley.

movement, without hesitation. The horizontal levels are weaker than in York; this cathedral is, and looks, one hundred per cent Perpendicular. The Minster stands in clear space on the outskirts of town, and the almost total disappearance of the conventional buildings gives it isolation and adds to its dignity. At the north-west and south-west oblique angles, the outlines are indeed noble, but the lack of a crossing-tower spoils what would otherwise be a masterly silhouette. Once again, we wish that modern largesse (and self-confidence) were available to complete the work.

Beverley is a collegiate church with the architectural lines of a major cathedral. However, there are also cathedrals which, while exhibiting the essential forms of a bishop's church, are in architectural character of collegiate or even parochial status. In Wales, for instance, the idiom of Perpendicular is simplified and scaled down – though still unmistakeable – to suit the purses of poor sees. Bangor, for

153

instance, is largely the creation of the sixty years 1470–1530. There is a powerful, even majestic, crossing, as there should be in a church built for episcopal services, but there is a two-storey elevation throughout, the west tower (1509–32) is low and squat, huge buttresses magnifying the spread, and the main arcading is plain to the point of austerity, without even an attempt at integral connection with the roof.

At Llandaff, the nave (1193–1229) is also plain, two-storey, though there is stiff-leaf carving on the capitals of the inner arches and the colonnettes which sweep up to the roof (a cathedral touch), but some of the mouldings of the arches plunge straight to the pavement without a capital at all – which, in the Gothic system of mouldings and corresponding compound pillars, they are aesthetically entitled to do. The invariable refusal of Gothic architects in Britain to take this logical step, so long as they had the money, makes it seem a certain stigma of impoverishment when we come across it. But it can be enormously effective, as in the nave at St Asaph (1320–52) where there are no capitals at all, and the arch-mouldings sweep from pavement to pavement in one uninterrupted movement, which gives it a modernist look (and is, accordingly, imitated by modern architects working in the Gothic mode). At St Asaph, however, the chancel is one of the plainest, except for a fine Geometrical-Decorated east window, and the tower (1391–2, by Robert Fagan) would, I fear, shame the meanest parish in Somerset. Llandaff, however, has a distinguished north-west tower (c. 1485–1500), lofty and pinnacled in the best Somerset manner, and distantly related to the tower at Gloucester. All three Welsh cathedrals lack the history and distinction of St Davids; but they are all worth visiting and studying, for it is illuminating to discover whether the Perpendicular style works when it is deprived of its frills and stone-carved veneer. The answer is that it works very well, on the whole.

The Geometrical-Decorated east window at St Asaph Cathedral, Wales.

Late Perpendicular seems to work well irrespective of the shape of the church, too. The collegiate church of Manchester, which was raised to cathedral rank in 1847, is practically square. The aisled six-bay choir (1422–50) runs straight into the aisled six-bay nave (1465–81), and each church-length aisle opens into a further aisle, cluttered with chantries. Neither the original builders nor their innumerable successors endured the tyranny of exact measurement, for the choir is a good three feet wider at the western end than it is at the east. This, together with other curiosities, does not seem to matter. Nor do the endless alterations. The college was disbanded during the Reformation, and refounded under Elizabeth, who made her mathematician-wizard friend, Dr John Dee, its warden. There was a lot of trouble here in the seventeenth century, and a whole series of restorations and repairs to war-damage over 150 years in the modern period. Much of the external appearance is due to the several efforts of J.P. Holden, J.S. Crowther, Basil Champneys and Sir Hubert Worthington, to name but four restorers and architects. But restoring what? There does not seem to have been a principal designer in the first place: the collegiate church just grew, like Topsy; but it grew at a time when designers were all so impregnated with the Perpendicular form, which was an all-embracing system of design, that the character of Manchester Cathedral has proved almost indestructible and has triumphantly survived all the vicissitudes it has undergone. In short, it is a big Perpendicular city church, fit to be a cathedral.

Perpendicular was ubiquitous in England and Wales, and even in Ireland, for two centuries. North of the border it tended to be a rare and exotic growth. Just

OPPOSITE Llandaff Cathedral, South Wales, from the south east.

The interior of Manchester Cathedral.

OPPOSITE The sixteenth-century oak ceiling in St Machar's Cathedral, Aberdeen.

as the long breach with France hastened its emergence in England, so the bitter hostility with Scotland, beginning with the wars and harryings of Edward I, produced a bifurcation of English and Scottish architecture, already marked by the time Perpendicular appeared. Scottish clergy tended to look more to France for their architectural ideas. So the equivalent of a big collegiate city church in England is Aberdeen's Cathedral of St Machar (not to be confused with the modern Episcopalian Cathedral of St Andrew and the Roman Catholic Cathedral of St Mary, 1860–77), which was essentially built in the years 1424–40, and was the work of Bishop Lichtoun.

Apart from some earlier fourteenth-century work in sandstone, St Machar's is built in granite, the only medieval British cathedral to use this hard, demanding stone in any quantity. As a result, though severely battered, part of it survives in working order. The massive central tower (completed in 1512) fell in 1688,

because (it is said) Cromwell's soldiers had removed stone from the choir to build a fort more than thirty years before. This may be so but the fact is that the choir was never completed, for work stopped at the Reformation; and no one troubled to rebuild the transepts when the tower fell; they are now in ruins. The fine west towers remain, crowned with two sixteenth-century sandstone steeples; and the West Front has its original seven-light window, which is stern and sober. Inside, however, and totally unexpected, is a magnificent early sixteenth-century oak ceiling, flat with panels, set up by Bishop Dumbar (c. 1530), and emblazoned with a series of heraldic bosses, of the Pope and the Emperor, St Margaret of Scotland, and most of the kings and princes of Renaissance Christendom. It is quite well preserved (the backing has been restored) and confirms the rule that carved bosses are more likely to have survived the assaults of puritans and soldiers, ignorant clergymen and ruthless restorers, than any other type of medieval decoration. Lichtoun's own tomb, in the desolate north transept, has been hopelessly mutilated.

Aberdeen was a case of a late-medieval cathedral being caught unfinished by the arrival of the Reformation, and thereafter suffering irreparable damage to its fabric. Another was Bath, though in this case the structure was finished in the end. Bath is a curious anomaly in English cathedral architecture, and to this day it is still officially called Bath Abbey. It is very likely that Bath, Britain's leading therapeutic centre in Roman times, was never wholly abandoned by its inhabitants, and certainly there was a college of canons there in the eighth century which was turned into a regular monastery by St Dunstan. Nothing remains of the Saxon church that we know of, but it was sufficiently dignified for King Edgar to be crowned there in 973. The monastery flourished in Norman times, and in 1088 the Bishop of Wells (a physician) got papal permission to transfer his see to Bath, which he turned into a monastic cathedral with himself as abbot. But the bishops returned to Wells in the twelfth century, and thereafter Bath Abbey, or Priory as it technically was, led an uneasy and eventually ruinous existence, though it was clearly of considerable size.

In 1499 Bishop King of Wells, Henry VII's secretary, had a dream about his church at Bath in which he saw angels ascending and descending a ladder to heaven, and heard a voice say: 'Let a King restore the church.' What he in fact did, however, was to demolish the church, and employ Henry VII's master-masons, Robert and William Vertue, to build a spectacular but much smaller replacement over the site occupied by the Norman nave.

The Vertues were experts in late-Perpendicular show-chapels. In the final phase of English Gothic, royal, prelatical and aristocratic munificence had tended to concentrate on collegiate foundations rather than cathedrals. The movement was started by Wykeham, who created the new kind of exotic-chapel architecture with his works at Winchester College and New College Oxford; and it was continued, on an even bigger scale, by the pious Henry VI, with his great chapels at Eton and King's, Cambridge. These dramatic new buildings converted the very ancient English feature of the long nave into a church in itself, but one composed mainly of glass and with a spectacular vault. Under Henry VII, who was building a gigantic chantry-chapel for himself at Westminster and a collegiate chapel at Windsor, St George's, the Vertues emerged as the leading exponents of glass-architecture and virtuoso fan-vaulting. They promised Bishop King an unprecedented prodigy at Bath: 'Of the vaulte devises for the chancelle there shall be none so goodely neither in England nor in France.'

What they designed for King is more than a chapel, for it has transepts and a central crossing-tower, and a bishop's choir; but it is something less than a cathedral, and very nearly became a ruin like its predecessor. When the Abbey was dissolved in 1539, only the choir and one of the transepts had been roofed and vaulted. It was in a poor state when Queen Elizabeth visited it in 1574, and it was through her efforts that the crossing was vaulted. The south transept vault followed in the early seventeenth century, and under Bishop Montague of Bath and Wells (1612–16) the nave acquired a wooden roof, the whole church a pavement, and a stone pulpit was set up. The church was not really completed until the nineteenth century, when the great system of fan-vaults was finally extended to the nave.

Despite this hazardous history, Bath is entirely homogenous and bears testimony to the excellence of the original design. It has to fight very hard indeed to carry its weight in Bath, which contains more first-class architecture than any other town of its size in Europe, not least in the quarter where the Abbey is placed. It is not enormous, either: the church is only just over 200 feet long (compared to at least 300 for a medium-sized cathedral) and the crossing-tower is a mere 162 feet to the top of its pinnacles. Yet the design works very well, not only from afar, where it rests at the bottom of the saucer formed by the ring of hills which encircle the city and so becomes the focus of attention, but in its immediate neighbourhood. Here its relatively small ground-plan is a crucial advantage. To put it crudely, the Vertues, by going for height (the vaults are not much less than eighty feet throughout), were able to pack a tremendous quantity of cathedral into a relatively small area. The design can therefore be taken in, with all its majestic simplicity, at very short range, so that the street vistas reveal it not as a mere indigestible chunk of stone scenery – the usual fate of cathedrals in heavily built-up areas – but as an intelligible and exciting artefact. No one can fail to see how cleverly it makes the most of its space: the tower is reduced to an oblong to avoid contracting its west-east profile, and the transepts follow suit, so that their narrow width makes their height seem almost incredible at close quarters – a very daring conception.

The Vertues, too, made very skilful play with a series of truly amazing buttresses, rising at the corners of the transepts in five high stages, along the four arms of the church in splayed flyers, like gigantic cleft twigs, and everywhere culminating in high pinnacles. The muscular strength of the buttress system (much more massive than engineering demanded) is deliberately stressed to draw the contrast with the gossamer frame of the structure itself, a glasshouse which was known as 'the lantern of the West'. It was as though the Vertues, so confident in their ability to imprison space in almost unlimited quantities, were mocking the laws of gravity by a light-hearted improvization on the well-tried Gothic theory of countervailing force.

There is so much fun in this design, such a lack of gravitas and high seriousness, that it plainly played a leading part in the first, eighteenth-century, phase of the Gothic revival, when architects like Wyatt and, still more, John Nash, were using 'Gothick' idioms for pure pleasure and sensation. Might it not have been designed for the Prince Regent himself? On either side of the great west window, Bishop King's dreamy angels float up and down their ladders, and it is hard to believe they were placed there to edify, inspire fear or love of God, or advance the cause of religion in any way whatever. Was not their function to delight or amuse? In the age of the Vertues, Erasmus was already mocking the

indulgence-cult and other aspects of mechanical religion, and the Renaissance was switching the focus of attention from eternity to man's place in the universe. There is no ocular trace of the Renaissance here but its spirit hovers over the values of the design.

The elegant frivolity of the scheme risks, indeed, distracting attention from its solid merits as a piece of prodigy-architecture. Why, for instance, does this West Front succeed where Winchester's lacks impact? Both appear to take the lazy way out – the cross-section – but the Vertues have got the proportions right by pushing the aisles down while pulling the big window up. They have made the turrets big and bold and thus justified their existence as a feature, drawing attention to them by the ladder-scheme (its real *raison d'être*). They have made clever use of the thick buttresses to bring them into the design of the front, and finally they have ensured that, at about sixty yards' distance, the point of maximum impact, the observer takes in the crossing tower pinnacles, beautifully framed by the gable-pinnacles of the front. Indeed, the exterior of the church as a whole is a brilliant lesson in how to make buttresses and pinnacles carry their full aesthetic weight without sinking the fundamental lines of the design. This emerges strongly if the visitor takes the trouble to obtain a roof-top view, especially from the westerly side, where the main bones of the structure, including the cunning stress on horizontal levels, bring out the sheer exuberance of the verticals and diagonals.

The Renaissance, of course, appears in places, notably in the great west door, which is early seventeenth century; but the main lines of the interior are unhesitatingly medieval, with no tongue in cheek and very little decoration of any kind, until the eye sweeps up to the spinning patterns of the vault-fans, where it is clearly meant to rest. The clerestory windows take up all the triforium space and more, and the east wall is all glass except for the lines of its design. As there is no lantern light at the crossing, the lighting is pretty uniform and there are no half-hidden mysteries in this sparkling and spotless church, except of course in the vault-shadows. Indeed, one suspects that, the vault apart, the Vertues really designed this church from the outside, as a townscape prodigy, since their skyscraper-transepts, which give the exterior such a tremendous lift, are, to put it mildly, too narrow within to serve much purpose. Leaving aside the heavyweight tomb of Bishop Montague (*c.* 1620), the one really spectacular item in the interior is the chantry of Prior Birde, with Bishop King the effective founder of the church. It dates from about 1515, and is wonderfully crisp and light; medieval, of course, but visibly fighting hard to keep the Renaissance at bay. It confirms to me, as does the interior as a whole, that by the reign of Henry VIII all the problems of the Gothic interior had been solved, and architects fought off boredom by daring displays of vaulting and by chantry-work, which was almost a form of jewellery – that great sixteenth-century art.

Certainly at Oxford, the last of our medieval cathedrals, the vault is the focus of vision (though by no means the only one). Oxford cathedral is an oddity, mainly because it was never designed to be a cathedral in the first place, or indeed in the second place. It began as a Saxon nunnery, allegedly founded by St Frideswide in the early eighth-century. Then, in the twelfth, it became an Augustinian canonry, and was provided with a set of late-Norman conventual buildings. Suppressing monasteries and convents was by no means an invention of Henry VIII's: it has been a royal device to grab or divert funds since the reign of Edward III, when many French priories in England were nationalized. It was

OPPOSITE The West Front of Bath Abbey; on either side of the great west window angels ascend ladders to heaven.

never very difficult to get papal mandates to suppress ailing foundations and make their incomes available for more workmanlike religious or educational ventures. Cardinal Wolsey was a large-scale operator in this field, and Thomas Cromwell was his expert executive – one reason why he was picked by Henry himself later. Wolsey's biggest foundation was what is now Christ Church, Oxford, and to clear the site he not only had St Frideswide's suppressed but knocked about fifty feet off its nave to construct Tom Quad, the principal court of the college. The rest of the church became the college chapel. When Wolsey died, Henry took over the foundation but later decided to turn the chapel into a cathedral, served by the college canons. By this time the church was roughly square-shaped, rather like Manchester, and only 160 feet 'long'; it seems to be, and indeed is, part of the collegiate buildings, and has no distinctive external personality, though its big stone spire, burly rather than elegant, is a hallowed part of the Oxford sky-line, the earliest (thirteenth-century) survivor of our cathedral stone spires.

Inside, however, the visitor gets a double shock. The first is provided by the original twelfth-century bay-order of the church. This is based upon what is now called a 'giant order' of columns, that is columns so high that they pass through two storeys. In this case, they are giant Corinthian columns, some of them with superbly carved capitals of about 1180–90, and the suggestion is that the Augustinian canons, who were eclectic in their architectural arrangements, may have been aiming at the effect created by some of the big Roman basilicas – a colonnade church, in fact. The design was too wedded to the fundamentals of the Romanesque three-storey bay to make structural sense of giant order columns. So each bay has not only a real arch on the top of each pair of columns, but a fake arch beneath, corresponding to the aisle-level and supporting the usual triforium, which peeps out from under the real arch. As the clerestory level was radically altered in the sixteenth century, when the vault was replaced, the result looks odd, though it is not unimpressive. It breaks the architectural rules but it has a heady character of its own, 'full of eastern promise', and strikes an exotic note in a cathedral composed of a structural dissonance anyway.

The second surprise, the choir vault, does not compound the error of the piers but, in a sense, resolves it by adding a structural prodigy of such blatancy that it harmonizes with the vertical obtrusiveness of the mammoth columns. In the late fifteenth century, as we have noted, architects focused their wits on the virtuoso vault. The lierne had resolved itself into the half-cone of the fan vault; but the lierne could also develop in the direction of a pendant by allowing the ribs to break through at the sides and continue behind the lierne as an arch (the pendant, in effect, being an audacious extension of the arch's keystone). So each pair of pendants corresponds to two arch-voussoirs, held by lateral pressure. Buttresses, unseen, counteract the pressure from the base of the arch. Once the exercise is actually thought out, it is much simpler than it looks; but it is a virtuoso ploy in stonemason's engineering all the same, and looks so spectacular that it is surprising it found so few Continental imitators.

The man who seems to have invented the pendant vault, later used with such *élan* by William Vertue in the Henry VII Chapel, Westminster, was a West Country designer called William Orchard, who first tried it out in the Oxford Divinity School, 1479–83. The vault at St Frideswide's (as it then was) was his second effort. It does not use the fan pattern but the lierne-star, and the pendants swoop down to form lanterns. It is a work of great skill and ingenuity, and one

OPPOSITE The nave of Bath Abbey, facing east.

162

can gaze at it fascinated for long periods without actually discovering how it works (the puzzle of course is resolved instantly one gets between vault and roof) and it has baffled generations of Bullingdon Club undergraduates. The danger, of course, was that it would degenerate into mere virtuoso display or, in conjunction with the pillars, suggest an architectural nightmare. In fact these two powerfully heterodox features, separated by over 300 years, are surprisingly congruous, the vault-buttresses even appearing to spring naturally out of the Corinthian capitals of the pillars, as though they were holding aloft a Romanesque barrel-vault rather than a piece of late-Gothic wedding-cake.

Perhaps the combination could only work in Oxford, which took to its bosom every variety of the Gothic, clinging to it long after the rest of England, even Cambridge, had embraced the Renaissance; clinging to it, indeed, with such obstinacy that it is almost, if not quite, true that Oxford never really abandoned Gothic in one form or another until the present century, and more's the pity. But Gothic, as a system of design for large buildings was dead in Britain by the time Oxford assumed its cathedral duties. The desire to build cathedrals had gone; even the urge to maintain them was weak, and when the great steeple of Old St Paul's fell in Elizabeth's reign, the City Fathers, richer than ever before, merely tidied up the mess, leaving the vast thoroughbred cathedral without its central feature, like a victim of architectural leprosy.

Yet if the age of cathedral-building was over, the idea of the cathedral survived, both as an architectural form and as an ecclesiastical institution. Why should this be? To obtain the answer we must look more closely at the way they were built, and the purpose they served.

6
How the Cathedrals were Built

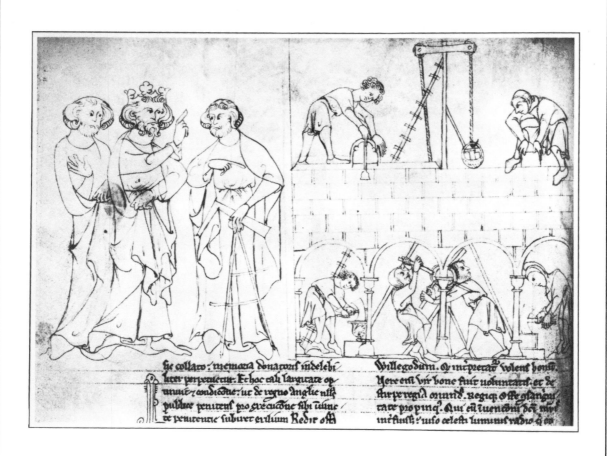

here is distressingly little documentary evidence about the actual building methods employed in cathedral-construction, and many of the secrets lie imprisoned in the buildings themselves. Something has been learnt from the ruined structures of medieval abbeys; something from damage to the cathedrals of north-east France during the Great War; and much was discovered during the restoration of cathedrals in the nineteenth century, especially in the work of Viollet-le-Duc in France and Sir George Gilbert Scott in Britain. What follows is a summary of our existing knowledge, culled from a variety of sources.

The first problem was levelling the site. It was usually about 150 by 100 yards, and was levelled by sighting or 'boning'; often a large cauldron of water was brought onto the site, which was then worked until the water-rim was level. The cathedral had to be orientated, and this was traditionally done by marking the sunrise on the feast day of the patron saint. Some of these have been examined by the Reverend Hugh Benson – for example, the orientation of Lichfield Cathedral is for sunrise on St Peter's Day, 1 August in the twelfth century; Oxford Cathedral is for Lady's Day, 25 March in the eighth century.

The next stage was the 'groundwerk' or foundations, and setting-out, using cords. A latt, or measuring-rod, was used for 'lattlaying'. We have some information about the preliminary work for Wolsey's foundation at Oxford, around 1515: the master-masons went out to the site 'to see the platte with the grownede' (to compare the plan with the actual ground). Six months later they were ordered to 'set forth the ground' ready for the foundation trenches. These were dug and filled with stone rubble or chalk, flints and other solid rubbish, rammed down hard. For high-quality work rubble-concrete and lime-mortar were used, and sometimes, on wet ground, square piles with iron points were driven in, and covered with planking to receive the stone. Most big medieval buildings had a plinth, its line consolidated with a row of stone slabs called a 'tablement', which had to be made level with extreme care, as it later became the standard for all other levels. For vertical distances between the levels, storey rods were set up and marked, the tablement projecting outside the wall-face to provide a footing for the rods. There was a rod for each storey, which was moved about as the building rose to keep the level constant, and for each new storey rod a new tablement was required; this effectively completed the storey and served as base for the next. The tablements in time became 'string courses', developed a mouldings system of their own and in due course assumed airs as a prominent architectural feature. Contracts refer to building 'true by level and line' – line being plumb-lines to keep wall-faces vertical. The storey levels which formed the basis of the ordered bay-unit design thus had a structural rather than an aesthetic origin. Levels had to be exact over large distances, especially the level at which the roof, and still more the heavy stone vaults, were sprung from the wall.

Medieval architects and masons knew nothing of solid geometry and other theoretical aids to structural engineering. So far as we know they never made perspective plans; nor, as a rule, did they make orthographic projections. John Fitchen, the leading authority on Gothic construction procedures, believes that the overall design and the solving of detailed problems were worked out in the course of constructing elaborate three-dimensional models, of both the whole and of key parts. But we have no evidence of complete models before the fifteenth century, and none has survived in Britain from the medieval period. Even on the

OVERLEAF A medieval manuscript illustration showing Henry III giving instructions to his masons as they work on St Albans Cathedral.

166

Continent, the earliest to survive is of St Maclou at Rouen.

Christopher Wren's great model of St Paul's Cathedral.

The merit of models, of course, is that they reveal not only what takes place during the constructional process, but how it is done and in what sequence. The speed and cost of the work was determined very largely by efficient sequences, especially as the level rose; so when the sequential problems had been solved on the model, a full-scale layout was made on the ground, not necessarily on the site. We know, for instance, that when the great roof of Westminster Hall was being prepared in 1395, all the trusses were laid out at 'the Frame' near Farnham. For experimental large-scale carpentry, like the Ely octagon and lantern, not only elaborate models but full-scale dress rehearsals were essential.

By the time the foundation-trenches had been dug, masons' and carpenters' huts had gone up on the site, and thereafter permanent dry areas were available for setting out plans of the major cruces in the construction process. As the building rose, setting-out areas were used within it. Sometimes these were improvised: thus, at Wells, a part of the chapter house floor was used for setting out the designs of the great saltires inserted under the crossing in about 1340. At York, however, the masons had a drawing-office of their own, by 1330, situated over the vestibule. It can still be seen, with settings-out on the floor, and templates hanging on the wall.

The master-masons were almost certainly fine draughtsmen, and most of them at some phase in their career had been accomplished figure sculptors. At various times they used lead pencils, chalk and metal stylus as well as ink on parchment or paper. Late-medieval accounts give us hints. At Westminster, in 1531, eight shillings was paid for 'two payre skrewis for tracerye roddis provided for the

maister mason to draw with in his tracery house'. Hardly any of these drawings survive from the medieval period, at any rate in England. In Vienna, a large collection of early architectural drawings has been found. We possess, too, a drawing from about 1250–60 of a rose-window at Strasbourg Cathedral, and a church-elevation of c.1250 from Rheims. A working drawing of the West Front at Clermont-Ferrand Cathedral exists, drawn to a scale of one in thirty. In England, the earliest architectural drawings, found in a sketch-book in the Pepysian Library at Magdalene, Cambridge, are mere fragments dating from 1350–1400. There are two drawings of King's College, Cambridge: one of a projected tower (c.1450) and the second of the north elevation, but both are show drawings for the patron, not working drawings. We also have Matthew Paris's famous illustration from his *Life of the Offas* in the British Museum's Cottonian Manuscripts, showing Henry III, the greatest and probably the most knowledgeable patron of them all, giving orders to his masons.

In the Bibliothèque Nationale in Paris there is a little skin-covered parchment volume, containing thirty-three sheets of drawings by an architect from Cambrai, Villard de Honnecourt, who probably designed Cambrai Cathedral. He travelled a good deal, going as far as Hungary, and his notebook contains sketches of Cambrai, Chartres, Laon, Lausanne, Rheims and Meaux, as well as other drawings. Some of them are stereotypes of hackneyed subjects, such as a king on a throne, Madonna and Child and so forth. But he also shows a sawmill, a screw-jack, how to cut a screw and a machine for forcing houses back into the vertical, as well as a large-scale mangonel. The sketch-book is a great treasure – it shows that Villard knew a little elementary trigonometry, for example – but it is sometimes exasperatingly obscure. Thus, he shows no flying buttresses on his drawings of the nave of Rheims Cathedral, though they certainly existed when he saw it; and sometimes he puts in features which did not exist, because he thought they should. There are a few medieval drawings and paintings actually showing Gothic buildings under construction, but they leave out most of the scaffolding and machinery because they were regarded as irrelevant to the purpose of the representation.

Undoubtedly vast quantities of drawings perished during the Reformation and with the advent of the Renaissance in architecture and design. By the time of Dürer, who also kept notebooks, the Gothic spirit was waning fast; it had nothing structurally to contribute to the new artillery-forts with which he and so many other sixteenth-century artist-engineers were obsessed, and which, indeed, marked a return to the Romanesque dependence on mass. However, there is another reason for the lack of documentation: the trade secret. All medieval artisans were secretive about their trades, but the masons were positively obsessed by the arcane, which was associated in their minds with the origins and history of their craft (mostly fabulous) and the mystery of numbers. They had elaborate pseudo-scientific theories of numbers, proportions and intervals, and they memorized number-series for their measuring-rods and lay-outs. As in ancient Egypt, another stone-carving culture, they had very strong *atelier* traditions, and canonical forms and ratios for almost any structural contingency. These were passed on by mouth and learnt by heart; as little as possible was put down on paper. There seems to have been no such thing as a builder's handbook before the sixteenth century.

The first problem the masons faced was getting the right kind of stone. Limestone makes the best freestone, and they could draw on the great limestone

OPPOSITE The room above the chapter house vestibule at York which was used by the fourteenth-century masons as a drawing-office.

belt which stretches from the Bristol Channel to the Wash. Architectural schools and masonic *ateliers* tended to develop in the region of big quarries, especially Doulting, eight miles from Bath, which was owned by Glastonbury, and Barnack, at the other end of the belt, owned by Peterborough. Other famous quarries were Bath and Ham Hill in Somerset, and Chilmark, from which Salisbury's stone was quarried. A further stretch of limestone went north from Nottingham to Newcastle. In Dorset there was Beer Quarry, which supplied the marvellous stone of Exeter, and the Isle of Purbeck. In the West Midlands and North-West there was no limestone, so Chester, Lichfield and Carlisle used sandstone from the Cheshire-Lancashire belt. South-East England had no suitable stone at all, and it was imported from Normandy (chiefly Caen) until the loss of the province under King John.

Stone was quarried by looking for natural cracks, which were then widened and split by wood wedges which were hammered home. On the site, reached as far as possible by river, stone was cut in the huts or lodges by 'banker' masons, then taken by wheelbarrow – one of the great early medieval inventions, replacing the two-man stretcher – to the wall-face where it was laid by a 'setting' mason. Until the eleventh century, it was rare for cathedrals to be built of anything other than field stone except for corner-stones or quoins, and wall- and window-opening frames. In the eleventh and twelfth centuries, rubble infilling was the rule. Thereafter, walls were built through with wrought stone or ashlar, with a rectangular face, a 'bed' on top and bottom, trimmed sides and a rough 'tail', though often the tail was trimmed too. The use of dressed stone, held by high-quality lime mortar burned on the site, enormously increased the carrying weight of piers, and enabled the thickness of the wall to be drastically reduced. Individual stones became larger: eleventh-century walling is usually of squarish stones, six or eight inches long; with the arrival of full Gothic in the thirteenth century, stones were rectangular, from fourteen to eighteen inches in length; and in the fourteenth and fifteenth centuries much bigger. The banker masons had to work out the details of the individual stones, which were sometimes very complicated in groin-vaults; for carving in place, banker-masons left a rough projecting stone-face for the carver-mason to deal with after it had been laid by the setter.

Stone (including its transport) was the biggest single item in cathedral building, but timber for scaffolding and roofs was a big item too. Inspecting and purchasing suitable trees, and sometimes whole woods, was an important part of a master-carpenter's duties, and sometimes he would be on the look-out for years for special timbers – for example: forty, fifty or sixty-foot oak lengths. Finding the right tree could avoid much labour in scarfing, and increase stability. Timber-spotting led to many tales of miracles, much cherished by monkish chroniclers, rather as, in Ancient Egypt, the finding of a large hardstone was often attributed to the intervention of a particular god.

Scaffolding is the aspect of medieval high-level construction about which we know least. We have documentary evidence as to the cost, but manuscript illustrations are suggestive rather than informative; thus a drawing in the Bibliothèque Nationale, 'Masons replacing a column-drum', shows them doing it without shoring the vault or cradling the column itself – a manifest impossibility. Close on-site inspection produces evidence of scaffold-holds and putlog-holes, usually invisible from the ground or carefully filled in, from which it is possible to conjecture scaffold-frames. Some scaffolds worked on rollers, like military siege-

OPPOSITE Medieval manuscript illustration of masons replacing a column drum. To make the picture clearer, the artist has omitted the falsework.

towers, and it must be remembered that master-carpenters, who were the engineers of the Middle Ages, usually owed their position, particularly in royal service, to their skill and ingenuity in devising war-machines. There was a big overlap in technology between building a cathedral and besieging a castle or town.

A great deal of thought went into the devising of scaffolding and centering which was economical in timber and quick to assemble and dismantle. As Viollet-le-Duc said: 'The real skill of the builder can be judged from the manner in which he places his scaffold. Well-designed scaffolding saves time for the workmen, gives them confidence and obliges them to be regular, methodical and careful.' Le Duc believed that in building high-vault cathedrals it was rare to use scaffolding straight up from the ground – which would have been enormously expensive and time-consuming – but instead scaffolding was raised by putlogs and stilts and took on new points of support at the higher levels, allowing the underpinning to be dismantled and used elsewhere. Scaffolding requirements were built into the detailed design of the cathedral, and met by the banker-masons working on individual stones in their lodges. In the Westminster accounts, which are very full, their are references to three tiers of scaffolding: *inferior*, *superior* and *supremus*. In 1490, for instance, Richard Russell was paid £60 for making 'lez grete scaffoldes in summitate navis ecclesiae' and 'le newe scaffoldes pro les syde yles'. The scaffold men were also responsible for erecting temporary protection for half-completed cathedrals during the winter and pauses in the campaign, which often lasted for years. At Westminster there were temporary penthouses and hoardings, sometimes roofed with hurdles and even tiled.

One factor in the arrival of Gothic was the development of lifting machinery, an important civil by-product of the Crusades, which dominated the advanced technology of the late eleventh and twelfth centuries. The Canterbury Revolution was brought about not only by the new designs William of Sens brought with him but also, according to the chronicler Gervase, to the 'ingenious machines for loading and unloading ships and for drawing cement and stones' which he caused to be constructed on the site. In addition to military technology, cathedral engineers could draw on wind- and water-mill machinery, especially the windlass, the spread and elaboration of which was the dynamic feature of the medieval economy in north-west Europe. The earlier types had compass-arm wheels: there is a portion of one at Durham Cathedral, and a complete one at Peterborough, with its frame and in working order. A windlass derived from the Peterborough type is still in the spire at Salisbury, and C. A. Hewett thinks this may date from the first building campaign (1220–58) and not from the building of the spire in the fourteenth century. A somewhat similar treadmill windlass is to be found in the crossing, above the vaults, at Beverley. In Norwich Cathedral there is a hand-operated wheel and windlass inside the spire, still in good working order; but it has threaded nuts and bolts, so is probably eighteenth century. Also from the eighteenth century is a vertical-mounted capstan in the south-west tower at Durham. Lifting machines sometimes had to be placed on platforms as high as 80 or even 100 feet above ground level (more in France), and the medieval carpenter-engineers appear to have mastered this type of machine by the thirteenth century. What they lacked was a machine to swing heavy weights horizontally at a height of 50–100 feet.

Certainly, Ruskin was quite wrong in arguing that the medieval builder was

OPPOSITE *St Barbara* by Van Eyck. In the background, to the right of the picture, can be seen the lodge of the masons working on the cathedral, and above it a crane lifting blocks of stone.

173

always 'true' to his material. Quite apart from the fact that many imposing medieval piers and walls had rubble cores, iron was used extensively for internal wall-supports and for clamps, stays, tie-rods, braces and dowels; vast numbers of especially-made iron nails were wrought on the spot. Where iron was used to pin stonework, it was first boiled in tallow to prevent rust. Sometimes tie-rods can be seen – for instance, those that link the piers at the arcade-springing in Westminster Abbey. A good deal of iron was used in the crossing-piers at Salisbury during the period when the great stone spire was built, that is, long before Wren had giant braces specially forged for the spire in the naval dockyard at Portsmouth.

Masons used a variety of devices to protect and strengthen exposed walling. Flaking could be virtually eliminated if the ashlars were correctly cut. Resin, linseed oil and pitch were used to prevent decay, and outer surfaces were often whitewashed every year. The quality of the mortar and its laying, by spreading the weight evenly across the entire surfaces of the ashlars, vastly improved the stability of walling. Medieval architects disliked building more than ten feet of wall-height in any one season, to allow settling to take place. Features which to us appear purely decorative often had a primary structural function. Thus, the blind arcading beloved of Norman designers, especially at lower levels, was used to strengthen rubble-core walls, notably of towers. Later, when dressed stone was used throughout in walling, the device disappeared, except as pure decoration.

In designing a cathedral, which might take anything from 38 to 150 years to build, the architect had to bear in mind not only the system of forces in the finished building, but the temporary conjunction of pressures at every pause in the process. A half-finished cathedral was liable to be a very dangerous structure. Abbot Suger describes the effect of a great storm on St Denis during the construction process. It occurred when work was still going on to build the high vault of the choir, and when the flying buttresses had been set up but not yet connected to the vaults to form a rigid frame – though their supporting scaffolding had already been dismantled. The winds were so strong that the buttresses visibly swayed and trembled, and the roof vibrated. Only a miracle, says Suger, prevented the buttresses from collapsing. Strictly speaking, then, the architect had to ensure that his stone framework had a balance of forces at any time during the construction period.

In addition to wind, the great enemies of the Gothic cathedral were fire and rain. It was the threat of fire which first led to the vaulting of castle-towers, and then churches. A good stone vault could preserve the interior of the church even if the roof was completely destroyed. Early medieval builders experimented with different types of roofs because, unlike the Romans, they had no cement. The wooden roofs of Romanesque churches were usually covered with tiles. St Martin de Tours used tin. Saxon York had a lead roof, probably the first in Britain; but lead was used at Norman Canterbury, for Gervase says it melted when the church was burnt. Nevertheless, when William the Englishman completed the new choir roof in 1184, he covered it with lead, which experience showed was the most effective material. This meant altering the pitch of the roof. In northern Europe, where rain was constant and snow seasonal, church roofs of tiles, shingles or stone slabs had high pitches for rapid drainage; but on a high-pitch lead roof, the sheets, which are enormously heavy and are always expanding and contracting with changes in temperature, tear away from their fastenings and roll down the slope like a carpet. As more lead-mines came into

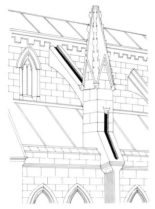

This diagram of one of the choir buttresses at Southwell Minster shows the way buttresses were used as aqueducts to avoid damage to the aisle roof.

production, English cathedrals switched to lead and lowered their roof pitches; for high-pitch spires the strips were laid on diagonally. Until about the end of the thirteenth century, English cathedral roofs remained steep – forty to fifty degrees as a rule. (Lincoln is much higher.) In the fourteenth and fifteenth centuries the pitch was lowered to the point where the roof cannot be seen at all from ground level (as with the naves at York), and battlements and parapets were put in to complete the skyline, a notable feature of Perpendicular.

The emergence of the cathedral battlement, a feature of towers as well as roofs, is only one example of a constant process whereby functional changes in structure bred new decorative devices and modes. Thus the corbel-table, as seen at Wells, Beverley and the east end of Norwich, became a kind of dripping eave-system to give projection beyond the face of the wall and so stop water dripping down it. This was a primitive system, which had the disadvantage that it made the roof difficult to inspect, and in the case of high roofs caused rain – and worse, snow – to crash down upon the aisle roofs below. The next development was to build the top courses of the wall hollow, with an inner wall, and open channel, and an outer wall, the gutter being constructed of non-porous stone and often covered with lead. The great Victorian Gothicist, Francis Bond, thought the origins of the gutter were military. It first appears at Ely Cathedral, and at Wells, for instance, a fourteenth-century gutter-parapet was superimposed upon the 1175 corbel-table. In the late fourteenth century the parapet became a battlement, in line with the trend towards battlemented country houses, a conscious archaism already. The next stage was to perforate the battlement merlons and often the embrasures too, a great feature of Perpendicular, especially for towers.

The gutter and gargoyle-spout, a Roman device, seems to have been re-invented in the thirteenth century. The object was to throw the rain-water as far as possible away from the side of the church. With this in mind, architects often used flying buttresses as down-hill aqueducts, a channel running down the strut of the buttress and through its balancing pinnacle – an example being the buttresses of c.1340 added to the thirteenth-century choir at Southwell. Spouts were sometimes used but on the whole English designers preferred an open system, which did not become clogged with leaves and dirt, and could easily be monitored.

They also used great ingenuity in devising external systems of chamfered stone, mouldings and drip-stones to protect the lower stonework and the arch-mouldings of doors and windows from the erosion of rain-dripping. These hood-moulds and aedicular drip-stones developed end-corbels of their own, which soon became animated as a leaf-carving, grotesque human head or animal mask. All external decorations on cathedrals began in this functional fashion; but, having established themselves as part of the external design, they tended to be repeated on the interior surface, where they had no function at all.

All medieval cathedrals had to be subjected to regular inspection to detect weather damage and deterioration of the fabric; so circulation systems, as we have already noted at Lincoln, were built in during the construction process. They are rare in Romanesque cathedrals, universal in Gothic ones. Indeed, we have to bear in mind, when examining the great second phase of cathedral building in the late twelfth and thirteenth centuries, that the bishops and monks who rebuilt the eastern arms of their churches, and sometimes the naves as well, were motivated not merely by aesthetic considerations, vainglory and the desire to provide prodigy-settings for their patronal relics, but also by the practical need

OPPOSITE A transept turret staircase at Lincoln Cathedral, showing the vaulted ceiling.

to make their churches fireproof, rainproof and sound, while accessible to inspection everywhere.

Medieval builders, especially in England, probably devoted more thought to their roofs than to any other aspect of the church. There were, of course, two distinct types of timber roof: the open timber roof, without a vault, and the high roofs designed to protect vaults. The latter might have as much as ten feet of clearance between the crown of the vault and the tie-beam, the lowest part of the roof structure. The tie-beams resisted the tendency of the roof slopes to spread apart at their bases, and kept rigid the roof triangle, transmitting the load from one side to another in accordance with the direction of the wind. They also served to transmit and neutralize the inward pressure of the flying buttresses, and became bases for platforms during the construction process of the vault. Mr Hewett, who has examined medieval ridged main-span roofing in forty cases, has an elaborate typology of roofs, which reveals a surprising number of radically

Diagram of the east end of an imaginary Gothic cathedral, showing the circulation system above floor level necessary for the maintenance of the cathedral fabric.

different schemes. It is often very difficult to date the timbers or to distinguish between the original framework and later additions. York is unusual in having no less than five of its original roofs intact; but then it has far less stone vaulting than most cathedrals of its size.

Vaulting was the great new engineering science of the Middle Ages, and it is clear that the trend towards ever more elaborate vaults, beautiful in themselves, was dictated not so much by aesthetic considerations as by the drive for more light and the need to cut down costs. John Fitchen, the great expert on vault construction, argues that architectural historians tend to ignore the importance of falsework and centering, and in particular the constant need to dismantle, shift and reassemble it from bay to bay, all these complex operations having to be carried out from below. The exigencies of centering were probably the biggest single factor in pushing forward new types of vault. Thus the simple barrel-vault developed into the banded barrel-vault, which could be built one section at a time (the bay unit) from a moving falsework and centering. The groin vault was developed to allow direct lighting of the nave, and with transverse boundary arches it permitted individual bay-construction, again from a moving falsework. The disadvantage of the groined vault was the complexity of the groin voussoir, a ten-sided shape, no two surfaces of which were parallel and four of which were curving. Hewing them required immense skill, and just fitting them, on a high platform, must have been a nightmare. The domed groin vault was developed partly to avoid weaknesses and partly to allow the masons to escape from the exigencies of strict geometry by cambering.

From this the masons moved on, empirically to be sure, for there is no evidence of actual theoretical studies, to the thin-shelled vault. They knew nothing of thin-shell theory but they learned by experiment that it was curvature rather than thickness which produced cohesion and rigidity in a vault. They also found that the rib gave the vault extra strength as a rigid arc. Hence they moved rapidly to a two-part system of ribs, built using centering, and vault-skin, which could be filled in, using a good deal of mortar to provide rigidity, after the ribs had set. The next step was to evolve the sexpartite vault which introduced a transverse rib to make use of the intermediate piers in double-bays as springing-points. The quadripartite vault, which marks the maturing of the Gothic system, followed logically; it ensured that a single bay of the high vault corresponded to one bay of the side aisles, the nave bays becoming rectangular, with their longitudinal span half their transverse span.

This vaulting system, which made possible the maximum combination of light and height, was locked into place by two masonry devices, the *tas-de-charge* and the flying buttress. The *tas-de-charge* was, strictly speaking, the lowest courses of the vault, which are laid horizontally and bonded into the wall, being corbelled outwards. It was the keystone of the vault because it effectively joined the ribs to the pier and transferred them into mouldings. Its corbelling reduced both the span of the vault and its thrust, and it contributed to the ordered convergence of the Gothic system by gathering all the thrusts of the vault together and transferring them straight to the buttress on the other side of the wall. The centrepieces of the *tas-de-charge* were enormous carved stones which posed the most serious problems the windlasses on the high platforms had to solve; but they were well worth their weight. The flying buttresses, in turn, were the final anchors of the system, which received the thrust of the vault on the outside, and transferred it to the ground. They were kept stable either by having a second tier, pushing the receiving tier downwards, or by high balancing pinnacles. Buttress pinnacles, indeed, which seem superfluous decoration, were in fact an essential part of the structure.

With a developed rib structure, centering was reduced to a minimum, and the weight of the stone skin between the webs was systematically reduced. Voussoirs did not necessarily have to be uniformly cut but could be laid in a sea of mortar, producing homogenous shells, for which the stones acted like a steel skeleton. Vault-skins might be as little as six inches thick, and were sometimes chipped down in size after the mortar had set, which might take a year or even eighteen months. The aim all along was to reduce weight and centering, and thereby time, materials and money; but there can be no doubt, however, that later vaulting proliferated ribs for purely aesthetic purposes. An example is the vault at Exeter: the additional ribs in the thirteenth-century choir are plainly structural, but in the fourteenth-century nave vault their purpose is decorative; this is also true of the later nave vault at Canterbury.

In the early Middle Ages, carpenters were at least as important as masons; in England, with its strong Saxon wood-building tradition, they were probably more important. Many masonry structural and decorative devices began as stone imitations of timbering. The balance of power shifted in the twelfth century, when wooden castles became obsolete and the arrival of Gothic engineering created a new type of master-mason, who had to be literate and numerate. The master-carpenters remained essential, however, because they built the latest war-engines, designed high-level scaffolding and erected roofs; in some buildings, such as the Ely lantern and the new Westminster Hall, they were effectively the designers too. In the fifteenth century, however, their role was squeezed at both ends: the smiths, who built the cannons, were taking over their work as military engineers, and the masons had by now completely emancipated stone-vault construction from its origins in carpentry. By the end of the Middle Ages, the best masons had pushed themselves high up the social scale, leaving the carpenters behind.

Of course the masons had been better organized for some time. There were skilled carpenters in every village. Masons were more mobile, moving from site to site, in time for the beginning of the building seasons, which usually lasted from 1 March to the end of October. Being more travelled – quite a high proportion had probably been abroad – they were more conscious of their status and rights and much more exclusive. From the monks they served they borrowed organizational concepts, forming themselves into chapters, and chapters into congregations. From St Augustine's *City of God*, one of the most widely-read and generally available books of the Middle Ages, they derived the idea of God as a maker of cities, a celestial super-mason; God was portrayed holding a pair of compasses, and measuring out the distances of the universe, rather as a master-mason designed a Geometrical-Decorated window. By the end of the twelfth century, leading masons were familiar with one or two classical texts: Vitruvius, for instance, copies of which were to be found in good monastic libraries, or the military handbook dealing with castles and engines written by Vegetius Renatus, *De Re Militarii*. But all masons, even if they could not read, knew that the origin of their craft went back to the Book of Genesis, and that the mysteries of their trade were as old as the Pyramids. Their handbooks were full of mythical history. They believed, for instance, that Charles Martel was a mason before he became king of France, that Euclid was taught by Abraham, that St Alban was the first to

A manuscript illustration of fourteenth-century masons at work, showing trowel, set square, hammer and level.

direct English masons – just as the English tinsmiths traced their origins back to Joseph of Arimathea – and that King Athelstan had founded the first lodge of their craft, awarding them ancient privileges in the process.

Medieval accounts distinguish between rough-masons or hard-hewers, and the freemasons who worked in freestone. Among the freemasons, the banker-masons, who worked in the lodges and formed the élite, had their distinguishing marks. The banker-mark was the mason's way of signing his work before the stone left the work-bench for laying. It is usually a capital letter, and may have stood for the mason's Christian name. Originally the system was imposed from above, probably during a mason's probationary period when he could not be relied upon to do absolutely satisfactory work. A graded mason was allowed to leave his work unsigned, which would explain why so many stones have no marks at all, but the idea of the personal mark seems to have changed its significance. A late-Medieval German masonic statute (1563) says: 'No man shall

180

Eric Kay, foreman mason on the restoration of Lincoln Cathedral, carving a patera (rosette ornament).

change, of his own free will and power, the banker-mark which hath been conveyed and granted to him by his guild. But if he purpose to change it, let him do so with the favour, knowledge and consent of the whole guild.' A good place to observe banker-marks is the Norman columns in the nave at Ely, but they are found in virtually all English medieval cathedrals. Some marks, however, are clearly position-marks (which are also found in carpentry).

At Peterborough, built in the Norman phase, as many as one hundred different contemporary banker-marks have been found, indicating that at least that number of masons were working on the site at the same time. No other occupation brought so many skilled workers together in the same place except cloth-working, which also developed a guild-system at an early date. There is no documentation about the early English lodges, perhaps because English masons were exceptionally secretive, but German records are abundant. However, there is a late fourteenth-century English *Articles and Points of Masonry*, which refers to 'Congregations', and statutes of 1360 and 1425 refer to general chapters of masons. The state kept a close interest in what the masons were doing, how they were organized and disciplined and what they were paid. They had their own courts on the sites of big operations. During the building of Caernarvon Castle, the master-mason, Walter of Hereford, petitioned in 1305 to have his 'free court of his workers at the said castle', as in the past; Edward I granted this and gave him 'the amends of transgressions of conventions and contracts made between the same workers.' The state, however, was ambivalent about the masons' organization. When Parliament, from the mid-fourteenth century onwards, tried to fix maximum rates for wages, it ran up against most opposition in the building trade. Indeed, a statute of Henry VI (1424) stated that 'masons shall not confederate themselves in chapters and assemblies' since the 'Statute of Labourers be openly violated and broken'.

Although a man like William of Wykeham might employ large bodies of masons both on work for the crown and on his own account, the cathedral programme was often in conflict with the king's castle (and palace) programme, especially in the period after the Black Death, when skilled labour was scarce. Impressment was constantly used by the crown in the fourteenth and fifteenth centuries, sometimes on projects which were not, strictly speaking, anything to do with national defence. The king's master-mason was often given authority to impress masons. Letters patent sometimes make exception for masons 'in the fee of the church', but exemption was not automatic. For the year 1479, the York Cathedral fabric roll itemizes 'the expense of a servant of Master Henry Gillow, riding to commune with Master Gervase Clifton for the excusing of masons working at St Peter's Minster, and requisitioned and taken by the officers of my Lord King for his works at Nottingham [castle].'

Crown documents in the reign of Edward III complain loudly and often – sometimes making the point that the King was personally furious – that his workmen, engaged on important state programmes, were being seduced by offers of higher (and illegal) wages by other lords, the clergy being singled out for special blame. There were times when the King's needs might virtually halt cathedral work, Edward I's vast castle-building programme in Wales in the years 1290–1305 being a case in point. At one stage during the building of Beaumaris Castle, there were on this site alone 400 masons, 30 smiths and carpenters and over 1,200 other workers, most of them impressed.

Cathedral chapters seem to have paid more than the crown, but they did not necessarily get better work. In 1344 a crisis report to the Chapter of York revealed an appalling state of negligence, idleness and indiscipline, involving the master-mason and the master-carpenter, as well as their workmen. The labourers had been going on strike, timber, stone, lime and mortar had been stolen, and incompetence and carelessness had led to damage which had had to be repaired at great expense. The fabric roll laid down new regulations for the workmen: 'All their time and hours shall be revealed by a bell, ordained therefor'; men should be at work 'as early as they may see skilfully by daylight and they shall stand there truly working all day, as long as they may see skilfully for the work.' There was a dinner-break of an hour at noon and they would have to keep rigidly to the set times of work. An offender was to be 'chastised by abaiting of his payment'.

One of the functions of the master-mason was to manage the men and get the best out of them. He no longer worked in the lodge but in the tracing-house. He

A contemporary depiction of the building of Vezelay Cathedral in France, showing the use of thatch to protect unfinished walling.

was contractor, surveyor and in practice the architect. An English-Latin phrase-book, written by the Bursar of Eton College and published in 1519, says of the master-mason: 'He is nat worthy to be called maister of the crafte, that is nat cunnyng in drawynge and purturynge' ('purturynge' meant making a three-dimensional model). The master's symbol was his square, which he holds in the famous Matthew Paris drawing. Another one is to be found on the incised tomb-slab, in Rheims Cathedral, of the master-mason Hugh Libergier. This square seems to have been a dual-purpose one: it had the 'general triangle' of 90, 60 and 30 degrees, and the 'Canonic Triangle' of 90, 58°17′ and 31°43′. The master used his square to set out work, ensure uniformity and to instruct subordinates. The square took the place of a scale, all relationships being in predetermined proportions. So once the bay width was determined, the square was used for the rest, thus obviating the need for detailed scale-drawings.

The Middle Ages saw a progressive rise in the status of senior craftsmen, especially masons. In the eleventh and twelfth centuries it is still possible to find cases of skilled masons and metal-workers who were serfs, and church moralists, who claimed that mechanics were descended from Cain – reputed to have built the first city – tried hard to keep skilled workmen in their place. Bishop Rodrigo of Zamora wrote: 'Oh, how many false masonries and stones there are, how many false devices are made by those who work in carving and wood-painting!' The mystic Hugh of St Victor, writing in about 1120, contrasted the mechanical and liberal arts:

The arts called mechanical are adulterine, because they deal with the work of an artificer, which borrows its art from nature. But the other seven arts are called liberal, because they demand liberty of mind (that is freedom for activity, seeing that they dispute subtly concerning the causes of things) or because of old it was only freemen (that is, nobles) who were wont to study therein, while plebeians and the sons of ignoble folk practise the mechanical arts.

Some moralists – St Bernadino of Sienna and Savonarola, for instance – continued to preach against the arts until the end of the fifteenth century.

Long before then, however, the craftsmen had emerged from anonymity. Thanks largely to the work of John Harvey, master-masons have been identified in about 300 cases. We know, for instance, that the early Norman work at Canterbury – nearly a century before William of Sens and William the Englishman – was by Elitherius, described as *praestantissimus artificium magister*, that St Albans was built by Robert the Mason and Durham by Richard of Wolverston. Some names are missing from the thirteenth century, but thereafter important work can usually be ascribed. Master-masons wrote and received letters, owned houses and manors and, quite often, quarries (just as master-carpenters owned lifting-machinery and scaffolding), and left wills bequeathing substantial assets. They had fine tombs: Richard of Gainsborough at Lincoln, for instance, and Thomas Wolvey at St Albans. From the thirteenth century the emergence of the architect is testified by contracts which specify the exclusive use of a master's services. They were received and treated as gentlemen. In 1393, Henry Yevele dined with William of Wykeham, Bishop of Winchester, at his Southwark palace on ninety occasions (as well he might: Wykeham himself had started out as manager of the King's dogs at Windsor). A famous entry in the hall-book at New College, for 25 March 1389, shows that the two greatest masons of their day, Henry Yevele and William Wynford, dined with Hugh Herland, the leading master-carpenter. At court, the master-mason was ranked with the esquires or the gentlemen, and he usually had a coat of arms (that of William Ramsay, chief mason to Edward III, was a compass between two rams' heads).

Where a master worked for the King, it is often possible to discover his wages from the surviving accounts. In Henry II's time, a skilled man like his engineer, Ailnoth, got three times the wage of an ordinary trained workman; James of St George, the favourite military architect of Edward I, was paid at ten times the rate. He was exceptionally well paid (the King had brought him to England from Savoy), as was Hugh Herland in the next century. The king gave such men clothing allowances, assigned them the profits from royal fisheries or mills, or gave them favourable leases of royal manors, the surest mark of high distinction. Cathedral payments varied in type. William Joy, the master-mason at Wells, got a retainer plus a weekly wage; John Lewyn, master-mason at Durham, got a fee plus clothing; Walter of Hereford got food and clothing, candles and firewood and an allowance for two servants and two horses; William Hurley, who came to Ely from London to help with the Lantern, got a straight fee. Many of these masters travelled extensively in England and in Europe, and held official positions or consultancies at up to half-a-dozen cathedrals, palaces and castles. The top architects were almost invariably professional pluralists or quangomongers.

Quite a lot is known about the careers of these men, especially Henry Yevele, whom John Harvey calls the greatest of English medieval architects. In 1353 he was made a Freeman of the City of London. In 1358 he was paid £221 for work done for the Black Prince over a period of eighteen months. In 1360 he became the King's Master-mason, and was described as 'devizer of masonry of the works'. At one time or another he was Master-mason at Westminster Abbey and Warden of London Bridge, and fulfilled contracts for Old St Paul's, the London Charterhouse and the Duchy of Lancaster, ending his life working at Canterbury and St Albans. Work which has been attributed to Yevele includes the naves of Westminster Abbey and Canterbury, Westminster Hall, the cloisters of the

Looking up through the timberwork of the spire of Salisbury Cathedral.

London Charterhouse, parts of the Tower of London, Cowling Castle, Queenborough, the tombs of Edward III, Cardinal Langham and Richard II, and various other works. However, it must be added that scholars are not all agreed on these attributions. The Canterbury nave, for instance, may have been designed by Thomas Hoo; the mason in charge at Queenborough was John Box; and Yevele may not even have been responsible for the nave at Westminster. One scholar who has recently examined Yevele's career, A. David McLees, argues that he rose to eminence through quarry-work and may have been primarily an administrator rather than a designer.

What applies to Yevele would apply to other men named in the accounts as responsible for work undertaken and completed. The documents we have are often maddeningly vague about who precisely did what. We know for instance that Canon Elias of Dereham, who was skilled in carving and metal-work, acted as an artistic adviser at Salisbury and Wells, when both these cathedrals had their own master-masons (Nicholas of Ely and Adam Lock). What, then, did Elias do? When Canon Edward of St Andrews was employed by Edward III to direct the carpenters working on the stalls of St Stephen's Chapel, Westminster, what precisely were his duties? The great medieval cathedrals were designed and built by professional experts: that much is quite clear, and the old illusion, beloved of nineteenth-century Catholic historians, that abbey churches were built by monks and cathedrals by the common folk, has long since been laid to rest. But what are we to make of this passage in the Gloucester records: 'In 1242 was completed the new vault over the nave of the church, not by the extraneous aid of professional workmen, as before, but by the vigorous hands of the monks who reside on the spot.' Vault-erection was very skilled and dangerous work. Again, when Geoffrey de Noiers' new choir was going up at Lincoln around 1191–1200, we are told that the Bishop, the famous St Hugh, 'oftentimes bore the hod-load of hewn stone or of building lime'. Was this to set a good example to the men? Skilled medieval workmen were no more willing than trade unionists today to permit unqualified men to do their jobs. Non-members of guilds could only get work outside town limits (for instance, in the 'liberties' of Southwark), or royal or cathedral 'peculiars' or other exempt jurisdictions. Even the intrusion of a fully-qualified outsider was sometimes resented. When Henry IV lent his master-mason to York in 1410, local men 'conspired together to kill him and his assistant' – and the poor assistant was actually murdered.

How was the money raised to pay for the cathedrals? Most of the work had to be paid for promptly, and in cash. One source, of course, was the chapter's own estates. Wealthy political bishops like Stapledon of Exeter or Wykeham of Winchester held benefices in plurality and forked out large sums themselves. Indulgences were sold. The 1349–50 fabric roll of Exeter records a payment of eight shillings for a scribe to write out 800 indulgences for sale on behalf of the building fund. York apparently employed professional fund-raisers, who took a percentage of the proceeds, and *quaestores*, who preached begging-missions. A very common device was to form guilds of benefactors, who guaranteed to raise fixed sums. Other methods which we know to have been used are as follows: the assignment, on a temporary basis, of a cathedral prebend to a master-mason, in lieu of salary, or its assignment to the building-fund; assignment of bequests to the building-fund, so that it had its own permanent income; assignment to the building-fund of donations to altars of absentee vicars or altar-priests; fees for burials within the cathedral, or for ringing the great bell at funerals; alms-boxes within the cathedral; donations of armour; thank-gifts of people who had recovered from serious illnesses (rich folk often contributed their weight in grain); fines on absentee clergy and 'conscience money' (for example, the value of dishonestly obtained possessions); special collections on Sunday; selling works of art; grand processions of cathedral relics, with indulgences in return for contributions; and the employment of famous preachers, celebrated for their ability to gouge money out of the most stony-faced congregations. Probably the biggest single source, however, was from the 'gate-money' charged for admission to the chancel or other 'clerical' part of the cathedral (the nave, and sometimes the transepts, were free to the public), to visit the shrines and relics they contained.

Nevertheless, without determined royal patronage, or a vigorous bishop to urge things on and see they were paid for, cathedral-building tended to languish for lack of cash. The rapid completion of Salisbury was quite exceptional. At Lichfield, major building operations stretched from 1195 to 1350; at York, they began in 1220 and continued, with intervals, for over 250 years. The great medieval cathedral was not unlike a modern airport – always being updated, never quite finished.

7
The Cathedral Clergy

cathedral was a church where the bishop had his throne, and the only place from which all of the church's sacraments could be administered. It was also a place where the church's daily, weekly and annual cycle of praise and supplication to God, the liturgy, was performed in all its plenitude and pomp. Of course it was more than that in the Middle Ages: it was a major centre of ecclesiastical power and administration, especially in Britain, where dioceses were few and large (17 in England, against more than 250 in Italy).

Britain was anomalous in this respect, but also in others. What exactly was its ecclesiastical structure? St Augustine had come to England with the mandate to set up an ecclesiastical hierarchy on the old Roman model, with two provinces ruled from London and York, each with its dependent dioceses. But Augustine had settled at Canterbury, with London as a mere bishopric. The Archbishopric at York had been founded separately; in early Saxon times, thanks to the vigour of St Wilfred, it had been a more weighty centre of Christianity and culture than Canterbury; under Alcuin, the school at York was the most brilliant in north-west Europe, and Alcuin had been summoned by Charlemagne to become master of his own palace school. Later, in the Viking times, the diocese had fallen on evil days and had been effectively run from Worcester. When the Normans came and the Conqueror appointed Lanfranc to Canterbury with orders to reorganize the English church, the new Archbishop tried to rationalize the structure by imposing his authority over the Archbishop of York. With the Conqueror behind him, he succeeded.

After the deaths of William I and Lanfranc, however, the Archbishops of York fought back, on the whole successfully. They had history on their side, and did not need to forge documents. The Canterbury monks did so, none too skilfully. The matter was fought out, sometimes with fists, at synods and ceremonies where both archbishops were present, and in 1123 the issue was taken to the papal curia in Rome. There, the Canterbury forgeries became apparent. According to the chronicle of Hugh of York (not, to be sure, a particularly objective witness) the Canterbury privileges, purporting to come from Rome, had 'no trace of the style of the Roman chancery, no seals or signatures'; the Canterbury delegation claimed that the bulls had been lost or had perished. When the cardinals heard this 'some smiled, others wrinkled their noses and yet others laughed aloud, making fun of them and saying that it was a miracle that lead should perish or be lost, and parchment survive.'

This undignified episode did not end the matter. The Archbishop of York took the side of Henry II against Thomas Becket, and was even accused of helping to organize the latter's murder. In 1176 at a synod in Westminster, presided over by the papal legate, the Archbishop of Canterbury insisted on taking his seat on the legate's right hand, as the place of primacy; whereupon York sat heavily on Canterbury's lap, 'irreverently pressing his haunches down upon the archbishop' says the Chronicler Stephen of Birchington (a pro-Canterbury source this time). The dispute dragged on, York claiming Scotland, Durham, Lincoln, Worcester, Chester, Coventry and Lichfield, and Wales. In the end, Canterbury made good its claim over Wales and most of the other sees. York lost Scotland, but got Cumbria instead. Canterbury established its right to crown the sovereign, but York retained its own primacy and none of its archbishops has made a profession of obedience to Canterbury since Lanfranc's day.

York had, however, its own problems of authority, especially over Durham, a

OVERLEAF A detail from the Bayeux Tapestry showing Stigand, archbishop of Canterbury until 1070 when he was deposed by William the Conqueror.

rich and fiercely independent see, whose bishop was a count-palatine and virtually the king's viceroy in the area. In February 1349, we are told, immediately after the singing of vespers in York Minster, supporters of the bishop of Durham entered the church and staged a demonstration against the authority of York 'by shouting insults, breaking wind and performing other enormities'.

Although Lanfranc did not settle the primacy problem, his other ecclesiastical reforms and changes were highly successful. When they were complete, the English cathedrals were divided into two groups. Eight were monastic: Canterbury, Winchester, Durham, Rochester, Norwich, Worcester, Ely and Wells (plus Bath); nine were served by secular canons: York, London, Lichfield, Hereford, Exeter, Lincoln, Chichester and Salisbury.

The idea of a monastic-cathedral was an English one, antedating the Conquest, and was at first accepted reluctantly by Lanfranc, mainly because he thought it would be easier to enforce celibacy among a monastic chapter, one of the prime objects of his reorganization. It was an awkward arrangement, mainly because the bishop, though theoretically the abbot, had in practice to delegate most of his abbatial authority to the prior, who was the effective head of the community and the establishment. Bishop and prior drifted apart, and the cleavage was reflected in their architectural dispositions. Thus at Ely, for instance, the Bishop's Palace is quite separate from the conventual buildings, and he had a different entrance to the church. The prior lived like a rival potentate, having his own hall, state guest-suite, chapel and kitchens; indeed, the prior's compound at Ely represents one of the most important surviving examples of a fourteenth-century great house.

These monastic chapters were great landowners, and in the earlier part of the Middle Ages – up to the middle of the fourteenth century in some cases – they farmed most of their own estates, 'high farming' as it was known. At Canterbury, the cathedral-monastery of Christ Church had developed, by the 1170s, a central treasury and annual auditing system which was a miniature version of the king's exchequer, run by three monks who were professional managers and accountants. To judge by their accounts, which survive, the monks were no less businesslike than secular proprietors. The system reached its peak under Henry Eastry, prior from 1285 to 1331, who went in for large-scale production for the market, especially of cheese, corn and wool (the monastery had over 20,000 sheep). He increased the cathedral income by twenty-five per cent, and paid for the stone screen around the cathedral choir. Another highly successful monastery was Westminster, which was still engaged in high farming at the end of the fourteenth century. It grew steadily in wealth throughout the Middle Ages (partly because of fresh royal grants) and in 1535, on the eve of its dissolution, was the second richest monastery, after Glastonbury. Durham also went in for large-scale farming, and about the year 1300 had an income of £4,500, at a time when the central expenses of the king's government and household came to about £10,000.

These huge incomes were spent partly on the cathedrals, to be sure; but partly also on the enormous establishments which the monks built up around them, usually to the south. No set of conventional buildings has survived in its entirety, but we can conjecture their ground-plans. At St Albans, for instance, where only the gatehouse is left, the monastic buildings occupied all the open ground to the south, four or five times the area of the cathedral; it was the same at Ely. The monks had the status of gentlemen, and were treated as such: at Norwich, for

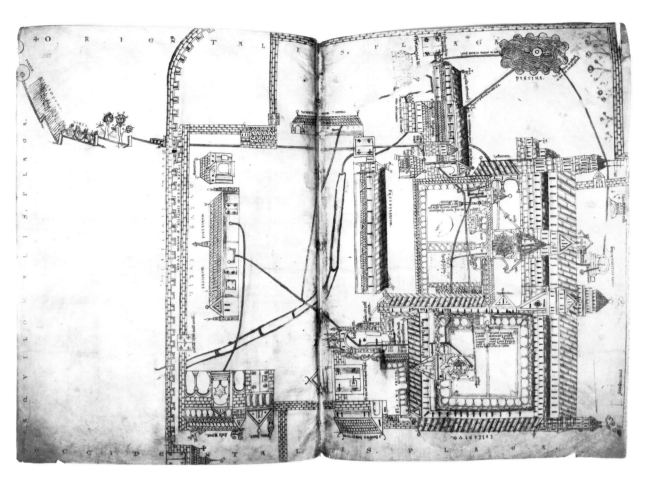

Diagram of the twelfth-century fresh water supply at Canterbury Cathedral and monastery.

instance, servants outnumbered monks by more than two to one. The buildings also housed corrodians, that is men who had bought an annuity from the monastery, which gave them free board and lodging for the rest of their lives.

The popular feeling towards monastic chapters, at any rate by the second half of the fourteenth century, was hostile. The townsfolk were denied access to the eastern arm of the cathedral, and had usually to be content with the nave, which was normally dirty, ill-decorated, unheated of course, and lacking any seating. Often it was a place where business was transacted. The monks were strict in keeping laymen, and still more women, out of their part of the cathedral. They were not liked as town landlords, especially as their presence in a town almost invariably restricted civic privileges, and they were most tenacious in exacting their own. In the course of the fourteenth century public opinion moved against them, sometimes violently, and monkish chapters built high walls and fortified gatehouses to deal with town mobs – there is a fine one at Ely, called the Porta, which was built in 1394, probably the nadir of monkish popularity.

It was Lanfranc's hope that the monastic cathedral chapters would be hives of learning and cultural activity. On the whole the hope was disappointed. Some had fine libraries: by 1500, for instance, Canterbury had a collection of 9,000 manuscripts, bound in 2,000 codices. Canterbury and Westminster also maintained distinguished series of historical chronicles, though neither was quite as elaborate or well-informed as the St Albans series. Henry III's favourite painter, William of Winchester, a monk from the Cathedral, did some fine work for the king at Westminster and Windsor. We hear of other artistic specialists

190

An artistic reconstruction of St Albans Abbey and monastic buildings in the late Middle Ages.

from monkish chapters. In the early fifteenth century, for instance, Thomas Semiston from Canterbury was acclaimed as the finest embroiderer in the country. But most of the men employed on decorating monastic cathedrals were laymen. The monks could not always provide even their own music. A contract survives from Durham showing the monks engaging a lay musician to play the organ, train the monks to sing plainsong, polyphony and counterpoint, and to compose every year a new mass.

In the later Middle Ages, the establishment of Oxford and Cambridge created invincible rivals to the old cathedral schools. Instead of trying to compete, the monks founded small halls or colleges in both universities, to train their abler novices. Thus the monks of Gloucester had their own hall, now Worcester College; and both Westminster and Durham founded colleges. It is hopeless to try to maintain that places like Rochester and Bath, or even Ely and Canterbury, made any significant contribution to art and education in the later Middle Ages. When Colet and Erasmus, those paladins of the English Renaissance, visited Canterbury together early in the sixteenth century, they were filled with contempt for the superstition and ignorance of the monks. It is true that the cathedral-priories ceased to be violently unpopular during the fifteenth century, as they ceased to be active landlords; but the public mood was no better than indifferent towards a class of men seen as *rentiers* or parasites; and it is significant of the state of morale in the monastic chapters that all submitted tamely to the Henrician dissolution.

The monastic chapters were, of course, governed by the Rule of St Benedict or

191

OPPOSITE The Bishop's Palace and moat at Wells.

the Rule of St Augustine. It was a different matter with the secular cathedrals. They were run by a body of canons under a dean, but there seems to have been great difficulty in defining exactly what a canon was, and how he ought to regulate his life. When the Conqueror arrived in England, at least one-third of the canons of St Paul's Cathedral were married, and it is likely that the canons of York also married and lived in the world. In about 1100, the Augustinian rule reached England, and thereafter there was a distinction between monks and canons, and between secular and regular canons. Both groups of regulars followed their international rule: the secular canons abided by the constitution and statutes of the cathedral where they served.

The model cathedral constitution was the work of St Osmond of Salisbury, one of the Conqueror's clerks. He served as Chancellor of England between 1074 and 1078, and for the next twenty years was Bishop of Salisbury. The statutes he drew up stipulated that the ruling body of the cathedral was to be a chapter (also called a brotherhood) of canons, controlled by four chief officers or principals. These were the Dean, who presided in the Chapter House, the Precentor, who was responsible for the choir and services, the Chancellor, who kept the minutes and correspondence of the chapter, the archives and library, and was the chief educational officer for the cathedral school and the training and examination of the clergy, and the Treasurer, who was in charge of the finances, vestments, relics and cathedral valuables.

The monks' lavatorium in the cloisters at Gloucester.

St Osmund also found time to establish a choir school for boys (which still exists) and to create a liturgical tradition which was much admired and still in use when the cathedral, under Bishop Richard Poore, was moved from Old Sarum to its present site. Henry III, who was a stickler for liturgical excellence and fine singing, and who took almost as much interest in Salisbury as in his own Westminster, encouraged other secular chapters to follow the Salisbury rite or the 'Use of Sarum' as it was known, and it was still regarded as standard when the first English Prayer Book was authorized by Parliament in the sixteenth century.

In St Osmund's day, the bishop was still effectively in charge of his cathedral, but bishops, and still more archbishops, were major pieces on the feudal chessboard and played an important part in the governance of the realm right until the days of Queen Elizabeth. The King's chief officers were usually bishops, who necessarily lived at court; even when they held no state office, they often lived in palaces or manor-houses far away from the cathedral. Most cathedrals had an episcopal residence nearby, the Palace at Wells being an outstanding example, but this was rarely the bishop's main residence. Thus the Bishop of Winchester spent much of his time at Farnham Castle in Surrey or in his Southwark Palace. The Bishop of London lived in Fulham Palace rather than the City. In the later Middle Ages these episcopal palaces grew more numerous and grander. In addition to Lambeth Palace, the Archbishops of Canterbury turned their manorhouse at Croydon into a sumptuous residence; in 1456 Archbishop Bourchier bought the manor of Knole and over the next ten years built a magnificent house there. Meanwhile, the Archbishops of York had built a number of palaces, notably at Southwell and at Sherburn-in-Elmet in the West Riding. They had a palace near Westminster called York House, later the nucleus of Whitehall; but in addition Archbishop Wolsey of York created Hampton Court Palace, which surpassed even Knole in size and splendour.

All this produced a certain remoteness on the part of the bishop. A bishop too closely connected with the cathedral tended to get involved in ecclesiastical quarrels. St William Fitzherbert had been Treasurer at York and was made archbishop in a disputed election in 1140. He did not get effective possession of his see until 1153, and the next year he died suddenly, just after saying mass; Archdeacon Osric was accused of slipping poison into his chalice. Osric was never convicted on this charge, but William was treated as a martyr, miracles were soon attributed to him and his grave became a shrine. In the early thirteenth century, the chapter pleaded his cause at Rome with great vigour, having noted the enormous prosperity which the Becket shrine had already brought to Canterbury, and obtained his canonization in 1227. So William joined St John of Beverley and St Wilfred of Ripon as a leading Yorkshire saint, and he is still commemorated by two fifteenth-century windows in the north choir aisle at York Minster, showing the translation of his body, and the halt and the blind at his shrine. In life he had been a source of discord, but in death he was pure gain for the chapter.

Indeed one is tempted to add that cathedral canons preferred their saintly bishops to be dead rather than alive. St Hugh of Lincoln, an active man with exacting standards, did not meet with the approbation of all the canons in his lifetime; but safely dead, buried, canonized and enshrined, he was one of the cathedral's principal assets. Again, Bishop Thomas Cantelupe of Hereford, who died in 1282, had his enemies in the close, but his tomb quickly became the object of pilgrimages and was probably the most valuable single relic in the west of

England until the cult of Edward II's body at Gloucester became fashionable in the 1330s. Cantelupe's shrine allowed the Hereford chapter to remodel the cathedral's aisles and helps to explain why it became such an important early centre of the Decorated style; but the canons of Hereford, who were poor, had no love for their bishops as such. They were in constant rebellion, and their tradition of recalcitrance was still being honoured in the nineteenth century.

One bone of contention between bishop and chapter was his right of visitation, to inquire into the functioning of the cathedral and the morals of the chapter – no mere formality when the bishop was as strict and energetic as the famous Robert Grosseteste of Lincoln. The bishops won their case on this issue, though they did not always exercise the right so established. From the early thirteenth century bishops were appointed by the king in consultation with the pope, a system of sharing the spoils, which meant in practice that the rich bishoprics went either to favourite royal clerks, who had little time to attend to diocesan matters, or to the pope's Italian favourites, who never as a rule set foot in the country. It is well known that Cardinal Wolsey, Archbishop of York, who was also Bishop of Winchester, never entered his archdiocese until his fall from power. His predecessor, Archbishop Bainbridge, never resided in York either. The record was even worse in poor sees, especially in Wales. As late as the eighteenth century, Bishop Hoadley, successively bishop of Bangor, Hereford, Salisbury and Winchester, neglected all four in favour of London residence, and never visited Bangor at all.

In these circumstances the dean and chapter gradually took from the bishop not only day-to-day control of cathedral life but the whole decision-making process. They took full advantage of the rapid development of canon law and the church's legal structure of appeals to Rome, which enabled king, pope, archbishops, bishops and chapters to sue each other endlessly over jurisdictional rights. If the chapter lost on visitations, they won on most other matters. In the early Middle Ages it is always the bishop who is credited with new building schemes for the cathedral. From the thirteenth century onwards, the dean and chapter took over the supervision of the cathedral fabric and the bishop's role was largely confined to raising money.

Hence it was the Dean who became the principal figure in the close. 'Not only in appearance but constitutionally, the medieval cathedral was a great ship with many decks or departments,' wrote Professor E.F. Jacob; and there was little doubt that the dean was the captain, the bishop being an admiral who was rarely on board. The statutes of York cathedral laid down: 'They say that in the church he is superior to everyone except the archbishop; and in the chapter he is superior to all.' In 1291, the Dean of York was worth £373.6.8d a year, which made it by far the richest benefice in England and Wales below episcopal rank. The dean had the right to install the new archbishop on his throne, and in York he lived a prelatical existence, his deanery being a fortified palace with its own gateway, enclosing gardens and an orchard. When visiting the estates of the chapter he was entitled to an escort of nineteen horses. Just before the Reformation, Brian Higden, dean from 1516–39, when going in state to the Minster on Christmas Day, was attended by '50 gentlemen before him in tawney coats garded with black velvet and 30 yemen behind him in coates garded with taffeta'.

At York the next richest official was the Treasurer, who received £233.6.8d a year in 1291. As it was a good benefice, it was often given to royal or papal favourites, who were absentees. The work would be done by the sub-treasurer

The Chancellor's Window at York, showing Chancellor Ripplingham instructing scholars.

and his five subordinates – two vestry clerks, who were in charge of the vestments, and three sacrists, who provided candles and oil-lamps, rang the bells and opened and locked the doors. The chancellor was the intellectual of the chapter, and usually a legal expert: the York Statutes said he must hold a Mastership of Arts, and in practice he was usually a Doctor. The Medieval church, amazingly enough, had no seminaries for training priests, and in default of them the chancellor gave lectures. In the so-called Chancellor's Window, in the nave at York (*c*.1330), Chancellor Ripplingham is shown instructing scholars, wearing his blue doctor's robe. The precentor was next in honour and dignity to the dean, at any rate in theory, for St Osmund laid down that he was to have direct charge of all the services, but he commonly delegated his duties to a succentor and the office was often held by a non-resident pluralist. Hence when Henry VIII created the secular cathedrals of the 'New Foundation', the statutes reduced the office to the status of a minor canon or chaplain.

Just as the number of monks in a regular chapter might vary from 50 to 100 (sometimes even more), so the canons of a secular chapter ranged from 24 (Exeter) and 28 (Hereford) to as high as 52 (Salisbury), 55 (Wells) and even 58 (Lincoln). The canons lived off prebends (from the Latin *praebenda*, provender), and their number depended partly on the wealth of the diocese. Lincoln, Wells, Salisbury and York (which had 36 canons or prebendaries) were rich, Hereford poorish and Exeter definitely poor.

However, a poor cathedral might in practice be better served, for its prebends were less likely to be sought by royal or papal benefice-hunters, who were almost invariably absentees. York was famous or notorious throughout Christendom, as having the biggest and most succulent plums. As Matthew Paris put it, the canons of York were 'gorged with rents and treasures'. The taxation returns of 1291 show that out of 36 prebends, no less than 24 were taxed as worth more than £20 a year, and the average worth was £48. The archdeaconry of Richmond stood at £200 a year, and no less than five canonries were worth more than £100, headed by Masham (£166.13.4d) and Wetwang (£120). These were baronial incomes, and their holders, if they chose to come to Yorkshire at all, were able to maintain one or more manor-houses on their prebendal estates. The medieval records of York cathedral are among the most extensive and best-preserved, which is the reason we know so much about what went on in the chapter. They show that in the later Middle Ages, the total income of the cathedral was well over £2,000, but between one-half and two-thirds went to absentees, many of whom were not even Englishmen.

The corrective to the system was the existence of the Common Fund, which had its own income from lands and was increased by the revenue of the church from collections, marriages, funerals and other services. The fund was shared only by the 'Canons in Residence', and to qualify for residential status and fees each canon had to do a preliminary or 'major residence' of six months, and thereafter attend for twenty-four weeks in the year. A recent study by Barrie Dobson, based on the York archives, shows that the claims of the canons-residentiary were closely investigated by the President of the Chapter, who was himself a resident canon and therefore had a presumed vested interest in keeping the numbers down and individual shares high. The President had secret interviews with the porters, sacristans and the vicars-choral to discover whether the canons making their 'major' residence had slept in their prebendal houses on the close every single night for the whole six months. The residential system was developed in the later Middle Ages as an answer to the problem of royal and papal provisions and the absenteeism it created, and it seems on the whole to have worked.

One unfortunate by-product of the residential system, however, was the hospitality rules, which varied from cathedral to cathedral but in general laid down that residential canons must do their share of entertaining, not only of visiting dignitaries but of the multitude of small fry who swam in the cathedral pond and were entitled to time-honoured 'treats'. Some Continental chapters, especially in Germany, had birth qualifications – a would-be canon had to 'prove his quarterings'. There was none of that in England, but both Chichester and Lichfield stipulated, in their statutes, that canons must be men of substance. A Lichfield statute of about 1300 lays down that a residential canon must be in a position to spend £40 beyond his fees 'of his own money, or of his patrimony of the Church of Lichfield or outside it, lest, like a drone among bees, or like a thief entering upon the labour of others, he should seem to eat the honey from which those labouring day and night in the vineyard of the Lord ought to be sustained, and should so destroy the apiary.'

Hospitality rules probably account for the small number of residential canons at York, despite the amplitude of the common fund. It was rare to have as many as six canons qualifying. Thus, a list of those present at an important ceremony at the cathedral in 1424 gives a total of eighty-two cathedral officers and functionaries. Of these only seven were canons. The rest was made up of sixteen parsons or chantry chaplains, thirty-six vicars, six deacons, five thurifers, seven choristers, two vestry-clerks and three sacrists.

Such minor cathedral office-holders constituted an important element in the

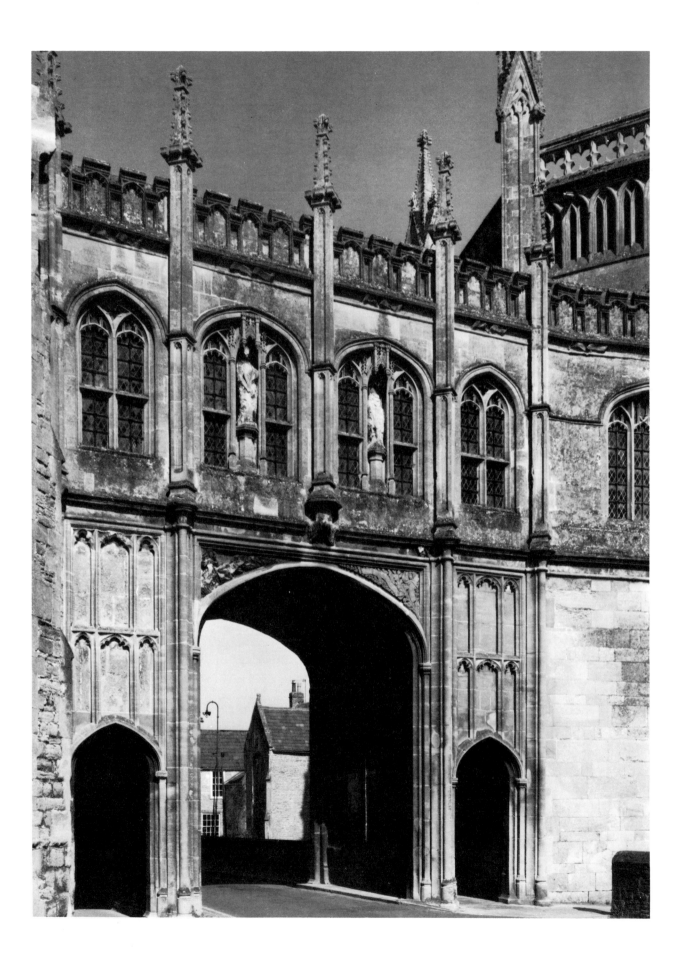

society of cathedral towns throughout the Middle Ages, and their existence is or was reflected in the geography of the close. The secular cathedrals, indeed, had almost as many attendant residential buildings as the monastic ones. Very few survive in anything approaching their original form. At Wells, however, the double staircase to the Chapter House leads, in one direction, to a bridge, which takes you over the Chain Gate and into a hall built about 1348, with a pointed barrel-roof, a big Perpendicular fireplace and windows from a variety of periods up to the early sixteenth century. This was where the vicars and other minor clerics dined. Nearby is the Vicars' Close, where they had their houses. In its own way it is a unique survival of medieval England, for it dates from 1348, when the vicars were organized on a collegiate basis and provided with accommodation; and it gives us some indication what a mid-fourteenth century street looked like, 456 feet long, with almost identical houses on either side. Naturally the houses have been modernized, but externally and collectively they still contrive to give a medieval impression. The group is completed by a library and chapel and epitomizes the old-style college plan which prevailed before William of Wykeham created the quandrangle pattern at New College and Winchester.

In the later Middle Ages, all secular cathedrals in England had similar groups of buildings, often surrounded by a close or wall. Thus in 1327, the canons of Salisbury were licensed by the crown to build a close round the cathedral and clergy houses, and much of this fourteenth-century wall, built from the stones of Old Sarum, can still be seen. The old prebendal houses and the collegiate

199

St William's College, York, where the chantry priests once lived.

buildings, however, have been replaced by the splendid late seventeenth- and eighteenth-century houses which inspired Trollope. At York, College Street is there to remind us of the minor clerical figures who once lived there. In what is now called St William's College, originally a house of one of the canons, the chantry priests lived a collegiate existence under the authority of a provost; there were still twenty-eight of them at the time of the Dissolution. There was also what was called the Bedern, for the vicars-choral, with its dormitory, chapel, hall and (like Wells) a private bridge to the Minster.

These vicars, who sang in the choir in place of the canons who were unable or unwilling to attend the services themselves, were by no means men of lowly or servile degree. They often came from well-known local families and behaved as if they owned the place, which in a sense they did since so many canons were non-resident. The court records of the fourteenth and fifteenth centuries cast a lurid light on their activities. They were accused not only of keeping women, but of harbouring them in the Bedern itself, where some of them gave birth to children.

Among other crimes and misdemeanours, the wearing of laymen's clothes and carrying of swords and knives are frequently cited against them. But like the canons themselves, they took full advantage of the church's legal system to appeal against the discipline of the chapter, to the archbishop and, if that failed, to the king and even the pope. The cathedral close was alive with the corporate spirit which gives such an edge to medieval litigation and was such an important safeguard against the tyranny of powerful individuals.

Cathedrals, indeed, were right at the centre of public life throughout the Middle Ages. It was not merely that bishops were great feudal landlords, and often the principal ministers of state; or that chapters were crowded with former royal clerks who knew how the machinery of government worked. When the king moved, as he did most of the time, his government moved with him, and the cathedral close, whether secular or monastic, was often the only suitable place to accommodate the whole court and, in the later Middle Ages, Parliament too. The spacious and noble chapter houses which became such a distinctive feature of

Mompesson House in Salisbury Close.

cathedral architecture from the thirteenth century onwards formed a natural setting for meetings of the king's council and the representative assemblies it spawned. Parliaments often met in the chapter houses of Gloucester, Winchester and Salisbury. During the 1330s, when the young Edward III was dealing with the Scottish problem, before turning his attention to France, he virtually transformed York into the seat of government and its close into a Whitehall; the Chapter House was turned into the chancery.

We get a last glimpse of the English medieval close, and its role in the state, in May 1520, when the Emperor Charles V paid his first visit to England, to his friend and ally, Henry VIII. The three-day state visit took place at Canterbury, where the Emperor was magnificently received by his aunt, Queen Catherine of Aragon, standing at the top of the marble staircase in the Archbishop's Palace. The two potentates spent the next three days in the close, giving banquets for each other and dancing every night, under the benevolent eye of old William Wareham, last of the old-style archbishops. A mere eighteen years later, Henry was dispatching his officers to Canterbury to break up the shrine of St Thomas and confiscate its treasures; and it is to the treasures of the cathedrals that we now turn.

8
Treasures of the Cathedrals

he treasures of Britain's cathedrals, despite the destruction by time, intolerance and ignorance, are still extensive. The hand of the destroyer fell most heavily on ancient stained-glass, as one would expect; though the smashing or removal of coloured glass was not necessarily the work of the Reformers in the mid-sixteenth century, or the Puritans during the Interregnum. Much twelfth- and thirteenth-century glass was removed in the fifteenth and early sixteenth centuries, when Norman or Early English windows were replaced by Perpendicular ones, filled with plain glass. The search for light continued long after the flames of iconoclasm had died down in the early eighteenth century, and not only in Protestant England: at Notre Dame de Paris, all the twelfth-, thirteenth- and fourteenth-century windows were replaced with white glass, as were the lower windows at Rheims.

Of the English cathedrals, the two great depositories of medieval stained glass, some of it in its original position, are Canterbury and York. Both were leading glazing-centres, as were Norwich, Oxford, Exeter, London and Coventry. At Canterbury, the surviving glass is concentrated in the east end. In the Corona are scenes from the Old Testament, some modern, the rest medieval and a few – the figures of Josiah and the Virgin in the north window – from the twelfth century. In the aisles or ambulatory of the Trinity Chapel, eight of the twelve windows still have their medieval glass, and this is a particularly important and interesting series, for it is entirely devoted to the miracles worked by St Thomas Becket – one man cured of nightmares, another of swollen feet, a lady delivered from epilepsy and another from the quartan ague, a madman restored to sanity – and pictures of the shrine itself. The colours still blaze intensely, in deep crimson, royal blue, amber and a brightish olive, the brushwork is delicate, and for once the windows are at eye-level and can be scrutinized closely.

In the north choir aisle there are further Biblical scenes, dating from about 1200: the story of the Magi, Solomon and the Queen of Sheba, Pharaoh and Moses, Joseph and his Brethren, the destruction of Sodom, the Presentation in the Temple and the Parable of the Sower and so on. These elements are the survivors of a complete Biblical set of twelve windows, which have been gathered together into two (the cathedral library possesses a fourteenth-century document which is a key to the complete series). Opposite, in the south choir aisle there are thirteenth-century scenes from the life of Christ and the Virgin which come from France and were inserted, with modern borders, quite recently. In the north-west transept there is a fine, large window donated by Edward IV in 1482, probably by William Nave, his master-glazier, beautifully painted but difficult to see well from the pavement. Opposite, however, in the south-west transept there are three rows of Romanesque glass panels, originally in the choir and Trinity Chapel, now easy to see, alongside much fifteenth-century glass. An outstanding feature of the early glass at Canterbury are the fine armatures of wrought iron, which keep the major sections in place and form an essential part of the decorative scheme, especially in the Trinity Chapel.

York was probably the first English cathedral to have glass of any kind; Edius Stephanus, Wilfrid's biographer, tells us that in about 670 he 'prevented the entry of birds and rain through the windows by means of glass, through which, however, the light shone within.' This, of course, was in the Old Minster, whose exact whereabouts have yet to be discovered. No Saxon glass survives, but York has a large quantity of twelfth-century Romanesque glass – the substance of

OVERLEAF One of the Becket miracle windows at Canterbury: Adam the Forester makes a miraculous recovery after being shot by an arrow through the neck, thanks to the intervention of Becket.

ABOVE LEFT The Sower, a window in the north choir aisle at Canterbury.

ABOVE Figures from the Jesse tree in the Corona at Canterbury.

twenty-seven figure scenes, fifteen fragments of scenes and bits of fifteen border-designs – which was re-set by fourteenth-century glaziers in the nave clerestory windows. What strikes one about Romanesque glass is its reliance for effect on dark and glowing colours, the strength and clarity of the composition, and the tenderness of some of the painted faces.

The earliest York glass which is still in place is in the transepts, especially the five grisaille lancets known as the Five Sisters (1230–50). This reflects a deliberate move towards lightness, under the influence of the Cistercians, who were very powerful in Yorkshire. Hence, in the thirteenth-century church, there must have been a striking and deliberate contrast between the dark, glowing choir, lit in Romanesque fashion with the stress on mystery and luminosity, and the brilliance of the transepts, where the sunlight streaming through the grisaille was designed to light up the carved ornamentation and reflect in the Purbeck columns. Such lighting systems have, of course, been utterly destroyed by progressive changes over the centuries; indeed, the Five Sisters windows themselves have had innumerable fragments replaced, much of it with inferior glazing and with a vast amount of consequential leading. As a result the original foliage pattern, which was astonishingly elaborate to judge from reconstructions, has been lost in most places, and the amount of light severely diminished.

Yet there is a great deal left at York in more or less its original state, and from most periods from the thirteenth century onwards. There is a delightful angel figure (c. 1440), with feathers down to his ankles, in the south transept and nearby a superb head of John the Baptist from the same period. The thirteenth-century glass in the Chapter House, though much restored, gives us some idea of what a

ABOVE Noah's ark and the Dove of Peace at Canterbury.

ABOVE RIGHT York: stained glass showing the donor of the window presenting it to the Minster.

unified lighting scheme was like in the Middle Ages, and contains some wonderful heads of St Peter in prison, for instance, and of disciples at the funeral of the Virgin. The nave has many fourteenth century treasures, including the heraldic window in the north nave aisle (1310–20), showing the first hints of perspective in roofs, battlements and turrets, and a brilliantly sketched head of the donor, Peter de Dene; the colouring is heightened by the introduction, for the first time in England, of yellow stain to highlight the white glass – a technique developed by the Arabs and brought to England through Spain. In the north nave aisle there is the Pilgrimage Window, dotted with animal grotesques, including a monkey's funeral and a monkey doctor holding up a flask of urine.

The chief glories of the York glass, however, are the enormous windows at both ends of the Minster. The Great West Window, by Master Robert and his atelier (1338–9), is a masterpiece of curvilinear tracery and contains some outstanding monumental figures, including a John the Evangelist of almost Renaissance elegance, as well as elaborate ornamentation. Much use is made of white glass and yellow stain (Master Robert was paid 12d. a foot for coloured glass, only 6d. for white) to bring out the main points of the design, and the colour scheme was carefully thought out. The Great East Window (1405–8) by John Thornton and his atelier, is even bigger, containing over 1,680 square feet of glass, and some brilliantly designed and painted scenes – notably the famous episode from Revelation when the twenty-four elders, shown first seated on their thrones, cast down their crowns before the throne of God. Two tracery lights have Thornton's monogram, together with the date, 1408. He seems to have been responsible for much of the glazing at the east end, and his particular manner,

206

using white and yellow-stain glass for the figures, contrasted with rich blue and ruby backgrounds, is known as the 'York Style'.

The fourteenth- and fifteenth-century glass is undoubtedly the finest at York, but the Minster has an early Tudor rose-window (*c.* 1515), with the red and the white rose united, and some superb panels by William Peckitt (1731–95), using enamels and pot-metals, the finest of which is a figure of Abraham with his sacrificial knife, in the south transept.

No other cathedral can rival York in the quantity and variety of its glass, but the following should be noted. Exeter's great east window, rebuilt in 1390 from one dated 1303, retains six lights of the earlier window, plus some good late fourteenth-century glass; and in the Lady Chapel there is some excellent sixteenth century glass which is mainly Flemish. At Gloucester there is the great east window, finished in 1357, showing saints, apostles, kings and many of the nobles and knights who fought at the battle of Crécy. This window was taken down and re-leaded in 1862, but is very largely the original glass, plain (with bubbles, making a silvery white), pot-metal blue, and red and yellow-stain, with brown enamel line-shading. The medieval glass in the Lady Chapel east window is pretty to look at but hopelessly jumbled up.

Wells has some beautiful fourteenth-century stained-glass in the south chancel aisle, some Renaissance glass in the south transept and jumbles of medieval fragments elsewhere. There are also mixtures of fragments in various chapels at Winchester, and in the famous east window at Carlisle. At Lincoln, there is some thirteenth century glass, including excellent borders, in the retrochoir, where it can be studied closely, and a magnificent rose window in the north transept, plus some fine grisaille and important fourteenth-century fragments at ground level. The Bishop's Eye, which is opposite in the south transept, is a sensational mixture of pieces from the late twelfth to the fourteenth centuries, including some major bits which are worth a close study. Finally, at Norwich, there is the Erpingham Window, which has a fifteenth-century frame filled with a superbly-arranged collection of medieval fragments, some of it from abroad.

We must bear in mind, however, that the Middle Ages were not the only great epoch of coloured and stained-glass. The nineteenth-century produced more religious glass than ever before (or since). Much is mediocre; a surprising amount is of high quality, and it is at last beginning to be studied with knowledge and sympathy. The work of Burne-Jones, especially at Birmingham, Oxford and Norwich, is well known, as is other glass designed for the William Morris Company. But the work of other Victorian artists, such as Arthur O'Connor, Henry Holliday, Thomas Willement, John Hardman and Harrington Mann, and firms such as Clayton and Bell, Lavers & Barraud, Heaton, and Butler & Bayne, is beginning to be appreciated. At Ely, where only fragments of ancient glass are left, there is an enormous amount of nineteenth-century glass, by Pugin and Hardman (south aisles), Clayton & Bell (south chancel aisle and south transept), Wailes (octagon, north transept, north aisle) and a dozen other designers and firms. What is more, in 1979 Ely Cathedral opened a stained-glass museum in the north triforium gallery of the nave. This has internally-lit display boxes, making possible the close study which is usually ruled out when the glass is *in situ*. The museum is a clearing-house for glass of all periods from demolished churches, fragments and redundant glass hitherto kept in storage; but most of it comes from the nineteenth century and provides the non-expert with the first real chance to come to grips with this rich vein of Victorian art.

A nave boss in Norwich Cathedral showing the devil thrusting souls into the jaws of hell.

OPPOSITE Gloucester Cathedral from the south east.

PAGES 210–1 The great east window at York Minster, showing the double mullions.

Next to painted glass, sculpture suffered most at the hands of bigots and restorers. Of the survivors, some of the outstanding concentrations have already been described. Wells remains our greatest national collection of medieval figure sculpture, most of it thirteenth-century, with Westminster coming a close second – though much of it is inaccessible and must be studied from photographs. For the study of English sculpture in the period 1275–1350, Exeter provides the most comprehensive collection. For capitals, Canterbury is incomparable. It has a magnificent collection in the crypt, all Norman work, mainly of various beasts and men fighting, and an equally distinguished set of early Gothic Corinthian leaf-carvings in the choir. There are also some early Gothic capitals in Oxford Cathedral. For the thirteenth and fourteenth centuries, the best collection is at Wells, with Lincoln the runner-up and Salisbury a good way behind as third. There is no competition for the leafwork carving in the Chapter House at Southwell, which is quite simply the finest in Europe.

Nearly all cathedrals, however, are well provided with carved (and often painted) stone roof bosses. The development of complex ribbed vaulting led to their creation in very large numbers – a leading expert, C.J.P. Cave, collected photographs of over 8,000 in English cathedrals and churches, 400 of which are reproduced in his book, *Roof Bosses in Medieval Churches* (Cambridge, 1948). As most of them are inaccessible, and not easily examined, at any rate in detail, from the ground, they have been left alone by puritan zealots, soldiers, bigoted deans and the narrow-minded, though many of them are profane, vulgar or even

obscene (they include phallic symbols at Worcester and Winchester). Collectively they constitute a complete repertoire of English medieval sculpture from the thirteenth to the sixteenth centuries, as well as an encyclopædia of medieval iconography and symbolism. There are particularly good ones at Lincoln and Exeter, but the outstanding collection is at Norwich: about 270 in the late fifteenth century nave (mainly scenes from the Old and New Testament), nearly 400 in the cloister (also Biblical scenes, plus the Life of the Virgin and the death and miracles of Becket), with a further 150 or so scattered through the cathedral.

There are carved bosses for wooden roofs also, two fine sets being at Southwark (very grotesque) and St Machar's Cathedral, Aberdeen (heraldic). However, the wood-carvers reserved their ingenuity and wit (often coarse) for the misericords of the cathedral stalls, that is the under-sides of the seats on which the monks or canons, who were supposed to stand throughout the liturgy, were allowed to lean or perch. These again were usually spared by the iconoclasts. There are believed to be over 700 carved misericords in English cathedrals, with good sets at Ely, Gloucester, Norwich, Bristol (including one known as 'The Spinster's Fate', in which she leads apes in Hell), Worcester (which has a naked woman riding a goat and another writing poetry), Carlisle and Lincoln, the last being a set of nearly 100, most of which are of high quality.

Carved choirstalls with spectacular canopies are found at Lincoln. The finest episcopal throne, a sixty-foot elegant giant, is in the choir at Exeter. One should not forget two early thrones of exceptional interest: St Frideswide's in Oxford Cathedral, and St Augustine's, of Purbeck marble, in the Corona at Canterbury, both of them thirteenth-century. Medieval doors in anything approaching their original condition are rarer than one might think. Some outstanding ones are: one in the Norman gateway to the precinct of Peterborough Cathedral (1177–94); the access doors to the cloisters at Durham; The West Doors at Ely, which are late twelfth-century; the Abbot's Door leading to the cloisters at St Albans, *c.* 1360, and an undated pair of doors, which once belonged to the St Albans West Front, now in the north transept. The finest set of all are two pairs

OPPOSITE ABOVE York Minster seen from the south.

OPPOSITE BELOW Detail from a fourteenth-century window at York showing a monkey's funeral.

Cloister bosses at Norwich.

Roof bosses in the nave at Norwich. ABOVE The Last Supper. A large proportion of this boss is painted gold. ABOVE RIGHT The blessing of Esau.

of doors (one larger than the other) in the Norwich precinct, giving access to St Martin's Palace – Perpendicular elegance and profusion at its best.

There are monuments without number in our cathedrals, some of which have already been described. Here I will just make a few suggestions. There are very few pre-Norman monuments of any kind, mainly because Norman bishops and abbots erased the memory of their predecessors, often as a matter of policy. At St Albans, Abbot Paul (1077–93), according to the chronicler, 'destroyed the tombs of his venerable predecessors the noble abbots, whom he was wont to call rude and unlearned, either despising them as English, or in envy, since almost all had been born of royal stock, or of the noble blood of great lords.' Norman tombs, too, were often ruthlessly pushed aside or demolished in the later Middle Ages. The outstanding survivor is the superb knightly effigy of that sad fool, William the Conqueror's eldest son, Robert Duke of Normandy, who was seized by his younger brother, Henry I, and spent the rest of his life in Cardiff castle; he lies in Gloucester Cathedral, not far from the equally melancholy (though much finer) tomb of Edward II. The finest collection of Royal tombs is, of course, in Westminster Abbey; I will say no more here, beyond suggesting that the best way to absorb the awesome solemnity of this regal mausoleum is to spend a night inside the Abbey, as I once did while making a film about the life of Richard II.

Other royal tombs are to be found in Worcester, where lies King John beneath a superb effigy, and the exceptionally fine early sixteenth century chantry tomb of Prince Arthur, Henry VIII's brother. Canterbury is second only to Westminster in its wealth of monuments. The Black Prince is there, beneath a tremendous copper-gilt effigy in full battle armour, and so is his nephew Henry IV and his Queen Joan, very delicate alabaster figures under rich vaulted tabernacles. There are also magnificent tombs of Archbishop Courtenay (d. 1396), Archbishop Chichele (d. 1443), Archbishop Bourchier (d. 1486), Archbishop Stratford (d. 1348) and Prior Eastry (d. 1322), the last two having particularly fine effigies. Other cathedrals which have tombs of outstanding artistry or historical importance are Bristol, Southwark, Salisbury and, of course, St Paul's, the last

A roof boss in Southwark Cathedral: the devil swallowing Judas Iscariot.

214

Misericord in Bristol Cathedral: a domestic quarrel.

containing the enormous iron funeral car of the Duke of Wellington, designed by Prince Albert, and the black marble sarcophagus of Nelson, made in 1524 for Wolsey and later intended by Henry VIII for himself.

Of funeral slabs, the most impressive, though neither is ancient, are both in Durham, St Cuthbert's at one end, St Bede's at the other. Becket has a tablet at Canterbury, on the spot where he was slain. There are many early medieval tomb-slabs, of bishops and abbots, all now anonymous, at Ely, Winchester and Peterborough, which also has a commemorative tablet to Mary Queen of Scots, who was buried there until her son James I brought her to Westminster. Brasses are comparatively scarce in our cathedrals, though there were once thousands, some of enormous size. The earliest surviving one, of 1315, is of Archbishop Grenfield in York Cathedral; and later fourteenth-, fifteenth- and sixteenth-century examples are found in Salisbury, Ely, Hereford, Wells, Exeter, York, Carlisle and Manchester. The rest were taken up for their metal, mainly in the sixteenth century.

Chantries suffered more than any other type of Cathedral furnishing, largely due to the Chantries Act passed in the reign of the boy king, Edward VI. This confiscated the funds bequeathed for their upkeep and those intended to pay the chantry-priests commissioned to say masses for the souls of those whose bodies reposed in the chantry-frames. Of course the chantry had become an abuse. They cluttered up the whole of the east end of the cathedrals, and had long since invaded the transepts and even the naves. Often they obstructed or militated against the basic architectural design, especially in the retrochoirs. On the other hand, the chantry funds served to pay for the upkeep of the cathedral itself, as well as the chantries. When the money was cut off, the fabric suffered, or opportunity was taken to have a general clear-out.

Misericord at Ely showing the devil seated between two gossiping women.

A typical case was at Wells, where the magnificent late-Perpendicular Lady Chapel (1478–88) had been endowed by Bishop Stillington, an absentee pluralist who only visited Wells once, in 1476 for four weeks, during the whole of his twenty-six-year episcopate. In 1552, under the Chantries Act, the whole chapel,

The head of the effigy of
King John on his tomb in
Worcester Cathedral.

chantry and all, 'wyth all the stones and stonework, ledde, glasse, tymbre and iron', was made over to Sir John Gate, the King's Collector of Lead, on condition that he demolish the building and leave 'the grounde fayre and playne'.

When the Chantries Act was passed, most cathedrals had at least twenty chantries; thirty or even forty were common. At York, one of the earliest, St Sepulchre Chapel, dating from about 1170, had a sacrist and twelve canons of its own by the late thirteenth century. In York surveys of 1546–8, it appears there were thirty-eight perpetual chantries, many of them having two priests each; there were sixty of all kinds. At Lincoln, Canterbury and Old St Paul's there were more, making a grand total for England and Wales of nearly 1,000.

Many of course, including some of the finest, were of wood, and of these none survives. Of the rest, York, Chichester, Lichfield and Rochester have kept none at all. Durham has only one, Bishop Hatfield's remaining out of a splendid array. St Davids has two fine ones, Bishop Vaughan's and Bishop Gower's. At Norwich there are two: Bishop Goldwell's and Bishop Nykke's, both fine. At Worcester there is the marvellous stone cage of Prince Arthur's. At Exeter there are three, belonging to Bishops Grandison, Oldham and Speke. At Wells there are two, Bishop Bubwith's and Hugh Suger's, the latter one of the best of all. Ely has a remarkable trio, the chantries of Bishop Alcock and Bishop West, and the superb chantry-tomb of Bishop Redman. At Hereford, there are the chantries of Bishops Stanberry and Audley, and at Lincoln four chantries or chantry-tombs, belonging to Bishops Fleming, Longland, Russell and Burghersh. St Albans keeps the famous chantry of Abbot Ramrigge and Oxford has the double-storey Stoney Chapel, a rare example in stone and timber. There is a fine chantry at Manchester, and another (John Gower) at Southwark. Westminster, of course, is in a class of its own, for the Henry VII Chapel is, as it were, a chantry-cathedral; and Winchester, as we have seen, has an outstanding collection of six. This is a meagre list compared with the hundreds we have lost, bearing in mind that in most cathedrals the chantry income was largely diverted to the general fabric.

Another major casualty has been the wall-paintings of the Middle Ages, many of them with three-dimensional gilt or silvered additions plugged into the wall-surfaces. In a typical medieval cathedral, virtually all the wall-space, the piers and the vaults, whether stone or wood, were covered with paintings and decorative schemes, of which only a minute fraction survives. At St Albans there are the remains of altar-paintings on the east sides of some of the nave piers. At Canterbury, two superb medieval paintings in the chapels of St Anselm and St Gabriel were revealed when twelfth- and thirteenth-century sections of stonework, which had accidentally protected them, were removed in modern times. Some cathedrals were whitewashed on the outside, with the mortar-lines picked out in red – hence Eadmer's twelfth-century description of England 'putting on a white robe of churches' – and nearly all were whitewashed inside at one time or another.

The effigy of the Black Prince
on his tomb at Canterbury.

No British cathedral has ventured to return to such thoroughgoing medieval decorative modes, though the Chapel of the Holy Sepulchre in Winchester gives one an indication of what this entailed. In a few places traces of the original decoration survive: the west or Galilee Porch at Durham, for example, and the vault-paintings at Salisbury, which have now been uncovered. At Salisbury, too, there are hints of colours in the vault of the Audley chapel. Many cathedrals have now embarked on ambitious schemes to restore the high colours and gilding of parts of stone and plasterwork, inspired by the work of Professor Tristram at

Hugh Suger's chantry on the south side of the nave at Wells.

Exeter in the 1930s. Thus the wooden roofs of the transepts at Ely, with their angel hammer-beams, are now a blaze of scarlet, gold and azure; and most are repainting and re-gilding their bosses and tombs. All this is welcome, as is the greater tolerance extended to nineteenth-century schemes of repainting, notably the magnificent wooden vaults at Ely, now discreetly faded.

Nothing now remains of the great medieval vestment collections. At York, we are told, the crown in the sixteenth century confiscated nearly fifty red-and-purple copes, dozens of green, blue, black and white sets of copes and mass-vestments, mitres encrusted with pearls, diamonds and sapphires, and vast quantities of altar cloths, hangings, canopies, carpets and curtains, of lace, silk, satin, velvet and embroidered cloth-of-gold. All cathedrals suffered, and these treasures have never been replaced, though some cathedrals have elaborate sets of modern vestments.

The Tudor monarchs also made off with much cathedral plate; and more was melted down in the Civil War, or stolen or confiscated after it ended. Over the past 200 years, small collections have been rebuilt, and some fine modern pieces acquired; in some cathedrals there are displays of plate on permanent exhibition in treasury museums. The most interesting and touching items are the funerary chalices and patens placed in the graves of bishops and archbishops. Thus Worcester has the thirteenth-century chalice of Bishop Cantiloup, Salisbury the chalice of Bishop Longspee. Lincoln has no less than three thirteenth-century chalices, belonging to Bishops Gravesend, Sutton and Grosseteste, and in the last case the bishop himself appears engraved on the paten. York has two thirteenth-century chalices, one of them of superlative quality, and a fourteenth-century chalice belonging to Archbishop Melton; but the rarest piece of all, the

The sixteenth-century vaulting of Bishop West's chantry at Ely.

217

LEFT The astronomical clock at Wells.

OPPOSITE The exterior of Abbot Ramrigge's chantry at St Albans.

only twelfth-century chalice known to exist in England, is at Canterbury, the death-gift of Archbishop Hubert Walter, once Regent of England.

Clocks first began to make their appearance in English cathedrals in the second half of the thirteenth century, and some of the earlier models are examined in the standard work by C.F.G. Beeson: *English Church Clocks, 1280–1850*. The earliest which still survives in virtually its original state (though with many replaced parts) is at Salisbury. The first reference to it is in 1386, when Richard Glover and his wife Alice were given a workshop near the close, in return for maintaining the clock in the bell-tower, which was of course a building separate from the cathedral. The clock, in a wrought-iron frame, was designed to signal the hours by striking a bell at the top of the tower. When Wyatt was told to pull down the bell-tower, the clock was moved to the first floor of the spire-tower, where it continued working until 1884, when it was replaced – a working-life of something like 500 years, though one assumes that many of its parts had already been replaced. Its historical importance was not established until 1929, and in 1956 it was completely restored, the missing parts being redesigned and made from conjectural historical evidence. For clock-enthusiasts and students of medieval technology it has enormous fascination, but for almost anyone its motions and the deep noises it emits have a sombre grandeur.

It looks as though the other great medieval clock-survivor, 'Jack Blandifer' in the north transept of Wells Cathedral, was constructed by the same mechanic; certainly, Bishop Erghum, who installed the Salisbury clock, was translated to Wells in 1388, and a few years later we get the first reference to the Wells clock. The markings are similar too. It is a much more elaborate and splendid affair than the one at Salisbury – heavenly bodies move round the earth in twenty-four hours and thirty days, and the outer circles of the clock give the day of the month, the hour and the minute; above the dial is a procession of four mounted figures, and

The figure known as 'Jack Blandifer' on the Wells clock.

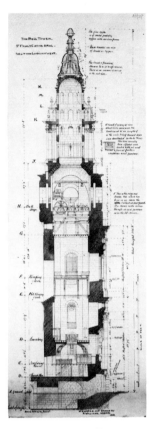

A section of the bell-tower at St Paul's Cathedral.

to the right Jack Blandifer, who strikes the quarters by kicking the earth which is a bell in the centre of the revolving circles. The clock also has an external dial, much simpler, with two figures which strike the quarter with their axes. The figures are probably late fifteenth-century, and the clock has been much mended and added to over the centuries. Indeed, its present movement dates from the 1880s, when the original works were sent to the Kensington Science Museum. Exeter Cathedral also has a medieval clock, with the sun and moon circling the earth, dating from the 1470s; but it, too, has a modern movement. British cathedrals abound in post-medieval clocks of all types and periods, too numerous to describe. One worth noticing is in the north transept at Gloucester, with its Art Nouveau case of Babylonian splendour (1903).

Gloucester also has one of the oldest bells in any British cathedral, its venerable 'Peter', dating from c. 1450, though weighing a mere fifty-eight hundredweight. The subject of cathedral bells is one of great complexity, for most old bells have been recast at least once in their history, and often several times. One of the most famous is Great Tom at Oxford, a medieval bell which originally hung in Oseney Abbey, and was recast in 1620. Another is Great Peter in York Minster, a very ancient bell recast in Victorian times. The monstrous Great Paul in the southern tower of St Paul's weighs seventeen tons, but it only dates from 1881. The business of erecting and hanging it, which was undertaken by the Royal Engineers with artillery tackle, involved removing a good deal of stonework and took three days; it has a fine deep tone and bears witness by sounding each weekday for five minutes on the hour.

Perhaps the best set of bells is in Exeter Cathedral. Its big bell, Peter, weighs four tons and was last recast in 1616; it had at least one earlier recasting, in 1448, and may originally have come from Llandaff Cathedral. Exeter's ringing peal is of thirteen bells; its tenor, 'Grandison', weighs over seventy-two hundredweight. Peal-weight is reckoned by the tenor, and this makes the Exeter peal the second heaviest in the country, after the new peal in Liverpool's Anglican Cathedral (tenor, eighty-two hundredweight). Their names, after Grandison, are Stafford, Oldham, Cobthorne, Doom, Fox, Pongamouth, Purdue, Pennington, Birdall, Earle and Thomas I and Thomas II. Names usually commemorate donors, but nearly all these bells go back to the fourteenth and fifteenth centuries and have been recast two or three times, with metal added. Some of them were cast or recast by the great seventeenth-century bell-founder Thomas Purdue of Closeworth, and they include his masterpiece, Stafford, held by many campanologists to be the noblest in the world. Cobthorne is also a very fine bell, and the set, though never used all together, produces some of the best-toned peals in the kingdom. Like the cathedral itself, the bells are the product of many centuries of craftsmanship and accretion.

The same can be said of Exeter's organ, whose history can be traced back to the Middle Ages through the cathedral's fabric rolls, as organs were built, added to, cannibalized and improved over the decades. During the Civil War, the parliamentarians 'brake down the organs, and taking two or three hundred pipes with them in a most scorneful and contemptuous manner, went up and downe the streets piping them; they meeting with some of the Choristers of the Church, whose surplices they had stolne before, and employed them to base servile offices, scoffingly told them: "boyes, we have spoyled your trade, you must go and sing hot pudding pyes."' At the Restoration, the chapter found and recovered a large number of the pipes, and employed a great builder, John Loosmore, to fabricate more and to build a new organ with them. This he did, enclosing it in a magnificent carved case bearing the date 1665. The case, with its floral and foliate carving, remains, but the organ was reconstructed and added to several times in the eighteenth and nineteenth centuries, and was last rebuilt (after wartime bomb-damage) in 1965. The present organ, then, has a definite, if tenuous, link with the medieval past.

At Salisbury, the organ-history was somewhat different. There too, references to the records beginning in 1480 show organs being added to, rebuilt and raided for the construction of new ones, the principal organ growing bigger and more splendid all the time. In 1643, the Dean and Chapter, anticipating the Demolition of Organs Act of 1644, thought it prudent to have the organ dismantled, and its parts safely wrapped up and hidden away. In 1661 it was re-erected and subsequently enlarged. In 1710 a new organ appeared, the first with four manuals, and doubtless the one on which Handel played when he visited Salisbury. This lasted until 1792, when George III celebrated his recovery from madness by donating a new one, constructed by his favourite organist, Samuel Green of Isleworth, who built more than fifty altogether, including eleven in other cathedrals. In 1877, this was given to a parish church, and yet another organ installed, deemed by Sir John Stainer (the composer and organist of St Paul's) to be the finest organ in the world, and certainly in England. This, in turn, was restored and updated in the 1930s.

Salisbury's claim has been challenged by Liverpool whose great organ, dating from the 1920s, was planned and designed in consultation with the cathedral's architect, Sir Giles Gilbert Scott, and is therefore an integral part of the fabric: its sonorities have been modified, over a period of half-a-century, to match the accoustics of the cathedral as it was built. It has five manuals and over 9,000 pipes, and is often cited as the largest church organ in the world. The big organ built for Guildford Cathedral, and installed in 1961, was also designed in relation to the basic architectural scheme of Sir Edward Maufe, and forms, in fact, a very effective part of the internal decorative strategy. It has no more than 4398 pipes, but it is a cunningly contrived double organ, a main organ and a French-inspired 'positive' organ which gives the perfect tone for Baroque music of the classical repertoire – both played from the same console and used separately or together.

All the English cathedrals have major organs, mostly from the last 150 years, though sometimes including earlier pipework. Two outstanding ones, both built by Harrison of Durham, are at York and Ely. The big organ at Lincoln, which plays such an important part in the main perspective of the interior, is notable for its exciting early Gothic revival case by E. J. Willson (1826), and the case at Worcester was beautifully designed by Sir George Gilbert Scott to match his stalls and bishop's throne. Finally, it is worth mentioning the fine case by Schwarbrick (1715), which encloses the organ in Birmingham.

English cathedrals are also famous for their libraries, though they vary considerably in antiquity and the value and interest of their contents. The library at Rochester, which I have already described, has preserved a degree of continuity since its foundations; so has Hereford's collection, with its famous chained books and its unique *Mappa Mundi*. The Exeter library, now housed in the Bishop's Palace, was begun by Leofric in 1072, and it still has twenty of his original sixty-six manuscripts. The collection includes not only the separate Exon Domesday survey, but the tenth-century Exeter Book, which contains the largest collection of Anglo-Saxon poetry in existence.

The organ-case in Liverpool Anglican Cathedral, designed in consultation with the cathedral's architect, Sir Giles Gilbert Scott.

In other cathedrals, however, there was destruction and discontinuity. York's first and greatest library, built up in the age of Alcuin, was destroyed by the Danes; a second was dispersed in the mid-sixteenth century. In 1628, however, Frances Matthew, widow of its great Archbishop Tobie Matthew, bequeathed to the cathedral his enormous and valuable library of over 3,000 books, the largest private library in England at that date, which includes twenty-seven six-monthly catalogues sent to him by the organizers of the Frankfurt Book Fair (1596–1623) where he bought many of his rarities. This formed the nucleus of what is today the largest and most active cathedral library in England, with over 65,000 books, including some great treasures, though the library's two unique Caxtons had to be sold in 1930 to raise money for repairing the fabric.

Two great monastic cathedral libraries, at Winchester and Ely, were wiped out by the Reformation. Both were refounded in the seventeenth century, and Winchester's, known as the Morley Library, now occupies the original monastic bookroom, added in 1150. But at Ely there is a sad tale: some of the original collection can be identified in the libraries of Corpus Christi College and the University Library at Cambridge. The cathedral library was re-established in

222

The famous chained library at Hereford.

1678, following a bequest by the dean, but this too was broken up in 1970, some of the books being sold, the rarer ones, plus the old cathedral muniments (contained in pigeon-holed chests dating from the reign of Edward IV) being deposited in Cambridge University Library.

A typical example of a good cathedral library is at Salisbury. The number of books, about 10,000, is not very large; but they include 200 manuscripts dating from the ninth to the fifteenth centuries and thirty *incunabula*, that is books printed before the year 1500. Among the outstanding items is one of four, and by far the best preserved, of the originals of Magna Carta, no doubt sent there by William Longspee, Earl of Salisbury, who was one of the witnesses to the document. There is a tenth-century psalter, brought to the cathedral by St Osmund himself. There are thirty books belonging to that great Wiltshire figure, Isaac Walton, bearing his signature and jottings. And, not least, there is the master-copy, in Sir Christopher Wren's own hand, of his report on the safety of the cathedral structure, including the tower and steeple, and his proposals to ensure it. Perhaps the most attractive item, however, which is always on display, is an immensely rich breviary, handwritten and illuminated in 1460. By that date printing had already arrived, and this must be one of the last major works carried out by an English professional scriptorium which we still possess. It was done by a team of scribes under a master-scribe who directed the placing of the borders and margins. The first scribe wrote all the words in black in the first section of four large sheets of vellum folded in half, then wrote the first word of the next section and handed it to the second scribe. He then put in the red words and the small decorations. The third scribe put in the large initials and the gilding and illumination, the completed section being checked by the master-scribe. He handed all the finished sections to the bookbinder, the book being sewn on leather thongs laced into wooden broads. It is an excellent but typical product of medieval collective workmanship, wonderfully skilful but with a slight note of mechanical weariness. By the date of its fabrication, the medieval pattern of life and art was already dissolving, and the Reformation was just over the horizon.

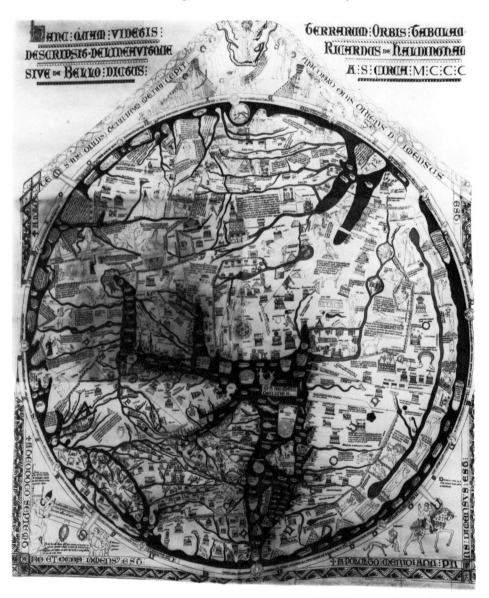

The Hereford *Mappa Mundi* or world map made by Richard de Bello in about 1280.

9
Renaissance, Reformation and Wren

he destruction endured by the ancient cathedrals in Britain did not come like a bolt out of a clear sky. Within Christendom throughout the Middle Ages, there was a strongly-held minority view, springing from the iconoclast movement but with its roots in Judaic Christianity, that severe limits must be placed on the natural exuberance of sacred art. The Cistercians, a reformed and austere branch of the Benedictines, originally forbade any form of decoration and ornament in their abbey-churches, and they made occasional efforts to return to their pristine severity: thus, in 1182, they decided that all stained-glass should be removed from their churches. The Augustine canons and the Premonstratensians also, from time to time, showed flashes of the puritan spirit. So, it is interesting to note, did discerning patrons. Matthew Paris tells us that the great Abbot John de Cella of St Albans was bamboozled by an over-ambitious master-mason, who 'added carvings that were impertinent, trifling and costly beyond measure'. Henry VI, in his very precise specifications for the building of King's College Chapel, 1447–8, insists: 'I will that the building of my same college proceed in large form, clean and substantial, setting aside an excess of too intricate works of carving and over-zealous mouldings.'

In the second quarter of the sixteenth-century, this latent puritan streak became, for a short time, the dominant religious aesthetic, and there was a period of active destruction. Religious ideology, however, was not the only factor. There was a collapse of belief, marked even in states which remained Catholic, in the apparatus of mechanical Christianity, the notion that grace and mercy could be bought by donatives and chantries, and this in itself weakened the spirit of late Gothic. In England, though the Renaissance in architecture came very late, Gothic degenerated into mannerism; a specific religious architecture ceased to exist. Men thought there were other and better ways to glorify God, notably through their own lives. In the second half of the sixteenth century, almost the entire stock of English private houses of all classes was renewed, and the rich built themselves palaces on an unprecedented scale; ecclesiastical building came almost to a halt. At Ripon, the sixteenth-century crossing-arches by Christopher Scune were left unfinished. At York, the cathedral's master-mason John Forman was the last of the English Gothic architects; when he died, just before Elizabeth's accession in 1558, he was never replaced.

In nearly all cathedrals maintenance was perfunctory. Absenteeism was almost as bad as ever – Elizabeth rewarded her old tutor, Roger Ascham, with one of the richest York prebends, Wetwang, and he treated it as a pension, never setting foot in the Minster. Nepotism was worse, as archbishops and bishops provided for their sons and plundered episcopal estates for their daughters' dowries. In addition, bishops and cathedral chapters were forced to give rapacious courtiers ruinous leases. Holinshed summed up the position in 1577:

… bells and times of morning and evening prayers remain as in time past, saving that all images, shrines, tabernacles, rood-lofts and monuments of idolatory are removed, taken down and defaced, only the stories in glass windows excepted, which for want of sufficient store of new stuff, and by reason of extreme charge that should grow by the alteration of the same into white panes throughout the realm, are not altogether abolished in all places at once, but provided and set up in their rooms.

When the spire of St Paul's fell from neglect, the roof was patched up but no attempt was made to rebuild the spire. Its forlorn stump was a symbol of the

OVERLEAF St Paul's Cathedral: looking into the choir from the nave.

OPPOSITE Seventeenth-century views of Old St Paul's Cathedral before and after its spire fell.

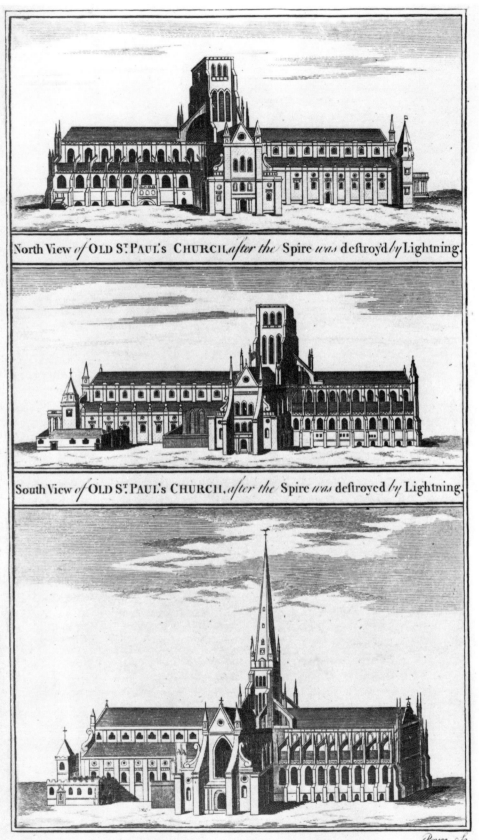

North View *of* OLD ST. PAUL's CHURCH, *after the* Spire *was* destroy'd *by* Lightning.

South View *of* OLD ST. PAUL's CHURCH, *after the* Spire *was* destroyed *by* Lightning.

Royce *Sc.*

South View *of* OLD ST. PAUL'S, *when the* Spire *was* standing.

careless attitude of Elizabethan England to its architectural heritage.

Worse was to follow in the seventeenth-century. Until the coming to power of Archbishop Laud, wrote Clarendon in his *History of the Great Rebellion*, 'The people took so little care of the churches, and the parsons as little of the chancels, that instead of beautifying or adorning them in any degree, they rarely provided for their stability ... and suffered them at least to be kept so indecently and slovenly that they would not have endured it in the ordinary offices of their own houses, the rain and the wind to infest them'. Laud tried to put the clock back, and made strenuous efforts to repair the fabric of both St Paul's and Canterbury; but his activities merely provoked the sectarians into a further wave of destruction once they came to power. In January 1641, Parliament set up a defacing and demolition commission, which toured the country. Bishop Hall wrote of its work at Norwich in 1643:

Lord, what work was here! What clattering of glasses! What battering down of walls! What tearing up of monuments! What pulling down of seats! What wresting out of iron and brass from the windows and graves! What defacing of arms! What demolishing of curious stonework that had not any representation in the world.... What tooting and piping on the destroyed organ pipes! And what a hideous triumph on the market day before all the country when, in a kind of sacrilegious and profane procession, all the organ pipes and vestments ... and service books and singing books that could be had were carried to the fire in the public market place.

Besides Norwich, the other principal sufferers in the Civil War period were Old St Paul's, Chichester, Peterborough, Worcester, Oxford, Winchester, Chester, Hereford, Exeter, Canterbury and Lincoln. Durham, which had fared disastrously under Elizabeth, lost its woodwork under Cromwell and its spires through neglect; Ripon lost its spires; Lichfield and Carlisle were savaged.

In Scotland, the damage was even greater and more lasting. St Giles, the Civic Church of Edinburgh, was the scene of a riot against the Laudian reforms in 1637, when Jenny Geddes threw her stool at the head of Dean Hannay. This fine cathedral-type church was built between 1387 and the mid-fifteenth century, with its big square tower and imperial-crown steeple added at the end of the fifteenth century, a monument to the Scottish version of French Flamboyant. In the Reformation, under Knox, it was called the Capital Kirk, and lost its forty-four altars, the statue of St Giles being thrown into the North Loch. It became an episcopal church for a brief span in the 1630s and again between 1660–88, and by the end of the seventeenth century was virtually bare of ornament. Since then it has become the Westminster Abbey of Scotland, harbouring the bodies of Regent Moray, the Marquess of Montrose, R.L. Stevenson and Jenny Geddes herself; the Church Assemblies meet there; Scottish judges worship there at the opening of the Court of Session; and Royal Proclamations are read at the Mercat Cross by the west door. But of its medieval past only the fabric, much restored, remains.

Other Scottish cathedrals lost even their fabric. St Andrews was once by far the largest and most sumptuous church in Scotland, built in the Early English and Decorated styles between 1161 and 1318, and enjoying a period of Flamboyant splendour, 1440–1559. It was attacked by Knox's fanatic following, and the period of the Civil Wars and the Covenanters completed its destruction; not until 1826 did the Barons of the Exchequer take possession of the ruins, and prevent the locals from using them as a quarry. By this time only parts of the east and west gables, the south wall of the nave, and bits of the choir (twelfth- and thirteenth-century work for the most part) were left.

OPPOSITE The choir of Christ Church Cathedral, Oxford, showing the pendant lierne vault.

PAGES 230–1 Lithograph by Charles Rivière of the west front of St Paul's Cathedral.

Ch. Rivière del et lith

CATHÉDRALE DE St PAUL

du Jardinet 12.

Paris - Maison Martinet

St PAUL'S CATHEDRAL

Dunblane Cathedral, which had a Romanesque tower from *c.* 1100, remained roofless for 300 years, and was only partly restored at the end of the nineteenth century. Elgin, a masterpiece of Early English Gothic (though in a Scottish mode), was built entirely in the thirteenth century, with twin western towers, a central tower and transepts, a six-bay nave and long eastern arm; though, after a fire in 1390, French influence crept into the Chapter House and the West Front. In 1567 the Scottish Privy Council ordered the roof to be stripped of lead to raise money to pay its troops, and in the late seventeenth century it became a ruin, though one of the noblest in the British Isles. Dornoch Cathedral survived as a parish church (or 'Great Church'), but stripped bare. It is simple, gaunt and of beautiful stone, with sixteen earls of Sutherland buried in its bowels; but its nave was completely rebuilt in 1835–7, and a whole wall was restored as recently as 1924. Dunkeld Cathedral was entirely a product of the fourteenth and fifteenth centuries (its great north west tower was finished in 1501) and a majestic church it must have been, before it lost its roof at the Reformation. It was pillaged and battered repeatedly in the seventeenth century, and is now a well-kept ruin, but some of its precinct buildings have been well restored by the National Trust for Scotland. Of the remaining medieval cathedrals, Kirkwall and Glasgow were saved by the public spirit and devotion of their townspeople, Iona has been rebuilt, Brechin is a parish church, and Whithorn, Fortrose and Lismore are ruins.

The ruin of the west front of Elgin Cathedral, Scotland.

The imperial-crown steeple of St Giles's, Edinburgh.

OPPOSITE ABOVE Liverpool Anglican Cathedral seen from the south east.

OPPOSITE BELOW Westminster Cathedral and its piazza, seen from the west.

In England and Wales, tribute must be paid to the vigour of the Restoration bishops. Intolerant they may have been in some respects, but they were dealing with intolerant people. At Exeter, for instance, Bishop Seth Ward had to eject a number of shopkeepers who had set up booths in the cloisters; he also had to defeat a proposal by the Nonconformists to divide the cathedral in two, with dissenters using one half and Anglicans the others. Ward threw out the partitions and spent the enormous sum of £25,000 on restoration work, 'for all the Leases belonging to the Ancient and Rich Church being expired, the renewing of them caused that plenty'. When Ward was translated to Salisbury in 1667, he immediately engaged Sir Christopher Wren to carry out a survey and make recommendations, the result of which was the saving of the spire.

By this date Wren was already hard at work at St Paul's. Old St Paul's had been by far the biggest church in Britain: 586 feet long, with twelve bays to the nave (two west towers outside it), a huge transept, and a twelve-bay chancel – much longer, in fact, than its replacement. The top of the spire had been 489 feet high. It was a gigantic compendium of English medieval architecture and, if it still existed, would supply many of the missing bits in the history of English Gothic. But it was in a mess even before the fire of 1561 which caused the central spire to fall down; thereafter the decline was steady.

In 1628, Laud became Bishop of London and set about saving St Paul's, or rather improving it. The Henricians and Elizabethans had not disliked Gothic – on the contrary, it was praised by such diverse minds as Leland, Stow and Camden – but the Carolines were definitely classical. Laud hired Inigo Jones, who refaced the outside walls of the nave and transepts with classical windows and cornices, turning the buttresses into pilasters; in front of the west façade he added a gigantic portico with columns sixty feet high. This extraordinary mongrelization of Europe's largest Gothic cathedral met with general approval from the *cognoscenti*. Mr Jones, wrote John Webb in 1655, 'reduced the body [of the church] from the steeple to the west end, into that Order and Uniformity we now behold; and by adding that magnificent Portico there, hath contracted the envy of all Christendom upon our Nation, for a Piece of Architecture not to be paralleled in these last Ages of the World.'

With the Restoration, a new commission was appointed to sit upon the church's future, and for the first time Wren made his appearance. At the Restoration he was still in his twenties, a man steeped in both the new post-Baconian scientific learning and the Anglican ethos. His father was Dean of Windsor, his Uncle Matthew Bishop first of Norwich, then of Ely. Wren was of the new breed of gentleman-architects who had replaced the old master-builders. He had been at All Souls, then Professor of Astronomy at Gresham's College, London; in 1661 he was appointed Savilian Professor of Astronomy at Oxford, where he designed the new Sheldonian Theatre at the invitation of Gilbert Sheldon, the former Warden of All Souls. Sheldon became Bishop of London at the Restoration, and he may have consulted Wren about St Paul's as early as 1660. At all events, when the Commission decided to embark on a major reconstruction programme, Wren was asked to submit proposals, and his report, in May 1666, urged in effect that the 'classification' of St Paul's, begun by Jones, be completed. He wote:

Among the many proposals that may be made to Your Lordships concerning the repairs of St Paul's, some may possibly aim at too great Magnificence which neither the Disposition nor Extent of this Age will probably bring to a Period. Others again may fall

OPPOSITE The ruin of Dunkeld Cathedral, destroyed in the seventeenth century.

Inigo Jones's drawing for the west front of St Paul's.

Inigo Jones's porch to Old St Paul's.

below, as to think of piecing up the old fabric, here with Stone, there with Brick & covering all faults with a coat of plaster leaving it still to the next Posterity as a further object of Charity. I suppose your Lordships may think fitt to take the middle way & to neglect nothing that may answer to a decent uniform Beauty or durable firmness in the fabrick & suitable to the Expence already laid out on the outside, especially since it is a pile as much for ornament as use.

The diplomatic tone of this report suggests that Wren was already skilled in dealing with an English committee, and aware he would never get away with anything more than a compromise. The last sentence indicates he intended, while keeping the basic structure of the old Gothic pile, to redesign it as a monumental piece of urban scenery, that is from the outside in. The inside would then follow suit, 'after a good Roman manner', as he put it, instead of 'the Gothick Rudeness of ye old Design'. The old central tower would go completely and the crossing would be enormously enlarged, to create a monumental central space, just like his uncle's cathedral at Ely: only, instead of an octagon and lantern, there would be a pineapple-type dome.

There can be little doubt that a creeping classification on these lines, though in a less drastic manner, would have been ordered by the Commission, but in September the Great Fire effectively brought down the old church. Wren saw his opportunity to abandon Gothic entirely and build a new classical basilica. He proposed 'a new fabric upon new foundations . . . to use the old but as you would use a quarry'. However, he had no official status at all until 1669, when he was appointed Principal Architect. Bishop Henchman, who had succeeded Sheldon, wanted a mere reconstruction job: a paper he wrote was headed 'Nine

236

Wren's design for the new St Paul's, based on the model.

Considerations against building a new cathedral, instead of repairing the old one'. At least two of the commissioners were Gothicists. Wren's first, basilican-type, design (the 'New Model') was universally criticized; his second, a Greek Cross design with a huge central dome (the 'Great Model') was admired by Charles II but disliked by most of the commissioners as too revolutionary (a twenty-foot scale model of this design is now in the Cathedral Library).

The third, or 'Warrant Design', was as Wren put it an attempt 'to reconcile as near as possible the Gothik to a better Manner of Architecture'. It had the long-armed ground-plan of an English Norman cathedral, keeping a dome indeed, but popping a Gothic spire on top of it. This bizarre design was accepted by the commissioners, and formally approved by Charles II. But the King, whose general political method was to avoid open warfare with his parliaments and his ministers and to do what he intended in secret, laid down in Wren's warrant that the architect should have 'the liberty, in the prosecution of work, to make some variations, rather ornamental than essential, as from time to time he should see proper'. Wren interpreted this discretion in the sense the King intended: as virtual *carte blanche*. In his autobiographical *Parentalia* it is noted: 'From that time the Surveyor resolved to make no more models, or publicly expose his drawings, which (as he had found from experience) did but lose time, and subjected his business many times to incompetent judges.'

However, this strategy did not mean the end of Wren's difficulties – far from it. For the first time we can follow the erection of a great British cathedral, from start to finish, in abundant documentary detail. The first stone was laid in 1675; starting as always at the chancel; the transepts were reached in 1681, the nave in

Wren's design for the restoration of St Paul's, showing the 'Pineapple' steeple.

237

1684, the foundations of the West Front in 1686. The chancel was consecrated in 1697, the west towers finished in 1708, the dome in 1710, and in 1711 parliament declared the building complete. Wren had been twenty-nine when his connection with the cathedral began, and he was seventy-nine when it was finished.

It was a half-century of constant struggle. Just to reduce the ruins, which had been solidified into cyclopaean masses by the molten lead, into clearable rubble taxed Wren's ingenuity. He used pickaxes, gunpowder and finally a giant battering-ram, forty feet in length and iron-tipped, swung by fifteen men on each side. Money was a constant problem. Two Coal Acts gave the St Paul's fund a lien of 3½d on each cauldron of coal brought to London from Newcastle; but Wren's own salary was miserly and sometimes withheld, a poor return for his fanatical devotion to duty. As Sarah, Duchess of Marlborough, put it to Vanbrugh, Wren 'allowed himself to be dragged up in a basket to the top of the scaffolding, two or three times a week to the hazard of his life, for a paltry £200 a year.' What she did not know was that Wren gave £60 of this to the building fund.

Wren did not hesitate to employ any new technology already available, but building methods were still medieval in some ways. He had the help of an Assistant-Surveyor, a Clerk of the Works and a paymaster. The masons, of whom the most celebrated was Edward Strong (others were Jasper Latham, Edward Pearce, Samuel Foulkes and John Tompson) employed their own men, as of old. As for the supply of stone, Wren's difficulties in this quarter open a window into the Middle Ages.

Portland Stone, 'the king of the oolites', had been Inigo Jones's favourite; he had used it both for his portico and the refacing of Old St Paul's. It could be hewn in huge blocks of uniform quality, and brought entirely by sea to the foot of St Paul's steps. The Portland islanders still had the medieval field-system, ancient marriage-customs and were in effect tenant-freeholders of a Royal Manor, enjoying special rights. All 200-or-so tenants had 'ancient rights' of quarrying, these being governed by the customs of the manor, disputes settled by the Court Leet after a 'jury viewing.' Purchasers had to pay a shilling a ton duty on stone, of which the Crown got 3d and the tenants 9d, paid into a 'Stone Grant Fund.' The commissioners of St Paul's had a royal warrant which allowed them to quarry stone and pay no duty. Naturally, the islanders were angry, particularly since the commissioners employed a series of undiplomatic or incompetent middle men. In 1678 the islanders rioted and broke up the commissioners' carts. Four ringleaders were summoned to the Privy Council in London and rebuked; but difficulties continued, the stone rose continually in price, and sometimes work on the cathedral had to be stopped for lack of supply. New carts had to be designed to carry the huge blocks; shipping was harassed by French privateers, and one vessel, with 150 tons of stone on board, foundered at sea. In 1696 a landslide led to 'a dismal destruction of the ways, cranes and peers in the Isle of Portland'; supplies ceased completely for nearly two years. Wren had to go to Portland himself before they were resumed. He also had to do battle with the Deputy-Surveyor of the Royal Gardens, who secretly bought 500 tons for Hampton Court.

The truth is, the Portland quarrymen wanted to supply the stone themselves, as they always had done, and this system was eventually introduced in 1702. But disputes continued. When, twenty years and two monarchs later, Wren finally got plenary powers from Queen Anne, he was still unable to enforce them against the 'ancient Customs'. He wrote to the quarrymen in 1705:

... Tis all one to me what your jury do. It shall not alter any measure of mine, except in endeavouring that the tunnage-money you claim by a pretended grant of the Crown, be disposed to better purpose than you apply it to, you having no more of right to it, as I shall easily make appear, and also represent to the Queen your contesting her right and your contempt for her authority, for though 'tis your power to be as ungrateful as you will, yet you must not think that your insolence will always be borne with ...

The quarrymen, resembling in their obstinacy and traditionalism a 'modern' British trade union, were not Wren's only enemies. From 1697 he was badgered by Parliament, which believed him dilatory. He had a row over the organ, by Bernard Smith, which not only cost £2,000 but was too big for the case, which Wren had designed himself; he refused to enlarge it, as he argued that his building was already spoilt 'by the confounded box of whistles'. After Henry Godolphin became Dean in 1707, the chapter turned against Wren. He was attacked in a pamphlet, and responded in kind. In 1718, aged eighty-six he was finally dismissd from the surveyorship. By that time the building was finished, though he was infuriated the next year when the commissioners added an open stone balustrade round the top of the cathedral. He commented contemptuously: 'Ladies think nothing well without an edging.' He retired to his house in Hampton Court, adding: 'As I am dismissed, having worn out (by God's mercy) a long life in the royal service, and having made some figure in the world, I hope it will be allowed me to die in peace.' His struggles, as monumental as his work, suggest that there are many untold and tragic personal stories behind the building of Britain's medieval cathedrals. However, Wren, unlike his predecessors – or, for that matter, Bramante and Michelangelo – at least lived to see his work completed. Until his death in 1723, he went once a year to visit St Paul's, and to sit under his dome. It was nearly 150 years before a memorial to him was set up inside the cathedral.

After all this, what in fact did Wren create? It is certainly not a Gothic cathedral; or a Roman basilica; or a Byzantine dome-church. In one sense it is a graceful blend of the Classical and the Baroque, and it proclaims its allegiance openly and fearlessly to the architectural ideology of both antiquity and the mature Renaissance. But once we begin to probe behind the decorative detail and look at the structure, we see the force of the proposition that Gothic never really died out in England.

Two years after Wren's birth, a Gothic church was built at Leeds (St John's); three years after his death another was put up at Fenny Stratford, and four years after that his own college, All Souls, was adorned with Nicholas Hawksmoor's Gothic towers. He himself must have been familiar with the new Gothic staircase-vault at Christ Church, Oxford. Wren's St Paul's is not a Gothic cathedral but it is very much in the English tradition. It has a cruciform shape, with the main parts – chancel, transepts, nave, crossing – kept distinct. It has the aisles Englishmen expect in grand cathedral architecture. Its nave is long, as in Norman times; its piers have a Norman massiveness too – not so very different from the masculine brute power of St Albans. It has an English-structure West Front, with towers placed outside the aisles as at Wells. From his first conception Wren retained the notion of a vast, Ely-type crossing, enclosing a stupefying volume of space. True, the lantern is again a dome, a huge and manifest dome, with the Gothic-spire element downgraded to a mere cupola, and a Renaissance one at that. Yet in mechanistic structure the dome is a concealed piece of Gothic, with an inner ceiling or vault of stone, and an outer roof of wood, covered in lead.

Also concealed (as at Durham) are flying buttresses; seen from above this Gothic bone-structure becomes apparent.

The Cathedral was a long time a-building and because of the fluid interpretation Charles II had set on Wren's brief, shifts in his architectural philosophy could be incorporated, to some extent, as the vast structure rose. When Wren travelled abroad in his thirties, he left no record of his admiration for any Gothic he saw; but of course in youth and early manhood he had been fluent in Gothic vernacular, steeped in it at Oxford, at his uncle's cathedrals and in his restoration work at Salisbury, Chichester and elsewhere. In 1713, when he was eighty, he wrote a memorandum on the restoration of Westminster, proposing a new spire and new Gothic fronts for the north transept and west end. The transept work was carried out in 1719 according to Wren's design and incorporated his notion of Gothic beauty. It was not 'correct' Gothic (there were no books on Gothic in Wren's day) and therefore Sir George Gilbert Scott in 1875 and J.L. Pearson in 1884 restored the transept front to what *they* believed the original builders had intended; but it is significant that, in his old age, Wren was thinking in Gothic terms, albeit a Gothic of his own imagining.

Ironwork by Jean Tijou on the north choir screen at St Paul's.

Nevertheless, it is misleading to stress too heavily the Gothic infrastructure of St Paul's. It is a display-church, a prodigy-cathedral, intended like its predecessors to excite from afar, to overwhelm by its gigantism from a viewpoint immediately beneath its West Front, and finally to present a series of shock-vistas within. However, it is not operating on a stream of pilgrims, on behalf of an ecclesiastical society-within-society, claiming a mediatory role between man and God and holding up the church as a kind of ladder to the empyrean. On the contrary, Wren built a display-church on behalf of a Caesaro-papalist state, in the Byzantine tradition. The openness and marmoreal frigidity of the interior are designed to be filled and warmed by huge state ceremonies, in which sovereign and high priest are coadjutors and society is present in corporative form, each in its ranks, lay and hieratic. No one can judge the architectural success either of St Peter's, Rome, or of St Paul's, London, until he has been present in the flesh (television is not a complete substitute) at one of the universalist occasions for which they were primarily designed. Only then, at a pontifical high mass or a royal jubilee thanksgiving, does the interior provide for the visitor the stunning perspectives of massed and ordered humanity, the majestic sonorities, the pyrotechnics of colour and, not least, the emotional homogeneity of a clerical state or a state church, militant, triumphant and above all present on parade, which alone justify the deafening histrionics of the interior. Of the two, St Paul's is now by far the more successful, even though smaller; St Peter's can accommodate over 20,000, but there is no focal-point where a ceremony can be effectively witnessed by more than a quarter of them. Wren was a practical man, as his success in getting the huge building aloft despite all the difficulties, mechanical and human, abundantly testifies. Acoustically and, still more, visually, his prodigy-church works. No normal man or woman who has attended a state occasion there leaves disappointed or indeed (in an Erastian sense) unedified.

As the artistic director of the great enterprise, Wren also showed himself an exceptional patron of talent. In addition to the fine masons already mentioned, Wren also employed, for the carving and statuary of the exterior, Francis Bird, C.G. Cibber, Jonathon Maine, and Christopher and William Kempster. Grinling Gibbons, discovered by John Evelyn at Deptford, also did some of his best work

OPPOSITE The interior of the dome at St Paul's, showing some of Thornhill's *trompe-l'oeil* painting of the life of St Paul.

for Wren on the outside, but still more in designing and carving the stalls. Wren had two very fine plasterers, Henry Doogood and Chrystom Wilkins, and in Jean Tijou, the French smith and ironworker, he employed a great artist to create the sanctuary gates in the north and south choir aisles, the altar rails and balustrades, and such fine details as the Dean's Staircase in the south-west tower. Indeed, the work of Gibbons and Tijou is on an artistic level with Wren's own overall design; no better can be seen anywhere in Europe.

Wren was not so lucky with the painters and mosaic-artists brought in to cover portions of the vast interior, including the dome itself. To decorate the dome the commissioners insisted on employing Sir James Thornhill, against Wren's wishes. The wrangles continued after Wren's death and, indeed, throughout the greater part of the eighteenth and nineteenth centuries, marked by confused arguments of principle and many changes of plan, and involving Sir Joshua Reynolds, Benjamin West, Nathaniel Dance and Angelica Kaufman, and, later, Alfred Stevens and G.F. Watts – with William Burges, Sir Edward Poynter, Lord Leighton, G.F. Bodley, Sir William Blake Richmond and John Tweed in minor roles. Thornhill's frescoes of the life of St Paul, done in monochrome with a trick architectural setting in the dome itself, are clever and undeniably impressive. The work of Alfred Stephens is, at its best (the Wellington monument), great art.

What the church lacks is a *baldachino* with the terrific virility and arrogance of Bernini's in St Peter's; but in almost every other respect, inside and out, St Paul's is a superior creation, a confident and unforced translation of a grand international style into an unmistakeable English vernacular. Its success, and the justification for Wren's ruthlessness, is that it does not make one regret Old St Paul's, for he gave us something better. Like all the greatest architecture, it has stamped its profile and proportions so indelibly on our minds that we cannot conceive of it being designed in any other way; when we actually look at the alternative proposals we recoil in horror or mirth. Indeed, it is a testimony to the strength of the design that, even today, St Paul's continues valiantly to defend the skyline it dominates from the barbarous encroachments of the abortive skyscrapers which encompass it. True monumentality will always overawe sheer size.

The case of St Paul's testifies to the underlying tenacity of Gothic notions even in the late seventeenth century and beyond, but it would be wrong to give the impression that enlightened men of taste, in the century 1650–1750, showed habitual reverence to the Gothic. On the contrary: the prevailing view, among the cultured upper class and right-thinking educated clergymen, was summed up by Sir John Clerk of Pennicuick, who wrote in 1727:

The Goths were those barbarous nations from the north of Europe, who overspread Italy and ruin'd the Roman Empire. They likewise broke or destroyed all monuments of antiquity, statues and ornaments of all kinds which fell in their way. They introduced a bad manner, not only in Architecture but in all other arts and sciences. We have been for upwards of 200 years endeavouring to recover ourselves from this Gothicism. Yet there are still too many amongst us whose bad taste neither example nor precept will ever rectify and therefore are to be left to themselves. For Goths will always have a Gothic taste.

This cleavage of taste, between the cultured élite and the Gothic-clinging populace, was strikingly illustrated in the case of All Saints, Derby, which became a cathedral in 1927. This was an old collegiate church dating from the early twelfth century, but with a magnificent late-medieval west tower. The

The nave of Derby
Cathedral, designed by
James Gibbs.

tower was certainly designed after 1475, by James Otes, the bulk of it being
constructed 1510-27, and collections for it were still being held as late as 1532. It is
178 feet high, in three stages, with large Perpendicular windows, and the angle
buttresses are carried up as pinnacles thirty-six feet above the parapet, which is
battlemented. The rest of the aisled Gothic church, which had been parochial
since the Chantries Act of 1547, had become almost ruinous by the beginning of
the eighteenth century. The incumbent, the Reverend Dr Hutchinson, had to deal
with parishioners who were even more traditionalist in their attachment to
Gothic than the St Paul's commissioners, and who wanted a mere restoration-
job. Even he did not dare to touch the tower; but he dealt with the rest by a
sudden and violent conspiracy. In 1723, in a single night, he and a gang of
labourers demolished the entire church save the tower; and he entrusted the new
nave and chancel to the ablest of Wren's successors, James Gibbs.

Gibbs was the brilliant creator of the Radcliffe Camera in Oxford, and of that
august and graceful church, St Martin-in-the Fields, which dominates the top
right-hand corner of Trafalgar Square. At Derby he designed an arcaded hall
church, with piers in Roman Doric, supporting entablatures from which spring
semicircular arches, part of a vault of great elegance and complexity, which in the
aisle bays even make a distinct genuflection to the Gothic. Gibbs, like Wren, was
a civilised architect, very conscious of his medieval predecessor's shade and
anxious to avoid offending it. He deplored the internal clutter of the eighteenth-
century church, whose private boxes, reflecting the age's obsession with the

freehold, often contained sofas, chairs and even fireplaces (Sir Gilbert Scott, in his *Recollections*, says he came across a case in which 'a noble family had an octagonal glazed pew, hung like a birdcage from the chancel-arch, and so well contrived that, by facing about east or west, his Lordship could attend either the nave or chancel service.'). At Derby, Gibbs insisted on a pre-Anglican simplicity, and wrote of his church: '... it is the more beautiful for having no galleries, which, as well as pews, clog up and spoil the insides of churches and take away from that right proportion they would otherwise have, and are only justifiable as they are necessary. The plainness of the building makes it less expensive and renders it more suitable to the old [tower].'

On the outside, he supplied a characteristic Gibbs touch by giving the wall openings an interrupted rusticated architrave. Inside, however, he made the focus of the church the magnificent wrought-iron choir-screens by the great Midland smith Robert Bakewell, whose genius was, perhaps, ignited by the example of Jean Tijou in St Paul's. One interior feature from the old church Gibbs was powerless (or perhaps unwilling) to exclude: the magnificent standing wall-monument to Bess of Hardwick, Countess of Shrewsbury (1608), the leading architectural patron of her age. In the event it is not obtrusive but adds to the dignity (and colour) of this noble church.

Almost contemporary (1709–15) was the Birmingham parish church of St Philip, which became a cathedral in 1905. This was the first English cathedral to be built with no obvious trace of Gothic in the design. Nevertheless, its main external feature, the great west tower, is a suggestive exercise in the English vernacular. The young architect, Thomas Archer, had travelled a good deal abroad, as well as studying the work of Wren, Vanbrugh and Hawksmoor, and seems to have been given a fairly free hand in presenting his own interpretation of English Baroque. His great tower has three stages. The ground floor is characterized by a generous rounded west window, with massive rounded pediment on coupled pilasters. This surges into a second storey where the coupled pilasters are echoed in Baroque-style corner buttresses, the bell-stage windows being recessed with concave pediments. The buttresses effectively turn the second stage into an octagon, and this is repeated in the top storey, where giant scrolled brackets lead the eye to the dome and cupola. If we compare this eighteenth-century tower with the sixteenth-century tower in Derby, we see how the Gothic love and understanding of the great tower is successfully translated into a completely different mode of architectural expression.

The interior is less successful, for it was Archer's first big commission and he did not dare leave out a gallery, which screens the aisle-windows. There were also important modifications to the chancel in the nineteenth century, adding a sumptuousness not to be found in the nave; this echoed the procedure in the late twelfth and thirteenth centuries, and may be justified in itself, but it was not part of Archer's design. His note of splendour, like Gibbs's, was struck by the sumptuous choir-screens, perhaps by Tijou, perhaps by Bakewell or perhaps by one of their pupils – at all events, excellent. Where the nineteenth century made an undeniable contribution was in the glass. With very few exceptions, eighteenth-century architects, patrons and ecclesiastics hated coloured glass: indeed, it was in the eighteenth century, not the sixteenth or seventeenth, that Salisbury Cathedral, for instance, lost most of its fine medieval glass. Archer did not ask for coloured glass. But in the nineteenth century Edward Burne-Jones designed and William Morris made it: behind the altar are the Nativity,

OPPOSITE Birmingham Cathedral from the north west.

245

Crucifixion and Ascension, of 1884–7; and in the west tower the Last Judgement of 1897 – Burne-Jones at his most powerful and direct, with strong, glowing colours. These windows give this entirely non-Gothic cathedral a high seriousness and devotional intensity which it cannot have possessed before.

This brings us to an important point, absolutely central to the problem of modern cathedral architecure. Why does Birmingham Cathedral need the Burne-Jones windows? Does any non-Gothic architecture lack the mystic or spiritual element without which cathedral devotion is incomplete? Is there, in fact, a natural or organic mode of cathedral architecture, and is that mode necessarily Gothic in some form? There are the questions which have dominated cathedral architecture for the last 200 years, and to which we must now turn.

10
The Gothic Revival
and Modernism

The notion of architectural 'style' was an Italian sixteenth-century conception. Once it was coined, the idea of styles – and conflicts between styles – became the common currency of architectural debate. Almost inevitably, Gothic (it was also called 'Barbarous', 'Germanic' and 'Northern') tended to be identified with universalist Christianity. Even in Italy, the home of the Renaissance, the notion that it was the 'right' mode of ecclesiastical architecture had its defenders. In the sixteenth century, major Italian artists designed Gothic façades for important churches, and even the most radical exponents of the Baroque owed something to Gothic. A great national debate raged over the unfinished Gothic cathedral of Milan, and the style of its west façade. Should it be Gothic? Baroque? A compromise? The argument lasted throughout the seventeenth and eighteenth centuries, despite eirenic interventions by the Vatican; and it took Napoleon himself to terminate it. In Germany, the debate centred around the unfinished cathedral of Cologne, with Gothic slowly assuming the colours of patriotism and the struggle against France: Gothic stood for the unity of Fatherland, Religion and Art, and to complete the great church at Cologne in the Gothic style was to build a memorial to the War of Liberation.

In Britain, Gothic never died. In the eighteenth century it was generally avoided for important ecclesiastical and secular projects. But in the half-century 1725–75, at least five provincial churches were built in the Gothic style (not counting Horace Walpole's Strawberry Hill, from 1750 onwards). In 1742 Batty Langley published his *Gothic Architecture Improv'd by Rules and Proportions in Many Good Designs*, a manual for architects and builders; and ten years later came William Halfpenny's *Rural Architecture in the Gothic Taste*. The return to Gothic at an intellectual level received an enormous impulse from the Romantic movement in poetry and painting, to whose exponents irregularity, asymmetry and wildness – characteristics attributed to Gothic by the contemptuous classicists – were terms of approbation. Both Wordsworth and Constable believed that nature unadorned was in some sense a form of religion: hence the theme of Wordsworth's poem 'Devotional Incitements', and Constable's practice of painting Salisbury Cathedral emerging from its trees. The return to nature almost inevitably led to a Gothic bias because Gothic was 'organic'. In 1806, John Claudius Loudon, in his *A Treatise on Forming, Improving and Managing Country Residences*, first put forward the notion that a building should be like an animal or vegetable organization, in its unity, integration and 'natural' growth. The only style which fitted this necessity, and was therefore universalist in its scope, was Gothic.

Hence, at the end of the eighteenth century, fashionable taste 'rediscovered' the Gothic cathedrals. In the decade 1795–1805 Turner did a set of Salisbury for Sir Richard Colt Hoare. In 1801 an industrious publisher, John Britton, who travelled about England on foot, published the first in his great series *The Architectural Antiquities of Great Britain*, the fifth volume of which (1827), entitled *A Chronological History and Graphic Illustrations of Christian Architecture in England*, was the first attempt to produce a coherent account of English Gothic and an irresistible architectural textbook. He accompanied this with his best-selling series, *The Cathedral Antiquities of England*, beginning with Salisbury (1814).

The rediscovery of Gothic coincided with the work of architectural theorists

OVERLEAF Sheffield Cathedral, showing modern additions in 'free Gothic'.

like R. Payne Knight and Uvedale Price, who linked architectural forms with human emotions and metaphysical concepts, rather as Hugh of St Victor had created the theory of light which helped to inspire the first Gothic churches in the twelfth century. Price's book, *Architecture and Building* (1798) was much read among young romantics, not least those of a religious bent. Whereas at Oxford the romantic religious revival expressed itself in doctrine, at Cambridge the stress was on ecclesiology. In 1839 two young Gothicists, J. M. Neale and Benjamin Webb, formed the Cambridge Camden Society for the study of ecclesiastical art. Two years later they began to publish a monthly journal, *The Ecclesiologist*, one of the very earliest practical journals of architecture, and a whole series of manuals for church architects, decorators and liturgists. Their influence was immense. During the eighteenth century, ceremonies at the altar in Anglican churches had almost ceased, the chancel had lost its central importance and was often used as a vestry. What the new ecclesiologists did was to bring back the chancel as the heart of the church, emphasizing the line of demarcation between the sanctified clergy and their mysteries, and the ordinary layfolk, by the restoration of altar rails.

Of course some clerics were outraged by this 'return to Romanism', just as they were appalled by the Tractarian movement in doctrine taking place at Oxford under Keble and Newman. In 1843, the new Bishop of Manchester visited a church remodelled on Ecclesiological Society lines and 'gave an exhibition of maniacal fury. He cast down cushions and altar-cloths; he screwed off ornaments and dashed them onto the pavement . . . and expressed a wish that the boys might break the stained-glass windows in the church.'

The younger clergy, and a growing number of bishops, reacted with more enthusiasm, however. The 'Cambridge Movement' was in the spirit of the age. One of Britton's collaborators, A. C. Pugin, produced a practical Gothic manual. After his death, it was carried on by his son, Augustus Welby Pugin, who became a convert not only to Roman Catholicism but to the notion that the Gothic was the only possible architecture for a true Christian church. He set out his ideology in a series of brilliantly-illustrated books, *Contrasts, The True Principles of Pointed Christian Architecture* and *An Apology for the Revival of Christian Architecture in England*, which, between 1836 and 1843, sold in enormous numbers and effectively completed the Gothic conquest of the English educated classes. By 1845 the Gothic revival was everywhere triumphant.

What effect did this gigantic shift in taste have on British cathedral architecture? We must distinguish between two aspects: the restoration of old Cathedrals, and the building of new ones. Restoration work, of course, began long before the Gothic Revival. Indeed, we ought to date it from the Restoration of the Monarchy in 1660, when all cathedral chapters spent large sums (even Rochester managed £13,000). Some of this early work was very well done, the 1699 campaign at Ely being an example; but Hereford, on the other hand, suffered more damage from its bishops than from the Civil War. It was Bishop Egerton who pulled down the chapels of St Catherine and Mary Magdalen in 1737, on the grounds that they were 'ruinous and useless', and it was ill-judged repair work at Hereford which led to the collapse of the west tower in 1786. At Durham, as I have already noted, the stone-scraping in the 1770s did irreparable damage to the decorative work on the exterior. We do not know much about routine restoration in the seventeenth and eighteenth centuries, but much of it was still going on in the mid-nineteenth century without benefit of expert advice, good or bad. Mr Sandall, the mid-nineteenth-century master-mason at Lincoln, testified in 1866: 'The way we now scrape to clean [the stone] was carried out before I had anything to do to the cathedral. When I came as a journeyman in 1846 and as master-mason in 1851, I was ordered to carry on the restoration as previously done, to wash and scrape away the dirt from the sound stone, cut away the bad and insert new stone, and to point the joints.' This process had been going on, largely unsupervised, for 200 years.

Some eighteenth-century work was excellent. Thus, from 1731–8, York was provided with a magnificent new pavement throughout, to a design by Lord Burlington and William Kent. Not all Kent's ideas were sensible, however: at Gloucester he proposed to flute the columns, as at Durham. At Winchester, Peterborough, Gloucester and Canterbury, much eighteenth-century woodwork was inserted, but this has since been removed. Extensive eighteenth-century work at Worcester has also been corrected. At Norwich, St Albans, Southwell, Ripon, Rochester and Peterborough, towers were repaired. At Newcastle in 1783–7 there was a wholesale clearance of pulpits and screens, pews, stalls, funerary monuments and brasses, which were destroyed or sold for scrap.

Of the eighteenth-century restorers, James Essex (1722–84) and James Wyatt (1746–1813) were the most important. Essex saved the West Front at Ely, which was leaning out of perpendicular (he was not allowed to destroy the porch), and he did an extensive job at Lincoln. He was much less ruthless than the deans and chapters who employed him, and was the first practising architect who mastered Gothic detail. Wyatt was attacked as 'The Destroyer' even in his own day, and generally abused then and since. At Hereford, where he had virtually to invent a new west end, following the fall of the west tower in 1786, he was attacked by Pugin: 'I rush to the cathedral; but horror; dismay! the villain Wyatt had been there, the West Front was his! Need I say more? No! All that is vile, cunning and rascally is included in the term Wyatt.' (Wyatt's West Front was replaced by another in 1908, designed by Oldrid Scott.) Wyatt also did extensive work at poor, battered Lichfield, and was again abused by Pugin: 'Yes, this monster of architectural depravity – this pest of cathedral architecture – has been here.'

However, we must be very careful, in asssessing Wyatt's work, to ascertain whether he was acting from his own notions or on the express commands of the deans and chapters. At Salisbury, for instance, where the detached belfry, two Norman porches, much old glass, the Hungerford and Beauchamp chapels, the reredos and many old tombs were demolished, he seems merely to have carried out the orders of the authorities. At Durham, too, the decision to demolish the Galilee Chapel had been taken before Wyatt even arrived, and he was instrumental in saving it. The destruction of the Norman Chapter House in 1795 was undoubtedly the work of the dean. Later, when taste changed, the clergy found it convenient to blame Wyatt. Indeed he is usually held responsible for the external scraping, completed before he had ever set eyes on the building. The historian must face the melancholy fact that clergymen do not always tell the strict truth; and it is astonishing how often, in cathedral handbooks, 'Cromwell's soldiers' or 'heavy-handed restorers' are now held guilty of vandalism which was, in fact, proposed, debated and approved in the cathedral's own chapter house.

In one respect the eighteenth-century restorers set a fashion which is still predominant: they began the demolition of the innumerable interior screens in British cathedrals, and prepared the way for the modern 'unbroken vista' we get at Salisbury, Worcester or Lichfield, for example, and to some extent at all

English cathedrals except Canterbury, Winchester and Exeter. So strong is the vista fashion that most modern cathedrals, even when designed in the Gothic mode, as at Truro, Liverpool and Guildford, omit the obstruction of a high bishop's choir, and permit an end-to-end view.

In most other respects, however, attempts have been made to erase or rectify the work of the eighteenth-century restorers. Some of them of course did not like Gothic at all. John Nash, who restored St Davids (which was later re-done by Scott) admitted: 'I hate this Gothic style. One window costs more trouble in designing than two houses ought to do.' And even when they liked Gothic, they tended to be eclectic, capricious and 'unhistorical'. The nineteenth-century ecclesiological movement was much more learned and systematic in its approach, but also more ideological and doctrinaire. Thus, whereas Pugin admired most forms of Gothic, including Perpendicular, the strict Anglican ecclesiologists regarded Perpendicular as decadent, worldly and mechanical. For them, 'Decorated' was the ideal style: the third edition of the most influential of their practical handbooks, *A Few Words to Church Builders* (1844), recommended that Decorated be used everywhere, especially in preference to Perpendicular, which 'employed meretricious ornaments' and 'symbolized worldly pomp instead of the Catholick faith.' As a result, some of the best nineteenth-century restorers replaced Perpendicular windows with Decorated ones, undoing, as they thought, the vandalism of the fifteenth and early sixteenth century. Was this not an act of nineteenth-century vandalism? That was certainly the prevailing view of British art historians until quite recently. So Kenneth Clark writes in *The Gothic Revival* (1928): 'It would be interesting to know if the Camden Society destroyed as much medieval architecture as Cromwell. If not, it was for lack of funds.' Again, Martin Briggs, in *Goths and Vandals* (1952) argues that the 1844 handbook 'led to most of Sir Gilbert Scott's acts of "vandalism"'. Most cathedral guides and the Pevsner *Buildings of England* series usually deal mercilessly with the nineteenth-century restorers, especially Scott himself.

George Gilbert Scott (1811-78) was a fanatically industrious man with a vast practice and many gifted pupils, including G.E. Street and G.F. Bodley, to say nothing of his sons John Oldrid and George Gilbert Scott Jr.* He made his name as an efficient and prolific designer of quasi-Elizabethan workhouses, of which he produced fifty-three at an average cost of £5,000. His first ecclesiastical commission was at Ely, where the dean was anxious to introduce a touch of Amiens in his 'dull' cathedral. Thereafter, of the twenty-six cathedrals of the Old and New Foundations, only St Paul's, Carlisle and Llandaff were untouched by Scott. At Bristol his advice was asked but not taken; at Norwich his work was confined to writing a report; and at Wells he worked with another restorer, Ferry. All he did at Lincoln and York was to design furnishings; but he did substantial work at Ely (1847), Hereford (1855), Peterborough (1855), Lichfield (1856), Durham (1859), Salisbury (1859), Chichester (1861), Worcester (1863), Gloucester (1864), St Davids (1864), Bangor (1866), Chester (1868), St Asaph (1869), Exeter (1870), Oxford (1870), Rochester (1871), Winchester (1875), Canterbury (1877), and at St Albans and Westminster at various times.

His work, therefore, was prodigious, and there can be no doubt that he knew more about the building history and the state of the fabric of English and Welsh cathedrals than any other man in his lifetime; indeed, apart from Viollet-le-Duc, no other nineteenth-century architect equalled his knowledge of Gothic building methods. He was not an ideologue. He emphatically rejected the view of the

Victorian statuary on the exterior of Lichfield Cathedral, restored by George Gilbert Scott.

* To clarify matters, George Gilbert Scott (1811–78) begat George Gilbert Scott Jr. (1839–97), who begat Giles Gilbert Scott (1880–1960).

Cambridge ecclesiologists that the Decorated was the only 'pure' and 'true' Gothic (they even wanted to pull down most of Peterborough Cathedral), and he refused to follow them when they later switched to Early English, or 'First Pointed' as they called it, as the 'true' style. He rejected, too, Pugin's bigoted identification of Gothic with spirituality. In his *Remarks on Secular and Domestic Architecture, Present and Future*, he argued that the division between ecclesiastical and secular architecture was unnatural and should be ended; good Gothic could accommodate changed habits and improved means of construction – hence his magnificent design for St Pancras station. That he had a strong historical sense was indicated by his *A Plea for the Faithful Restoration of our Ancient Churches*, which he published as early as 1850, the beginning of scientific restoration. In 1862, he addressed the RIBA on the theme of 'The Conservation of Ancient Architectural Monuments and Remains', making the case for a historical and conservative approach. Right at the end of his life, attacked by William Morris, who had founded the Society for the Preservation of Ancient Buildings in 1877, he defended himself vigorously in his *Personal and Professional Recollections* (1879), which devotes a whole chapter to the anti-restoration movement. He claimed he was always a conservative restorer but he rejected the extremist position of doing nothing at all except to make safe. He did not minimize the damage:

> The country has been, and continues to be, actually devastated with destruction under the name of restoration. For years and years the vast majority of the churches to be restored have been committed to men who neither know nor care anything whatever about them, and out of whose hands they have emerged in a condition truly deplorable, stripped of almost everything which gave them interest or value; whilst it must be admitted that the best of us have been blameable, and that even our conservatism has been more or less destructive.

Scott admitted his own mistakes, which he blamed on 'bad judgement' and 'the urgent influence of clients' (ie, clergymen). He had a large number of assistants, some of whom he trusted too much. On the other hand, he is often blamed for earlier work (Hopkins's at Worcester, for instance, and Cottingham's at Hereford), which he had been brought in to retrieve. Jealousy of his great success (he left £130,000 at his death) was responsible for many of the attacks on him. His methods were, on the whole, sensible and served as the basis for twentieth-century restoration: stabilize the structure; replace stonework only when absolutely necessary; do not strip plaster from walls, and remove whitewash carefully; keep a careful watch for old painting; existing roofs to be kept, and repaired; re-use old screens; floors to be levelled and dried, but old slabs and tiles to be replaced; windows not to be altered back to match the originals, as they are part of building history.

These rules meant very high (and expensive) standards, and Scott's employers would not always allow him to stick to them. But his best work, at St Davids, Exeter, Salisbury and Chichester, was very careful and sound, based on massive historical knowledge, imaginatively applied. Examination of his work at Ely, Hereford, Lichfield, Peterborough, Gloucester and Ripon clears him from most of the charges levelled by his critics, then or since. His worst mistake was to yield to the pressure of the Dean at Rochester, and restore the east end perpendicular window to lancets; as against this, at Exeter he was responsible for retaining the choir-screen against 'immense opposition' from the Dean and others. He has also been attacked for his undoing of Wren's work on the north transept front at

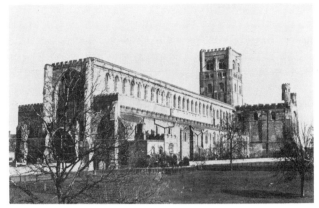

Westminster: the best answer to this is his *Gleanings from Westminster Abbey* (1862). His work on the Westminster Chapter House was a model.

St Albans Abbey from the south west, before and after the reconstruction of the west front by Lord Grimthorpe.

Many of the Morrisonians who went for Scott believed him responsible for the truly awesome mess at St Albans. Thereby they merely revealed their ignorance. The ruin at St Albans was the work of centuries, during most of which time it had been in the possession of the town, a notoriously corrupt borough. When, in mid-Victorian times, the idea was mooted of turning it into a cathedral for a see to be carved out of the sprawling London diocese it was in an appalling mess. There was a right of way through the nave, the rest of the church being closed except for services; earth was up to the sills of the windows in the Lady Chapel, the two porches were bricked up, the south wall of the nave was out of perpendicular, the western bays of the nave windowless, and the west end itself in ruins. Scott reported that it would cost at least £46,000 to provide a bare restoration. No one in the church had or would provide the money, and St Albans itself was only too glad to accept the offer of Lord Grimthorpe, a millionaire railway director and enthusiastic church layman, who had been chancellor of the York diocese for twenty years.

Grimthorpe's main object was to get the great abbey back into working order as a centre of cathedral worship, and in this he succeeded brilliantly, spending £140,000 of his own money on it, and laying down the tradition of activism which is still alive today – St Albans is, without doubt, the 'busiest' of Anglican cathedrals. But Grimthorpe was also an amateur architect and restorer, and after Scott's death he rebuilt the West Front to his own design. It is poorly conceived and quite unhistorical.

Morris's censure of Scott was thus based on ignorance; indeed, at Tewkesbury, which provided the immediate pretext for the attack, Scott's assignment was mainly to remove post-medieval additions, and it is clear that Morris had not troubled to inform himself of what was happening there, let alone investigated the details of Scott's career as a restorer or his principles and methods of work. Another ill-informed critic was Ruskin. In 1873–4, when Scott was President of the RIBA, Ruskin was awarded its Royal Gold Medal; he refused to accept it on the grounds that architects were vandals and their president the worst of the lot. Yet Ruskin, who understood little about medieval architecture, and carried the 'organic' theory to the point where he believed that the decay of stone was a sign of the 'life' of a building, was opposed to restoration as such, preferring that a building should collapse in ruins rather than that new stone be used.

Other anti-restorers took this view. The antiquarian Charles Boutell wrote in

1871: 'Rather than that the restorers, with ample means and unrestricted powers, should work their will on the abbey church of St Albans, let it share the fate of Kirkstall, of Fountains, and Netley and Tintern, and their sister ruins.' Some of Morris's supporters agreed with him. None of the leading men in the Society for the Protection of Ancient Buildings were churchmen, or concerned with the needs of living congregations. As the Dean of Canterbury put it: 'Mr Morris probably looks upon our cathedral as a place of antiquarian research or for budding architects to learn their art in. We need it for the daily worship of God.' It was claimed that a member of the SPAB, down to 'inspect' the restoration work at Exeter, urinated near the altar screen which Scott fought so hard to preserve. Be that as it may, the society was quite ineffective until it accepted the principle of restoration and, in consultation with the authorities, began to work out practical rules about how it could best be done. In all essentials, these followed Scott's own precepts. As he indignantly pointed out, he had been practising them for more than thirty years before Morris even interested himself in the subject, and often in the face of much philistine hostility. He has a much better case than Morris and the SPAB to be considered the father of modern restoration, and it is unfortunate that so many guide-books fail to do him justice.

The case of St Albans showed that it was not just a matter of restoring old cathedrals, but of providing new ones, to meet the demands of an ever-growing, half-Christianized population. In 1861, the president of the Ecclesiological Society, A.J.B. Beresford-Hope, wrote an important book called *The English Cathedral in the Nineteenth Century*. For the vast new urban populations, he pleaded for large, spatially-unified churches, a plea to which architects like Pearson, who specialized in big parochial churches, responded. But Beresford-Hope did not think the parish system alone was enough to evangelize the urban masses. 'Every town above a certain cypher of population', he wrote, 'ought to have in it one head clergyman, who should preside over the evangelization of the whole community. There is a name 1,800 years old for such a head clergyman, and it stands to reason he had better use it, and be entitled bishop.... The religious institution which will undoubtedly grow out of rational and business-like endeavours to evangelize large populations, whether it is called so or not, will virtually be a cathedral, and it had therefore best be moulded openly and honestly into a cathedral shape.'

At the time Beresford-Hope wrote, his plan had already been adopted in Manchester, where in 1848 the collegiate church of St Mary, which I have already described, was raised to cathedral rank. I have also glanced at two other upgraded parish churches, Birmingham, which became a cathedral in 1905, and Derby (1927). St Albans began to function as a cathedral in 1877. Bury St Edmunds was also raised to cathedral rank, though not until 1914; but here the old abbey had virtually ceased to exist even as a ruin. Only its Norman gateway still stood, and this was turned into the cathedral bell-tower; St James, the upgraded parish church, has no tower, but it boasts a spectacular Perpendicular nave, designed by John Wastell, who built the splendid Angel Tower at Canterbury and worked on the vaults of King's College Chapel, Cambridge. Scott restored the chancels in the 1860s, and rebuilt the marvellous hammerbeam roof, now magnificently painted and gilded. He also designed the pulpit and the chancel mosaic. Further colour is added by Flemish stained-glass of the early sixteenth century, and some excellent glass by leading nineteenth-century designers, Clayton & Bell, Kempe and Hardman.

The nave of Bury St Edmunds Cathedral, facing east.

The imperial-crown spire of Newcastle Cathedral, seen from the castle.

At Newcastle-on-Tyne, St Nicholas was raised to a cathedral in 1882, and deserved to be. It is fundamentally of the late fourteenth, early fifteenth century, with Norman vestiges, but it is nearly 250 feet long and, at the crossing, the tall piers give a real sense of cathedral scale. Distinguished, too, is its tall west tower, with its imperial crown spire, which reaches up to close on 200 feet. It is the only crown of its type in England, and earlier than the ones on St Giles, Edinburgh, and King's College, Aberdeen. The church also has an elegant Palladian library (1736) and some good, cathedral-like tombs.

Wakefield, too, raised up in 1888, is also in the cathedral class by virtue of its dimensions. Its exterior is entirely Perpendicular and its magnificent spire of 1420, which is 247 feet high, is easily the highest in Yorkshire. Inside, it is a bewildering mixture from the twelfth to the fifteenth century. The south front had been rebuilt in 1724, much aimless work had been carried out inside, then and later, and in the years 1858–74 Scott had patiently to undo the worst work of his predecessors and sort out the muddle. It now looks right, and it also looks like a cathedral within, for in 1904 J.L. Pearson added transepts and a new choir and retrochoir. He had to work within a very restricted space, but he contrived to combine a sumptuous reredos with a simplified version of the forest-glade effect we have examined at Wells and Lincoln.

The spire of Wakefield Cathedral, the highest in Yorkshire.

Chelmsford, raised up in 1913, is also full of interest, though to the casual eye it does not look like a cathedral. Here is another mainly fifteenth-century big parish church, with a superb south porch and a dignified tower with powerful buttresses. But a great deal of it is post-medieval: a lantern-spire of 1749, a north aisle and transept of 1873, and major additions at the east end and elsewhere, from 1878 to the 1920s. The interior, too, was much altered at the very beginning of the nineteenth century. However, the detail is nearly all very good of its kind, and the church is already with time beginning to acquire a more homogenous look.

Sir Charles Nicholson, who designed the new east end at Chelmsford, also took on the extension work at the church of St Peter and Paul at Sheffield, when it was made a cathedral in 1914. Again, it is basically Perpendicular, with a big crocketted crossing-spire. Its Shrewsbury Chapel (1530), where lie some of the great earls (including Bess of Hardwick's harried husband) gives it distinction, as does Nicholson's Chapel of the Holy Spirit, a notable and noble Gothic survivor in the age of the Bauhaus. Bradford, which became a cathedral five years later, is also modern Gothic added to Perpendicular (the powerful millstone grit west tower is 1493–1508). Sir Edward Maufe's Song Room was joined to the tower in the 1950s, and a good deal of work at the east end, including a lady chapel, was not finished until the mid-1960s. The real treasure of the church, however, is the dazzling stained-glass of the 1860s in the chancel – Burne-Jones in his best form, and good work by Rossetti.

Chelmsford Cathedral.

Of the three cathedrals created in 1926–7, Leicester's St Martin is the simplest to describe, though it is an uneasy mixture of styles. It looks Victorian, even if its history goes back to the twelfth century. The arcades are thirteenth-century, as one might guess; and there is quite a lot of Perpendicular work; but the spire on the tall crossing tower is the work of Raphael Brandon in the 1860s; the north aisle is by G.E. Street, the south aisle by Pearson, the south porch by G.F. Bodley, and the north porch and the chancel chapels are also Victorian. Blackburn is even more confusing: a pre–Victorian Gothic revival church of 1820–6 by John Palmer, reconstructed by Thomas Rickman after a fire in the 1830s. Beginning in

The much-restored
Cathedral of St Thomas at
Portsmouth.

The new spire of Blackburn
Cathedral.

1926, it underwent a process of modernization, cathedralizing and redesigning in what was termed 'simplified Gothic', a process, with interruptions, which culminated in the placing over the crossing of a corona with pinnacles and long spire (by Lawrence King) in 1961.

St Thomas's at Portsmouth is more complicated still. It was originally collegiate and Transitional; then a parish church in the Decorated period. It was badly damaged in the Civil War, and had its nave rebuilt in a provincial version of Wren. Its tower dates from the 1780s, there were several restorations in the nineteenth century, and in the twentieth century it has been considerably altered and enlarged, in styles varying from Sir Charles Nicholson's painstaking Thirties Gothic to 1960s reinforced concrete, which already looks unfashionable. Very few cathedrals can have had such a weird building history. It is worth visiting as a mere curiosity – as well as for important Gothic survivals, and an exquisite Virgin and Child plaque by Andrea della Robbia.

Blackburn and Portsmouth illustrate vividly the problems which arise when unsuitable existing churches are transformed into cathedrals by piecemeal changes. Lack of the hardihood to demolish and build afresh can be a fatal virtue (or weakness). The real charge to be brought against the Victorians is not that they restored cathedrals too heavily; it is that they devoted too little of their boundless energy and skill to building entirely new ones.

Indeed, the only Anglican cathedral to be built in England during the Gothic revival – the first cathedral since St Paul's – was at Truro. The design posed many problems, for the new diocese was poor and the site itself restricted. When the commission went to John Loughborough Pearson RA, he must have felt the eyes of the architectural world were on him. He had started as a follower of Pugin in the 1840s and had later been influenced by the more specific and accurate Gothicism of Scott. More than any other architect he had responded to Beresford-Hope's plea for congregational churches. Yet his real speciality was vaulting, and he took a manifest delight in the technicalities of Gothic. What he built for the Cornishmen, therefore, was not a congregational hall church

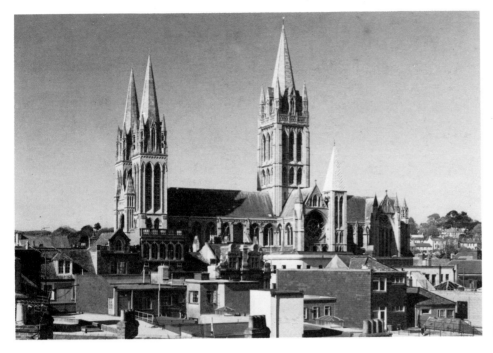

Truro Cathedral, designed in 1880 by John Loughborough Pearson RA.

(his St Augustine's, Kilburn, and St John's, Red Lion Square, were functional in this sense), but the brilliant evocation of the ideal Gothic cathedral.

Pearson was obliged by his mandate to incorporate the Perpendicular remains of the old Truro church of St Mary. This inspired him to a complex exercise in Gothic historianism – to trace the evolution of Gothic architecture in England. Thus the crypt moves from Norman to Early English; the nave is mainstream Early English on the plain side; the choir and the east end are Decorated. The St Mary element supplies the Perpendicular. The concept has an academic flavour, and Pearson has been accused of academicism in this work. In fact it is a most ingenious piece of planning. Pearson had only 300 feet of length to work with; but both from outside, where the roof ridge is continuous, and from the inside, where the vista is quite unencumbered, the cathedral looks much longer than it actually is. On the exterior, the three slim and fairly plain towers, their buttresses and pinnacles echoed in the buttress-and-pinnacle system of two sets of transepts and the east end, give an overwhelming sense of thrusting verticality. Hence, though the nave, with a breadth of sixty-five feet, has a height to the crown of its vault of only seventy feet, and the spires which crown the towers are stocky, the cathedral looks surprisingly tall as well. It is true that Pearson could have given Truro tall, slender spires, as he did at his excellent church of Dalton Holme in the East Riding. But this would have meant doing the same for the ten echoing pinnacles, and the effect, though spectacular, would have come close to mannerism and absurdity. As it is, Truro is beyond question a prodigy-church: a gigantic cathedral presented in miniature. From a distance it looks vast; and even close up it retains the peculiar cathedral dignity one finds at, for example, Lincoln, which I think inspired it. Inside, these optical illusions cannot of course be maintained in full; but it never loses its confident sense of the grand manner, not least because Pearson insisted on vaulting it throughout, and doing so with great care and solidity.

Where Pearson erred was in underestimating the ferocity of Cornwall's winds. He rightly built the cathedral in hard granite – one reason why it looks bigger

than it is – but he thought he could get away with creamy Bath stone for the dressing and string-courses. They have worn badly, and the contrast with the granite is unfortunate. Inside, however, there are no errors of judgement or taste, and the stained-glass, by Clayton & Bell, is late-Victorian artistry at its best.

If, however, British architects of the nineteenth century were given only one opportunity in England to design churches in the Anglican cathedral manner, they had plenty of opportunities elsewhere, notably in the British Empire. There was also Scotland, where the Episcopalian Church commissioned and built cathedrals at Aberdeen (St Andrew's), Glasgow (St Mary's), Inverness (St Mary's) – a handsome and vigorous piece of work, in rose-coloured stone from Conon, which has the familiar medieval note of an octagonal Chapter House – Dundee (St Paul's) and Perth (St Ninian's). Sir George Gilbert Scott was involved in two of these, at Glasgow and Dundee, but it was not until the 1870s, when Pearson was designing Truro, that a competition for a vast new Episcopalian cathedral at Edinburgh, made possible by a generous endowment, gave him the chance to produce his perfect Gothic cathedral.

The result is St Mary's, Edinburgh. It was built mainly in the 1870s and 1880s, but with a square-and-polygonal Chapter House of 1890 and its two western spires added in 1919. Scott genuflected to Scottish history and sentiment to the extent of incorporating details from ruined Elgin and Jedburgh in the west door, echoing Dunblane in the triforium, and Coldingham Priory in the choir clerestory. But, in general, this huge church, inside and out, is a compilation of what he believed to be the best and truest features of Gothic, during its finest period in the second half of the thirteenth century. He poured into it the experience, knowledge and enthusiasm of a lifetime spend in restoring Gothic to vigorous life.

That, indeed, is the keynote of this massive church: vigour. The West Front ripples with muscles for Scott obtains the needful depth-effect with strong corner-buttressing of the towers and deeply recessed lancets, their powerful overhead arches echoed in the gabling of the centrepiece and the great overhang of the west door. Seen from in front the three bulky spires get into menacing formation and exert a masculine grandeur in total contrast to the slender femininity which is the impact of the similar arrangement at Lichfield. Scott took enormous trouble over his huge crossing tower and its spire, which weighs 6,000 tons. The dexterity with which he transforms the square of the first storey into the dramatic octagon belfry, with the corner buttresses turning into pinnacles, and then all eight features echoed in the aedicules of the octagonal spire, is masterful. This is, indeed, architecture in the grand manner; and though Scott does not aim at any transfixing effect in the interior – he is content to let the perfect double-bay design and pure vaults, swelling into a great controlled space at the crossing, speak for themselves – he provides a number of great external vistas, so that the 300-foot stone Gothic finger, which is admonitory rather than exalting, threatens to dominate the Georgian amoralism of the new town. From the south-east, the real size of the central finger becomes unmistakable: it is using the same architectural syntax as Salisbury, but the voice is stronger, rougher and more direct. When St Mary's is viewed from the east, looking up Melville Street, not only the strength, but the verticality of the massive church is fully displayed: the central spire dominates its western brothers in a tremendous triangle of forces, with the strict verticals of the east end lancets thrusting upwards with controlled power. One has the feeling of an intercontinental rocket at the moment of take-off, with

OPPOSITE The West Front of St Mary's Cathedral, Edinburgh, by Sir George Gilbert Scott.

weight and power in momentary equilibrium. These east end vistas are particularly illuminating, for they allow pointed contrasts with the enframing Georgian civility of the street architecture; they make it clear why the classicists found the Gothic savage. In some moods it is, and at St Mary's, Scott, who was undoubtedly a man of fierce personal faith, of which his art was only one facet, allowed himself an uncompromising statement of totalitarian Christianity.

Of the other major Victorian architects, William Burges's great cathedral at Cork lies outside the scope of this book, as does his brilliant winning design for the cathedral at Lille, which was never built. William Butterfield, however, was lucky in that the Earl of Glasgow provided funds for his collegiate church at Millport, on the island of Great Cumbrae, which in 1876 was consecrated as the Cathedral of Argyll and the Isles. Butterfield, like Scott, was a man of intense faith, but his cathedral is not, like Scott's, a manifesto of Gothic ideology, but rather a celebration of the collegiate process. In its clustering of roofs (a device he learnt from Pugin), his use of trees and hill contours, and above all his employment of local island stone, with the craggy mountains of Arran as a consciously-employed background and skyline, it is a deliberate reminder of the Celtic origins of British Christianity, set on the rim of the known world. The scheme is very effective, partly because the craftsmanship is superb throughout and partly because Butterfield designed the community enclave as a unity – the cathedral is only a part of the roof-scenery, for instance. But it is not what we normally understand by cathedral architecture.

The Roman Catholic architects of nineteenth-century Britain were in one respect more fortunate than their Anglican brethren. In searching for an architectural and spiritual synthesis, they were in no way inhibited by doctrinal limitations, and they did not have to combat or conform to anti-ritualist pressure-groups. Pugin, who became a Catholic at the very threshold of his career, was able to say without qualification: 'I feel perfectly convinced that the Roman Catholic church is the only true one, and the only one in which the grand and the sublime style of church architecture can ever be restored.' Then, too, the Catholics were working on a *tabula rasa*. Much as they might regret the passing of what they saw as their medieval heritage into Anglican hands, they had the opportunity which confronted the Normans in 1066 – to create an entirely new set of cathedrals on virgin sites.

Unfortunately there was a drawback: money. In A.W. Pugin, the Catholics had an architect whose enthusiasm and ingenuity rivalled and in some ways surpassed even Scott's, and who had a spark of pure genius which Scott's earthbound frame did not harbour. But Pugin, by his totalitarian approach to design, which insisted that every element of furnishing as well as every detail of a grand design should conform to the highest standards of craftsmanship, was by his nature and creed an expensive architect. Only on one occasion, at St Giles, Cheadle, the finest nineteenth-century church in England, was he given the money to realize his vision in full and in depth. Pugin designed, or was a determining influence, in six churches which are now cathedrals: St Chad's, Birmingham (1839), St George's, Southwark (1840), St Barnabas, Nottingham (1842), St Mary and St Thomas, Northampton (1844), St Mary, Newcastle-on-Tyne (1844) and Our Lady of Help, Shrewsbury (1851–6). But all these cathedrals had to be built cheaply, and in most of them he was under pressure from the bishops to get the fabric completed as fast as possible.

At Birmingham, Pugin had just enough money for a big church, but not an elaborate one, and he was under orders to get it up in two years. It is therefore of mass-produced brick, and in the circumstances the design is a striking success. Outside, it has the nervous and strident spikiness of some of the best red-brick Gothic of the Baltic shore, the steep roofscapes providing shocks and tingling excitement from all points of the compass. Inside, he has spectacular hallchurch effects, an enormous room which achieves all the practical aims of modern Catholic round-churches without any of the ugliness and vulgarity – indeed, Pugin's tall and slender columns, which make the buildings a church rather than an arena, seem to emphasize the space rather than limit it – the true touch of a master-architect.

At Southwark, Pugin was allowed only £20,000 for the cathedral (for comparison, William Butterfield's parish church of All Saints, Margaret Street, cost more than £70,000). The concept is noble all the same, but what financial stringency failed to achieve was accomplished by Nazi bombs and the subsequent cheap rebuilding – the ruin of a vision. Externally the church is now a mere negation; internally, the sense of space and light, the sensitive yet confident carvings and mouldings or arches, pillars and window-tracery, are all that remain to testify to Pugin's wealth of ideas.

Of Pugin's other cathedrals, Nottingham, a cruciform building in Early English, with an 150-foot crossing-steeple, is the best. It has prominent transepts, a square east end (but with chapels and ambulatory) and looks a cathedral all over. Here, Pugin had just enough money to design the altars and furnishing himself, and even to put in seventy-six stained-glass windows, so some elements of the concentrated but ubiquitous richness he sought are there – but not enough. At Newcastle, the external effect is very fine, though the 220-foot spire (by J.A. Hansom), a sharp needle with spiky spirelets, is not the one Pugin designed. But the big gables and windows of both fronts, in restrained Decorative, work beautifully; inside, the atmosphere is austere. At Northampton, Pugin merely designed a small church, later enlarged by his son, and largely rebuilt after the Second World War. It cannot be counted as a Pugin cathedral concept. On the other hand, Shrewsbury, though merely suggested by him (his son did the actual design), is a brilliant exercise in demonstrating how, even without a tower, a tall nave with well-conceived gables can create an astonishing effect of soaring.

When Pugin died in 1851, Catholic architecture was left without a galvanic figure until the emergence of Scott's brilliant Catholic grandson, Giles Gilbert, but they continued to build at great speed. Cathedrals went up at Wrexham, at Plymouth and at Middlesbrough, where Goldie & Child produced a long, Wight-bay church which looks impressive even without a tower. At Salford, a complex design by Weightman & Hadfield unites an enormous steeple modelled on Newark, a choir derived from Selby and a nave reminiscent of Howden – a combination which actually looks much more homogenous than it sounds. At Lancaster, E. G. Paley designed a fine, high nave and an enormous, 250-foot spire. At Arundel, Hansom, using ample funds (which Pugin would have envied) provided by the Dukes of Norfolk, produced a glittering and glowing exercise in early French flamboyant, which fills modernists with contempt but delights and edifies simpler (and humbler) visitors. At Leeds there is a modest but well-designed and well-built church in the simplified and scaled-down Gothic of the Edwardian era, a true period piece; and in Portsmouth a slightly earlier but much more ambitious attempt was made to render the *c.*1300 English Decorated in dark red brick, not unsuccessfully.

The interior of
Giles Gilbert Scott's
cathedral at Oban.

By the time Portsmouth was finished in 1906, Giles Gilbert Scott was already active, and to him went the commission for the last (1931–51) of the small Catholic cathedrals: Oban. This is a distinguished piece of architecture, which ought to be more widely known. Like Truro, it is of granite (grey to pink); like Truro, it is small but looks far bigger than it is. It is right on the edge of the sea, and leans into the wind, its powerful west tower hammered down to the rocks, as it were, by twin west porches. Inside, everything is plain except the altar, a blaze of colour. It has tall simple columns and high simple rafters, which need a proper vault. But it looks spacious and cathedral-like – no one could ever mistake it for a mere parish church – and it powerfully conveys the message that it serves a scattered community of seafarers.

Meanwhile, the one really major work the Catholic Church had to offer in Britain, the new Westminster Cathedral, had been entrusted to J.F. Bentley (1839–1902), a Catholic convert and an expert designer of fonts, altarpieces and other church furnishing, who had never carried through anything approaching a commission on this scale. When Bentley got the job in 1894, it was strongly hinted that the Ultramontane spirit of English Catholicism wanted something Italian or

The choir of Westminster
Cathedral.

Byzantine, rather than Gothic, and he accordingly went on a tour which took him
to Ravenna and Venice, as well as other Italian art centres, but did not include
Istanbul, the obvious place. The ecclesiastics who commissioned Bentley were
obviously thinking in terms of a vast congregational church, where everyone has
a good view of the high altar; so much was stipulated. But instead of opting for a
Byzantine round church, they laid down the ancient English stipulation of a long
nave. Bentley might, therefore, have given them a Roman basilica, like St John
Lateran. Instead, he lined up four domes in a row, called the first three double
nave-bays and the last the chancel, and then built downwards to support them.
The church, then, is clearly designed from the inside outwards. Outside, to make
it interesting, Bentley added a 284-foot campanile tower to the north of the West
Front, which itself is composed of a giant Italianate porch with a spectacular
series of domed pinnacles, diminishing in size as they recess and climb upwards.
    Bentley's great strength was in detail, and in his feeling for surfaces, glitter and
natural polychrome. Throughout the cathedral he made the most striking use of
contrasting brick and white stone. On the West Front the device succeeds
brilliantly. The horizontal layers it provides bind the immense and complex

263

design firmly together, strike an effective contrast with the impressive verticality of the tower, and convey to the spectator, standing 100 yards to the west, an overwhelming impression of depth as well as height, for the layering brings home to him the fact that the front contains many planes. Now that the clutter to the west has been cleared away, the red-and-white piazza pavement completes the design, and provides us with a truly sensational architectural panorama, quite one of the sights of London.

The effect of the interior leaves one ambivalent. That Bentley achieves a sense of confined space on an enormous scale is undeniable; in this respect, the unusual grouping of the four linked domes works very well. But Bentley dealt in luxury effects, of dazzle and polychromy. He intended the entire interior to be faced with high-grade coloured marble up to a height of thirty feet, and above that to be decorated with a vast series of colour-and-gilt mosaic pictures. He designed the lighting, which is low, to be reflected and enhanced by these myriad surfaces, so that the echoing internal spaces would be shaped and made mysterious by innumerable pin-points of light, even in the most distant recesses. The marble and the mosaics, for the most part, do not exist; only in the Lady Chapel has the scheme, as Bentley planned it, been completed. Like Pugin before him, his aims have been frustrated by poverty. Instead we have an internal darkness indeed, but not the one Bentley planned: soft-edged, indeterminate, formless, almost foggy, the lights, both natural and electric, struggling through it mistily, while the walls, instead of regurgitating the radiance, swallow it greedily.

By the time that Bentley was commissioned to build Westminster, the belief that Gothic was the compulsory mode for cathedral architecture had already been abandoned, though the clergy still thought themselves compelled by custom and decorum to have a rectangular nave. But in the twentieth century, and especially since 1945, mandatory modes have disappeared completely, and with them the idea of ordered architecture of any kind. The designer's liberty has tended, increasingly, to be constrained solely by function and finance. Against this changed background, five major English cathedrals have arisen. Let us examine them, in didactic rather than chronological order, to see what they can teach us about the creation of a successful cathedral-church.

In 1918 the Perpendicular parish church of St Michael in Coventry was raised to cathedral rank. The choice was excellent, for St Michael's had an exceptional steeple, nearly 300 feet high, and its surface area, around 25,000 square feet, was very large for an ordinary town church. But of course it was not an ordinary town church; for those old enough to remember it before the war, it was one of those half-dozen grand aldermanic churches (Newark and Ludlow, for instance) which are, as Queen Elizabeth I said of St Mary Redcliffe in Bristol, so 'goodly' as to be 'fit for a cathedral'. In November 1940, it was largely destroyed by blast and burning. After the war there were three choices: to demolish it and build anew; to rebuild it in replica, with suitable changes to remedy the very real defects of the original; or to rebuild and modernize at the same time.

Our medieval predecessors would clearly have opted for the first choice. There is a good case for the second, as has been shown time and again in eastern Europe, especially Poland. The third was the course unsuccessfully urged by the 'Gothic' minority on Wren's St Paul's commission. But even they would not have dreamed of proposing what, in a mood of post-war sentimentality, was actually done: that is, to make secure and preserve the fragmentary ruin, including the spire, and to adjoin to it, as the bulk of the church, a rectangle conceived and adorned in the height of what was then (1951–60) considered fashionable taste. In strict liturgical parlance, the ruin is the forecourt or narthex of Sir Basil Spence's rectangle. But to the observer it seems part of the church as a whole; and, accustomed as he may be to the progressive, or even abrupt, changes of style which characterize virtually all our medieval cathedrals, he finds here two contrasting modes, so radically different in their aesthetic assumptions, that they will shout against and brawl with each other so long as they stand. No conceivable ingenuity on Sir Basil's part could have overcome this fundamental handicap. However, it must be said that he compounded his problem by composing his design of some of the more meretricious features of the 1950s modernist vernacular (or should one say slang?).

His cathedral, nevertheless, has many admirers. What seems to appeal to them is the bold concept of saw-tooth walls, the dramatic entrance-porch with its high plain columns, and the west wall, which is entirely of glass. To the right of the porch is a spectacular composition by Epstein, one of his last works, showing St Michael expelling Satan from paradise. Inside there is a remarkable baptistry, the font consisting of a huge uncarved boulder, brought from Bethlehem, and a polished marble plinth, which is designed to be seen against a concave stone grille set with jewel-like stained glass, designed by John Piper and made by Patrick Reyntiens. There is also some impressive coloured glass in the aisle windows, which by virtue of the saw-tooth design all face the altar, though at the diagonal angle. This sometimes produces a notable lighting effect, and it cannot be denied that much thought and ingenuity has gone into the whole design and its separate,

The new Coventry Cathedral, adjoining the old.

but integrated, decorative features. However, the most important of them is the Graham Sutherland tapestry of Christ, which is over seventy feet high: and one's impression of the entire cathedral interior depends to a great extent on an estimation of this enormous and controversial figure. Coventry is very much of its time and place and will always have value as a period-piece; whether it has sufficient *gravitas* for a cathedral is a matter of opinion.

At Guildford, by contrast, a virgin site and a very fine and prominent site too greeted Sir Edward Maufe, who had won the competition for the cathedral of the new see created in 1927. The situation is so prominent and commanding, rivalling Lincoln, that it demands a stone skyline cathedral, designed from the outside. It got something different: a modernised version of St Albans. The brick is of clay dug from the hill itself; and it is notorious that brick architecure, especially in the Gothic mode, abhors simplicity of line, demanding instead a multiplicity of sharp and ambitious angles and a general mood of spikiness, as a visit to the Baltic will show. Maufe chose instead stern simplicity: right angles and a curious combination of lancets with a Perpendicular frame. He has a low west transept, of sorts, which makes his west end look like a medieval staircase east end; and the lateral view, where the aisles dissolve into the general silhouette, and the transepts seem the same width as the indeterminate central tower, is almost featureless, as though the cathedral had been delivered in a big protective box, and nobody has yet bothered to unwrap it.

The nave and aisle of Guildford Cathedral.

This last image is the key to the design, for once inside the brick carapace, one can see the cathedral Maufe designed: and it is sublime. The brick is gone, replaced by stone and plaster, and all the simple forms come to brilliant life: immensely tall arcades, without capitals, and with only the merest clerestory apertures under the arching vaults, but ample lighting from the aisle lancets. The choir lacks a great east window, having instead one small eye; but the full view down to the lancets of the West Front, taking in the cavernous high vault of the crossing-tower, is spectacular, reminiscent of York, for the nave is wide for its height. The joy and power of the interior makes up for the missed opportunities of the skyline, for Maufe proves once more, in a modern reinterpretation, what medieval Gothic shows again and again, that the grandeur of enclosed space – which is the real essence of cathedral architecture – does not depend on dimensions but on imagination.

Nevertheless, at the risk of contradicting myself, I must add that sheer dimensions can be of decisive assistance. For the really grand interior effects, which make the scalp tingle and the heart leap, size is a necessity. This, I think, is one of the many lessons to be learnt from Britain's greatest twentieth-century building, the Anglican Cathedral at Liverpool. The site chosen was magnificent and audacious, effectively dominating the arc of the vast city, and therefore demanding a silhouette of confident power and great size, The choice of architect was audacious too. In 1901, Liverpool was bitterly divided on sectarian lines, and for the Anglican establishment to pick for this monumental work a twenty-two-year-old Roman Catholic demanded courage. But courage has been the keynote throughout the gestation of this cathedral. It took courage, for instance, for Giles Gilbert Scott to opt for Gothic at a time when the revival had lost much of its force, but Gothic organized on new principles which make radically different and dramatic allocations of space. It took courage, too, for him to make a decisive revision of his design after the work had already begun.

Scott's original idea was based on the glorious opportunism which gave Exeter

OPPOSITE A portion of the interior of Coventry, showing Graham Sutherland's tapestry of Christ.

a two-tower transept (the central space came later). At the same time, the external effect was to have the harsh and uncompromising power of Albi – not a bad notion for intolerant Liverpudlian sectarianism. He soon realized, however, two towers do not make a strong silhouette even in placid Exeter, let alone on a Liverpool hilltop. So the two-tower transept became an immense central tower, spanning a space between two equal transepts, and turning the heart of the cathedral into a square, from which nave and chancel protrude at either end. The effect of the change externally was that the central tower, firmly based on its long, high plinth, seems to have the whole of Liverpool, not normally a subordinate city, at its feet, and brings to mind not mild Exeter but the palatine absolutism of Durham. Indeed, the more one looks at this great cathedral from outside, the more Durham haunts one's thoughts.

Inside, however, the note that is struck is not of brutal or even sophisticated power, but of awe and civilized mystery. Scott took a risk in working with pink-grey sandstone, for externally it may weather badly. Internally, however, the colour is so magnificently warm, and so endlessly subtle, as to justify any hazard. As at Exeter, the stone seems magic: the eye lingers over the vast wall-spaces, and follows the line of column and the curve of arch with a never-ending pleasure which is almost sensuous and tactile, as though one were stroking satin. The cathedral is a very complex building indeed; like Canterbury, it takes a lot of knowing before all its parts are impressed in correct order on the brain. It is also embellished, already, with an exceptional number of splendid artifacts, in stone, metal, wood and glass, the products of a native craftsmanship which one believed no longer existed. But the major decorative features, such as the high altar, the organ, the bishop's throne and choirstalls, the stupendous font, and many of the side-altars, are integral parts of the original design, through which the architect has imposed intelligible patterns of thought. It is important, in viewing this church internally, to sit quietly and to look hard at the parts and the details of these parts, until their structural and decorative relationships become firmly established; the design of the church is a high-powered cerebral exercise; it requires patient and deliberate mental exertion to attune oneself to it, and move along Scott's lines of thought.

The essence of the design is a series of exercises on the enclosure of space. Scott grasped that a cathedral is, in one sense, a metaphysical concept: it brings God to man by showing him that the infinity of space, by which we conceive of deity, can be captured or harnessed in a way man can grasp. That is why size, or at any rate scale, are so important in cathedral art. At Liverpool, Scott was given a brief which allowed him to use size whenever or wherever he wanted: but he used it intelligently, too. Externally, he keeps the bay system as a useful form of punctuation. Internally, he thinks in terms of spaces: the nave space, the western transept space, the central space, the eastern transept space, the choir space. One moves from one space to another, barely conscious, at first, of the vast columns and curves which provide the demarcations, aware only of changes in light and chiaroscuro, or a different ring in footsteps. One's eyes explore the shape of the interlocking spaces Scott has enclosed, gradually penetrating to the distant corners and eyries, and then perceiving and tracing to their source in the pavement the soft stone bones of the structure.

The cathedral is arranged so that the sensations of space become more intense as one moves from west to east, and this has only recently become possible with the completion of the nave. But even moving from the high altar westwards, the experience is overwhelming. In most prodigy-cathedrals, to step from the choir into the crossing is an emotional descent – the crossing must be entered from the nave. Here the crossing works either way. Moreover, to move from the enormous crossing into the vast, shadowy nave involves stepping down into a nether-world of unknown dimensions, an emotional experience in itself. By a stroke of genius, between the nave and the crossing, Scott has placed a stone bridge carried over a vast low arch. He borrowed this cunning device from Gloucester, and it serves a number of functional purposes admirably. What it also does, however, is to increase the sense of distance which separates the high altar from the west end, and vice versa; and it greatly intensifies the verticality of the east end when seen from the west. The bridge, of course, provides a different level of space-perspectives in both directions. A third level of internal perspectives, including some spectacular downward views from a height of 120 feet, radiate from the gallery of the corona, under the crossing-tower. There are, too, some totally unexpected and dramatic vistas, upwards as well as laterally, in the side aisles and particularly in the ambulatory; a stunning glimpse into the chapter House through its superb ogee arch doorway; and a bridge for downward views into the sumptuous Lady Chapel which, again, recalls the virtuoso treatment of space at Gloucester. Scott's design has been criticized as traditional and nineteenth-century. The truth is that it offers new interpretations of the Gothic mode which could only have been possible for a man living in the twentieth century and aware of its technology. It is a venturesome and audacious experiment in high cathedral space-enclosure; and as one stands in its crossing, and is made humbly aware of man's puny stature, one is grateful to those who had the fortitude, during two world wars and the destructive cynicism of the modern age, to carry through Scott's vision to its triumphant realization.

When the Catholics of Liverpool saw Scott's noble cathedral begin to arise, they were filled with a spirit of emulation, and in 1930 they entrusted the task of building a cathedral to Sir Edwin Lutyens, the undisputed head of his profession, and the greatest English architect since Wren. Sir Edwin, who had the boundless optimism of the Edwardian Age, produced a design even more stupendous than Scott's. It was cruciform, but barely so. Nave, transepts and chancel, though they existed, had their individuality blunted by angle-chapels at all the corners; and the whole was surmounted by a gigantic dome, with a diameter of 168 feet, against 137 for St Peter's, Rome, and a mere 112 for St Paul's. The concept, in so far as it had progenitors, was Byzantine rather than Baroque; but in truth it sprang straight from the deep well of Lutyens's own imagination; it was *sui generis*, though conceived on a scale even he had never hitherto considered practicable. The length was to be 680 feet, the width 400, the height to the top of the dome 510 feet; and the surface area to be covered no less than 233,000 square feet, making it the grandest cathedral in the world.

Work on this sublime monster went on from 1933 to 1940, when it stopped for-ever. By that time an enormous crypt had been built, a house of many labyrinthine marble mansions, which actually rises some twelve feet above ground-level, and thus formed a monumental plinth on which the vast brick-and-stone edifice was to be solidly seated. Alas, only the model of it remains, and that in a damaged condition. In the 1950s, Cardinal Heenan despaired of raising the money to complete Lutyens's colossal scheme, and instead held a competition for a new and cheaper design, the salient feature of which had to be perfect visibility for a congregation of 2,000. The competition was won by Sir Frederick Gibberd, with

a circular design nearly 200 feet across, sitting on the crypt-plinth, or rather part of it, framed by sixteen boomerang ribs or trusses, made of reinforced concrete, and bound together at the top by concrete rings, which support a glazed lantern. The lantern ends in spikes, and contains some remarkable deep-coloured glazing, made by Patrick Reyntiens to a design of John Piper. This feature, which has some merit, is balanced by a grotesque concrete main porch of unspeakable ugliness. However, what must strike the student of cathedral architecture most forcibly is the effect of the interior as a whole. Although its span is nearly twice as big as the Hagia Sophia in Istanbul, the greatest church of antiquity, it conveys no impression of space: space, indeed, is not imprisoned but has made its escape up through the spiky lantern. One feels one is in half a collapsed balloon, or a precarious tent; and when the church is full, and various activities are taking place in the centre, the ambience is crowded and restless rather than sacramental. Indeed, the congregation tends to become a mere audience, and intrude on the theatre-in-the-round taking place in their midst, a case of the demotic overwhelming the hieratic.

Unfortunately the notion of a circular church is, superficially, an attractive one to modern clerics, anxious to swell their dwindling congregations; and the circular plan was promptly adopted for yet another Roman Catholic cathedral, this time at Clifton, near Bristol. The design, by Perry Thomas Partnership, was realized in the late 1960s, and already bears the imprint of fading novelty which marks that meretricious decade. At least the church at Clifton has no mark of Cain, like the Liverpool porch; and is, comparatively speaking, tucked away and unobtrusive. The real tragedy of the Catholic Cathedral at Liverpool is that it occupies a prominent position, in the heart of the city, and not only invites but loudly insists on being compared with its Anglican rival. The comparison is not only an aesthetic but a moral one, and the two communities know it. Though the Liverpool Catholics enjoy a higher living-standard than at any time in their history, they are aware that they were judged insufficiently generous, by their own pastors, to support the completion of Lutyens's noble tribute to Almighty God. And they can see with their own eyes that the Anglicans had the will and courage to press on where they themselves faltered. It is a hard cross to bear, harder than any conceivable financial burden; for no Liverpool Catholic can be unaware that triumphant Anglicans refer to their modernistic bauble as 'Paddy's Wigwam'.

However, the building of a cathedral is a story without an end. Who knows? It is not impossible that Lutyens's masterpiece will yet be built by a more robust and confident generation. In the nineteenth century, churchmen thought, and often said, that the age of cathedral-building was over. We are now in the last decades of the twentieth century, and we know this pessimism to have been unfounded. It is disproved not only by the gigantic ocular evidence of Scott's great church but by the equally visible fact that most of our medieval cathedrals are now in better condition, perhaps, than at any time during their long existence. In the last resort, cathedrals are not built by money but by faith, of which money is merely an outward manifestation. I grew up under the lengthening shadow of a vast Catholic church, whose conception and design and very fabrication was the product of the galvanizing energy of one priest. My father gave him artistic advice, when he was in the mood to listen to it; and I saw this noble pile rise stone by stone. It was the backdrop of my boyhood. Like the canons of Seville, this eager priest was judged mad by his sober colleagues. But he had faith, and his

Detail of the interior of the Catholic cathedral at Clifton, near Bristol.

OPPOSITE Liverpool Roman Catholic Cathedral, showing the central lantern and external altar.

church, which is now a pro-cathedral, is there to justify it, and him. It is not given to many men to build a cathedral alone. Cathedrals are collective efforts, and the individual sinks to insignificance in the immensity of their fabrics and the teeming fruitfulness of their long lives. But for all that, faith is an individual emotion, one man's gesture of confidence in his maker; and without the faith of individuals, a few known, most unknown, the collective process which raised our cathedrals from the dust would not have been set in motion. I salute these faithful Christian forebears as I end this book.

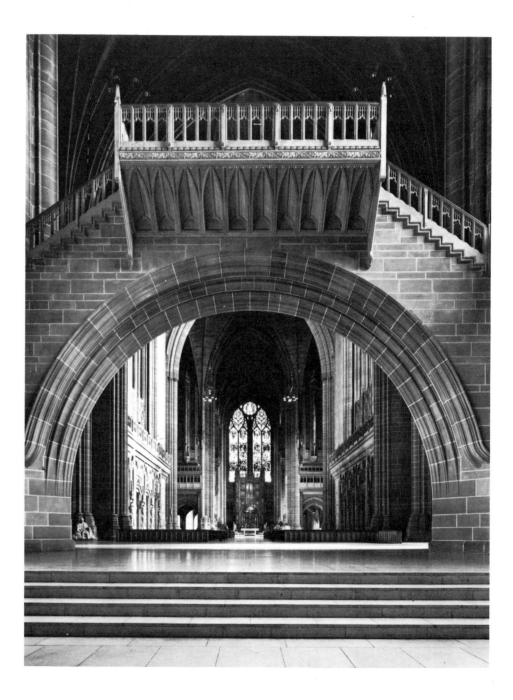

Looking east through the stone bridge in Liverpool Anglican Cathedral.

Glossary of Technical Terms

Abutment: solid masonry countering thrust of arch or vault.
Aedicule: door, window or other opening framed with columns and other ordered features.
Ambulatory: processional aisle circling apse.
Annulet: decorative ring round shaft.
Apse: semicircular or polygonal end to chancel.
Arcade: range of arches supported by piers or columns; **blind arcading** is similar pattern on wall.
Ashlar: hewn masonry blocks (as opposed to unhewn stone).
Baldachino: fixed high altar canopy on columns.
Ball-flower: decorated period ornament of three petals enclosing ball.
Baluster: small pillar or column.
Basilica: rectangular aisled church with clerestory lighting.
Bay: unit section of walling.
Boss: ornamental cover of join in rib-vaulting.
Bracket: supporting stonework to carry projecting horizontal.
Buttress: solid stone or brick projection to give support to wall. **Angle-buttresses** are two meeting at 90 degrees angle, usually on towers. **Flying buttress:** arch or half-arch transmitting vault- or wall-thrust to ground.
Campanile: detached bell-tower.
Canted: sloping or tilted.
Capital: head of column.
Centering: wooden frame used to support arch or vault until mortar has set.
Chancel: portion of church east of crossing.
Chantry: chapel within church or cathedral for saying masses for the soul of donor.
Chapter House: assembly-chamber for governing members of ecclesiastical foundation.
Chevet: from French 'bed-head': semi-circular apse with radiating chapels.
Chevron: zig-zag moulding.
Choir: central portion of chancel where service is sung.
Clerestory: windowed top storey above aisle roof.
Corbel: supportive block of stone projecting from wall. A corbel table is series of corbels immediately below roof-eaves.
Corinthian: Greek decorative capital invented in fifth-century BC Athens; characterised by acanthus leaves.
Cornice: top section of entablature (that is, horizontal toppings of column).
Crocket: leaf-shaped decoration on sides of spires, pinnacles, etc.
Crossing: central space of church at meeting of nave, chancel and transepts.
Crypt: church cellar.
Cupola: polygonal or circular turret crowning roof or dome.
Cusps: projecting point in Gothic tracery.
Decorated: English Gothic style, c. 1280–1350.
Diaper: square or diamond patterning.
Dogtooth: diagonal pyramid patterning.
Early English: English Gothic Style, c. 1190–1290.
Engaged column: column attached to wall.
Entablature: upper part of an ordered façade,
Feretory: relic shrine behind high altar.
Flamboyant: French late Gothic, marked by wavy lines.
Fluting: vertical channels on column.

Flying shore: horizontal prop or support.
Foliated: leaf-shape carving.
Galilee: vestibule at west end of church; also called narthex.
Gallery: upper or middle storey of church; also called tribune and triforium.
Grisaille: grey or monochrome decorated glass.
Groin: edge where two faces of vault meet; hence **groin-vault**, which predated ribbed vaults.
Hallchurch: wide church where nave and aisles are of roughly equal height.
Hammerbeam: wooden beams projecting from wall to provide support for upper members of roof.
Herringbone: diagonal laid brickwork.
Hoodmould: projecting moulding over exterior arch, etc, to throw off rainwater.
Impost: wall-bracket supporting end of arch.
Lancet: tall, narrow window, characteristic of Early English.
Lantern tower: tower over crossing to project light downwards.
Lintel: horizontal beam over opening.
Minster: misleading term originally meaning a monastic church, later applied to any large collegiate church. York and Beverley are both correctly referred to as Minsters, but by usage only.
Misericord: bracket on underside of hinged choir-seat.
Moulding: contours around projecting features, windows, arches etc.
Mullion: vertical post dividing window into 'lights'.
Narthex: vestibule at west end of church.
Nave: church west of the crossing, for the lay congregation.
Newel: centre-post of circular staircase.
Ogee: concave/convex arch characteristic of Decorated. A 'nodding ogee' is a projecting ogee arch-hood, of chapter stall, choirstalls, etc.
Order: architectural rules or discipline governing the use of columns, and by extension any set of architectural rules of decoration.
Paten: plate for communion bread.
Pediment: low pitched gable above doors, windows; usually decorative only.
Pendant: elongated boss.
Perpendicular: English Gothic style, c. 1330s– c. 1530s.
Perron: low flight of steps.
Piano nobile: principal floor, usually on first storey.
Pier: main support for arcade; square or composite (compound) in cross-section. The compound pier is a collection of shafts.
Pilaster: decorative pier attached to wall.
Pinnacle: upright ornament on spire, tower.
Plinth: projecting base of structure.
Portico: projecting central entrance to façade.
Presbytery: area of high altar, east of choir; also called sanctuary.
Pulpitum: screen dividing choir from nave.
Puthole: holes to support scaffolding during construction.
Quatrefoil: four-fold lobe of cusping in arch or circle.
Quoins: dressed stones at corners or angles.
Rebus: pun on word or proper name, much used in late-Perpendicular decoration.
Reredos: backing of high altar.
Retable: decorative altarpiece, often a painting mounted on or above altar.

Retrochoir: portion of church behind high altar.

Rood-screen: partition in front of nave, usually supporting cross or rood above.

Romanesque: pre-Gothic style of tenth-twelfth centuries; in England, after 1066, usually called Norman, especially of period 1066–1154.

Rose-window: circular window with radial tracery.

Rustication: decorative walling where visible plane of ashlar is left undressed to produce rustic effect.

Saltire: St Andrew's Cross, that is equal-armed diagonal.

Sanctuary: area of high altar.

Scallop: sea-shell ornament.

Shaft: main trunk of column; sometimes coupled or clustered in a compound pier; a reed-shaft is very narrow.

Soffit: underside of arch.

Spandrel: wall-surface between two arches or on either side of arch.

Springing: level from which arch rises from its support.

Stiff-leaf: conventionalized leaf-carving, chiefly Early English.

Strainer-arch: arch inserted to keep walls vertical.

String-course: projecting horizontal band on wall.

Tabernacle: ornamental case for Blessed Sacrament.

Tas-de-Charge: Horizontal bottom course of arch or vault

bonded into the supporting wall.

Tracery: intersecting rib-work in windows or blind arcading; **bar-tracery,** c. 1250, slender shafts intersecting mullions.

Transept: transverse arms of cruciform church.

Trefoil: three-fold lobe or cusping in arch or circle.

Tribune: middle or gallery storey.

Triforium: arcaded passage or middle storey; also called tribune or gallery.

Tympanum: area between arch and lintel of doorway.

Vault: stone or wooden ceiling below roof. In simplest form, **barrel** or **tunnel vault.** A **groin vault** is formed when two tunnel vaults intersect at right angles. **Rib-vaulting** occurs when the groins are reinforced by projecting stonework. A **quadripartite vault** divided a rib-vaulted bay into four parts. **Sexpartite vault** divides a quadripartite vault into two transversely, so each vaulting bay has six parts. **Tierceron** is a secondary rib connecting the springing or central boss to a ridge-rib.

Lierne is a rib which does not lead from either springing or central boss. **Fan-vaulting:** ribs of equal length and curvature springing from same point.

Volute: spiral scroll, usually on Ionic capital.

Voussoir: wedge-shape stone in arch.

Select Bibliography

In general, the most authoritive guides to the architectural history of our cathedrals are Nikolaus Pevsner (editor): *The Buildings of England*, 46 vols (London 1951–76), and the *Victoria County Histories*. For brief guides to individual cathedrals, the Pitkin 'Pride of Britain' series is usually excellent; the volumes in Bell's Cathedral Series are also still valuable. The best one-volume survey is John Harvey: *Cathedrals of England and Wales* (London 1974 edition), which includes the ingenious index system I have used in Chapter One. Also excellent are:

Alec Clifton-Taylor: *The Cathedrals of England* (London 1977)

Kenneth Hudson: *Exploring Cathedrals* (London 1978)

Hugh Braun: *Cathedral Architecture* (London 1972)

Harry Batsford and Charles Fry: *The Cathedrals of England* (London, new edition 1960).

For architectural styles, there are, for the earliest periods:

Richard Krautheimer: *Early Christian and Byzantine Architecture* (London 1965)

Kenneth J. Conant: *Carolingian and Romanesque Architecture* (London 1959)

A. W. Clapham: *Romanesque Architecture in England* (2 vols, Oxford 1965).

For Gothic:

John Harvey: *The Gothic World* (London 1950)

Hans F. Hofstatter: *Gothic* (London 1970)

Francis Bond: *Gothic Architecture in England* (London 1905)

Arthur Kingsley Porter: *Medieval Architecture its Origins and Development*, 2 vols, (New York 1909)

Jean Bony: *Gothic Architecture Transformed: the English*

Decorative Style (London 1979)

John Harvey: *The Perpendicular Style* (London 1979

For later developments:

Rudolf Wittkower: *Gothic Versus Classic* (London 1974)

George Germann: *The Gothic Revival in Europe and Britain* (London 1972)

Stefan Muthesius: *The High Victorian Movement in Architecture* (London 1972)

Roger Dixon and Stefan Muthesius: *Victorian Architecture* (London 1978)

H. C. N. Williams: *20th Century Cathedrals* (London 1964).

For architects:

John Harvey: *The Medieval Architect* (London 1972)

English Medieval Architects: A Biographical Dictionary down to 1550 (revised edition 1979)

B. G. Morgan: *Canonic Design in English Medieval Architecture* (Liverpool 1971)

Jean Gimpel: *The Cathedral Builders* (London 1963)

W. R. Matthews and W. M. Atkins: *A History of St Paul's Cathedral and the Men Associated with It* (London 1957)

John Summerson: *Sir Christopher Wren* (London 1953)

M. S. Briggs: *Goths and Vandals* (London 1952)

A. W. Pugin: *The True Principles of Pointed or Christian Architecture* (London 1841)

Phoebe Stanton: *Pugin* (London 1971)

Peter Ferriday (ed.): *Victorian Architecture* (London 1963)

George Gilbert Scott: *Personal and Professional Recollections* (London 1879)

English Church Architecture (London 1881)

Peter Ferriday: *Lord Grimthorpe 1816–1905* (London 1957).

For building technology, the works I have found most useful are:

John Fitchen: *The Construction of Gothic Cathedrals: a study of Medieval Vault Erection* (Oxford 1961)

L. F. Salzman: *Building in England down to 1540: a Documentary History* (Oxford 1952)

Pierre du Colombier: *Les Chantiers des cathédrales* (Paris 1953)

Norman Davey: *Building Stones of England and Wales* (London 1976)

Nathaniel Lloyd: *A History of English Brickwork* (London 1934)

Douglas Knoop and G.P. Jones: *The Medieval Mason* (Manchester 1933)

C.A. Hewitt: *English Cathedral Carpentry* (London 1974)

R. F. Tylecot: *A History of Metallurgy* (London 1976)

H. O'Neill: *Stone for Building* (London 1965).

For cathedral organization, finance, life and worship:

Kathleen Edwards: *The English Secular Cathedrals in the Middle Ages* (London 1967 ed.)

Lionel Butler and Chris Given-Wilson: *Medieval Monasteries of Great Britain* (London 1979)

Christopher Brooke: *Medieval Church and Society* (London 1971)

Henry Kraus: *Gold Was the Mortar: the Economics of Cathedral Building* (London 1978)

Barbara Harvey: *Westminster Abbey and its Estates in the Middle Ages* (Oxford 1977), which is one of a number of recent studies on ecclesiastical finance.

G.G. Coulton: *Art and the Reformation* (Cambridge 1953)

Ronald Finucane: *Miracles and Pilgrims: Popular Beliefs in Medieval England* (London 1977)

Jonathan Sumption: *Pilgrimage, an Image of Medieval Religion* (London 1977)

J. G. Davies: *The Architectural Setting of Baptism* (London 1962)

G. W. O. Addleshaw and F. Etchells: *The Architectural Setting of Anglican Worship* (London 1948)

H. de S. Shortt: *Salisbury Cathedral and Indications of the Sarum Use* (Salisbury 1973)

C. Wordsworth: *Ceremonies and Processions of the Cathedral Church of Salisbury* (Cambridge 1901)

James Floyd White: *Protestant Worship and Church Architecture* (New York 1964)

Geoffrey Hill: *English Dioceses: a history of their limits from the earliest times to the present day* (London 1900).

Among specialist studies, there are:

J. Baker: *English Stained Glass* (London 1960)

C. Woodford: *English Stained and Painted Glass* (Oxford 1954)

Alban D. Caroe: *Old Churches and Modern Craftsmanship* (Oxford 1949)

Harry Forrester: *Medieval Gothic Mouldings: a Guide* (London 1972)

G.H. Cook: *Medieval Chantries and Chantry Chapels* (London 1963)

A. Caiger-Smith: *English Medieval Mural Painting* (Oxford 1963)

Lawrence Stone: *Sculpture in Britain: the Middle Ages* (London 1972)

Margaret Whinney: *Sculpture in Britain, 1530–1830* (London 1964)

C.J.P. Cave: *Roof Bosses in Medieval Churches* (Cambridge 1948)

W. H. Aylmer Vallance: *Greater English Church Screens* (London 1948)

F.E. Hoard and F.H. Crossley: *English Church Woodwork* (2nd ed. 1927)

F.H. Crossley: *English Church Monuments, 1150–1550* (London 1921)

Katherine A. Esdaile: *English Church Monuments, 1510–1840* (London 1946)

C.F.C. Benson: *English Church Clocks* (Chichester 1971)

J. J. Raven: *The Bells of England* (London 1906)

J.G.M. Scott: *The Bells of Exeter Cathedral* (Exeter, nd)

H.L.C. Stocks (ed.): *British Cathedral Organists* (London 1949)

E.H. Fellowes: *English Cathedral Music from Edward VI to Edward VIII* (London 2nd ed. 1970)

Frank Harrison: *Music in Medieval Britain* (London 1958)

F. Wormald and C.E. Wright: *The English Library: studies in its history before 1700* (London 1958)

W. H. Mackean: *Rochester Cathedral Library* (Rochester 1953)

N.R. Ker: *Medieval Libraries of Great Britain* (London 2nd ed. 1964).

Further specialists studies are to be found in the *Journal of the Society of Architectural Historians, Archaeologia*, the *Archaeological Journal, Medieval Archaeology* and the *Journal of the British Archaeological Association*, whose *Proceedings*, dealing with individual cathedrals, are particularly valuable and up-to-date.

Among cathedral histories, there are:

H.K. Westlake: *Westminster Abbey*, 2 vols (London 1923)

Norman Summers: *A Prospect of Southwell* (London 1974)

H.N.C. Williams: *Coventry Cathedral* (Coventry 1974)

Gilbert Thurlow: *Norwich Cathedral* (London 1972)

Walter Hussey: *Chichester Cathedral* (Chichester 1970)

Robert Runcie (ed.): *Cathedral and City: St Albans Ancient and Modern* (London 1977)

E.A. Freeman: *History of the Cathedral Church of Wells* (London 1870)

V. Hope and J. Lloyd: *Exeter Cathedral* (Exeter 1973)

D. J. Steward: *The Architectural History of Ely Cathedral* (London 1868)

G. E. Aylmer and Reginald Cant: *A History of York Minster* (Oxford 1977)

Robert Willis: *The Architectural History of Canterbury Cathedral* (London 1845).

For Scotland:

David MacGibbon and Thomas Ross: *The Ecclesiastical Architecture of Scotland*, 3 vols (Edinburgh 1896–7)

Hubert Fewick: *Scotland's Abbey and Cathedrals* (London 1979)

For Catholic cathedrals:

Bryan Little: *Catholic Churches Since 1623* (London 1966).

Index